Construction Disputes—Liability and the Expert Witness

General Editor
Andrea Burns, LLB (Hons), CMA

Contributors

Professor Phillip Capper, MA (Oxon), BA (Dunelm)
Kim Franklin, LLB, ACIArb, Barrister
Richard Hawkins, FRICS, FCIArb
His Honour Judge John Newey, QC, MA, LLM, FCIArb
Norman Royce, FRIBA, PPCIArb
Anthony Speaight, MA (Oxon), Barrister
Anthony Thornton, QC, Assistant Recorder, MA, BCL (Oxon)

Butterworths
London, Edinburgh
1989

United Kingdom	Butterworth & Co (Publishers) Ltd, 88 Kingsway, LONDON WC2B 6AB and 4 Hill Street, EDINBURGH EH2 3JZ
Australia	Butterworths Pty Ltd, SYDNEY, MELBOURNE, BRISBANE, ADELAIDE, PERTH, CANBERRA and HOBART
Canada	Butterworths Canada Ltd, TORONTO and VANCOUVER
Ireland	Butterworth (Ireland) Ltd, DUBLIN
Malaysia	Malayan Law Journal Sdn Bhd, KUALA LUMPUR
New Zealand	Butterworths of New Zealand Ltd, WELLINGTON and AUCKLAND
Puerto Rico	Equity de Puerto Rico, Inc, HATO REY
Singapore	Malayan Law Journal Pte Ltd, SINGAPORE
USA	Butterworth Legal Publishers, AUSTIN, Texas; BOSTON, Massachusetts; CLEARWATER, Florida (D & S Publishers); ORFORD, New Hampshire (Equity Publishing); ST PAUL, Minnesota; and SEATTLE, Washington

A CIP Catalogue record for this book is available from the British Library.

ISBN 0 406 11101 4

Typeset by Latimer Trend & Company Ltd, Plymouth
Printed and bound in Great Britain by
Mackays of Chatham PLC, Chatham, Kent

Top Row (left to right) Anthony Speaight, Phillip Capper, Anthony Thornton QC, Richard Hawkins, Norman Royce.
Bottom Row (left to right) Kim Franklin, His Honour Judge John Newey QC, Andrea Burns.

Preface

It has been an honour and a pleasure to be editor of this work which I hope will be useful for all persons practising in this interesting field of construction disputes. It is not a book which is solely intended for lawyers, but also experts and would-be experts in various professions involved in the construction industry. I would just like to say a little about each contributor and their chapters.

1. *A Guide to Construction Liability by Phillip Capper*

Phillip Capper is one of the leading authorities on liability in construction disputes and this is a first class introduction to the law from the point of view of liability both in contract and in tort.

Phillip Capper is a Special Adviser at Masons solicitors in London. He is also the Masons Professor of Construction Law at Kings College, London and a Fellow of Keeble College, Oxford. Before joining Masons he was Chairman of the Faculty of Law at Oxford University. He is also a well-known lecturer and writer on building contracts, negligence and design liability, and many other aspects of construction law.

2. *The Nature of Expert Evidence by Anthony Thornton QC and Kim Franklin*

Anthony Thornton and Kim Franklin consider together the question of the nature of expert evidence taking material from various sources. Both are practising barristers and specialise in construction disputes.

Anthony Thornton QC is eminent in his field, having taken both a BA and a BCL in law at Keeble College, Oxford. He started in specialised practice after being called to the Bar by the Middle Temple in 1971. He took Silk in 1988. He edits the 'Construction Law Journal' and was appointed an Assistant Recorder in 1988. He is a member of the Bar Council and of both the Official Referees' Users' Committee and Bar Association. He contributed to the title 'Building Contracts' in Halsbury's Laws of England. He also gives lectures on building contract law and practice.

Kim Franklin graduated from Warwick University with an Honours degree in law in 1983 and was called to the Bar the following year. She did her pupillage in various sets of chambers including those of Donald

Keating QC, dealing exclusively with construction and civil engineering disputes. She practises from the Temple, primarily in the Official Referees' Courts and arbitration. She is a regular contributor to 'The Architect's Journal' and 'Construction Law Journal' and gives lectures on building contract law and practice.

3. *View from a Solicitor by Andrea Burns*

My chapter describes the role of a solicitor in a construction dispute with particular reference to instructing an expert and the various stages at which he or she will be consulted.

Having obtained an external Honours degree in law from London University, I was fortunate to join Gouldens, where I was articled to the Senior Partner, Hugo Scott. I became a Partner at Gouldens and then joined Robert Fenwick Elliott in October 1987 practising under the name of Fenwick Elliott & Burns. I am married to a chartered surveyor.

4. *The Expert As Advocate by Richard Hawkins*

Richard Hawkins describes the role of an expert who also acts as advocate in arbitration proceedings. He is a chartered quantity surveyor and gained experience in arbitration when he spent some five years with the practice of James R Knowles where he ultimately managed the Winchester office of the practice. The majority of his career has been spent with building contractors, both large and medium sized. Early in 1989, however, he joined a property developer known as Downland Estates Limited where he controls the project management section and advises on contractual matters.

5. *View from Counsel by Anthony Thornton QC and Anthony Speaight*

Anthony Thornton and Anthony Speaight together consider the interrelation of the roles of counsel and the expert witness.

Anthony Speaight is a barrister practising in the field of construction disputes from the Temple. He graduated from Oxford University with an MA degree and is a member of the General Council of the Bar. He is the author of *The Law of Defective Premises* (1982) and editor of 'Architects' Journal Legal Handbook'.

6. *An Official Referee's View by His Honour Judge John Newey QC*

The judicial viewpoint has been admirably treated by Judge John Newey QC, an Official Referee, well accustomed to construction disputes.

Judge Newey was educated at Ellesmere and Queen's College, Cambridge and has MA and LLM degrees. He served Central India Horse from 1942 to 1947 and was awarded the US Bronze Star in Italy in 1944. He was called to the Bar by the Middle Temple in 1948 and took Silk in 1970. He became a bencher in 1977 and an Official Referee in 1980. Since 1971 he has been Commissary General of the City and Diocese of Canterbury. In 1989 he became a Fellow of the Chartered Institute of Arbitrators. He is married with five children.

7. *View from an Arbitrator by Norman Royce*

Norman Royce, a consultant architect and arbitrator, has given a very learned and also humorous account of the role of expert evidence from the viewpoint of an arbitrator.

Mr Royce did his architectural training at the Bromley College of Art and the Architectural Association. He is a Fellow and past Vice President of the RIBA. He is a Fellow and past President of the Chartered Institute of Arbitrators and also past Chairman of the London Court of International Arbitration. He is a Founder and Consultant to Royce Hurley and Stewart, Chartered Architects, and served in the Royal Air Force as a pilot in Europe and the East. His hobbies are gardening and flying.

October 1989 Andrea Burns

Contents

Table of statutes

References in this Table to *Statutes* are to Halsbury's Statutes of England (Fourth Edition) showing the volume and page at which the annotated text of the Act may be found.

Page references printed in **bold** type indicate where the Act is set out in part or in full.

Table of statutory instruments

List of cases

CHAPTER 1

A guide to construction liability

Professor Phillip Capper MA (Oxon), BA (Dunelm)

INTRODUCTION

Buildings and civil engineering works are high-value, long-life, multi-owner products. Design expectations often now involve leading edge technology, which can be unrealistic in relation to traditional construction methods. Some defects are almost bound to occur and are expensive to repair. Owners are likely to try to recover those repair costs and associated consequential losses of rent and profit, by seeking to shift the responsibility on to those involved in the design and construction process.

The fact that there is both multi-party involvement in design and construction and successive multiple ownership of the product has meant that few of these parties are in a contractual relationship with each other. Thus in the judicial climate which prevailed from the early 1960s until the mid-1980s indulging extension of negligence liabilities, the construction industry saw a remarkable growth in tort-based liabilities to third parties.

Traditional building procurement involves a disparate team, with employer design and supervision, nominated sub-contracting, and third party monitoring of building control and quality. This is a fertile seed-bed for legal claims, both during construction and after, because multiple lines of involvement obscure the location of responsibility, and provide a wider choice of solvent 'suable' defendants. During construction there will be claims for loss and expense arising from delay to the progress of the contract works or disruption of productivity. After construction there will be claims that defects could have been avoided.

Contractor margins are tight. Profitability may depend on successful pursuit claims for loss and expense during construction. The rate of contractor failure by insolvency is relatively high compared with other industries. The party who may be primarily responsible for defects could therefore be unavailable or not worth proceeding against.

Against this background, any insured or financially secure organisation becomes an attractive target for claims, and a very suable defendant. Hence building control local authorities arguably became a form of partial underwriter for defects over a decade from the mid-1970s to the mid-1980s. However, building control compliance is statutory and mandatory for public health and safety, and was until the mid-1980s an exclusively public sector function. By contrast, consulting professionals and contractors chose to sell their services, inducing reliance thereon by third parties, and so remained more likely to attract liability. Hence there were public policy reasons for limiting the liability exposure of the control authorities without necessarily signalling any general retrenchment of liabilities. The courts' renewed concern, emerging in the mid-1980s, not to extend the liability of public authority regulatory agencies was arguably a matter of public policy about the necessary immunity of certain public functions. This reasoning would have no necessary application to professional and contracting services offered competitively in the private sector, and so would not of itself have signalled any general retrenchment in legal liabilities found to be owed to third parties.

Nevertheless, the English courts did begin in the mid-1980s a new trend of caution, tending to restrict negligence liability and overrule some of the extensions of the previous decade. Hence, local authorities' liability in respect of building control functions (which exploded in the mid-1970s) was limited to present or imminent threats to health or safety of the occupier (and even then not an owner-builder). The recovery of purely economic losses which were not immediately consequential on damage to the person, or to property in which the claimant has a legal interest, was also considerably restricted.

This latter restriction is subject to an important exception. There has remained a well established category (called negligent misstatement) allowing recovery of pure economic loss arising from a lack of reasonable care by a defendant who held itself out as offering specialist or professional advice, or making an express or implied representation with special expertise, in circumstances where it knows or should have contemplated that it would reasonably be relied on. This is not a duty that would be owed to the world at large merely because of the publicly known or perceived position of a defendant. The claimant would have to be in a sufficiently proximate relationship to the defendant. However, case law has recognised the extension of this duty to third parties not in a contractual, or client, relationship with the defendant so long as the reliance by the claimant was reasonable, and reasonably to be contemplated by the defendant.

The main objection to the recovery of economic loss is that it opens the floodgates to claims from an indeterminate range of claimants. Where, however, the context of claimants is self-limiting, as in a construction project, then the particular project creates proximity and the argument against recovery may be weakened.

A further trend emerging in the case law of the late 1980s is a renewed emphasis upon the various parties' own contractual framework of risk allocation. Their free assent to such arrangements has not only defined their contractual rights and obligations. The courts have even come to recognise that the contractual structure of risk should also delimit the extent of risk exposure to third parties. Hence liabilities even in tort could be reduced significantly if the extent of reliance were managed by appropriate wording in the contractual terms of engagement and, where relevant and admissible, earlier correspondence. This is as much a matter of positive but realistic portrayal of the limits of the scope of the service intended, as it is perceived in the client's and others' minds, as it is with the language of actual warnings or disclaimers.

The supply of everyday goods or services typically involves a quality or fitness obligation. Contrast this with the typical duty of professional advisers, engaged for their expertise. They are not normally taken by

English law to warrant that the advice will lead to a successful result. They merely have to take reasonable care in the giving of advice.

Users who want rights to a certain level of quality or freedom from defects in goods and services (which are not otherwise dangerous or damaging) must get a contract to that effect with whoever they wish to make responsible. If there is a contract, the obligations may be implied, by statute or because a judge would regard them as necessarily implied.

In English law only the parties to a contract are entitled to the rights it creates. Third parties cannot take advantage of the contractual duties. This puts a natural limit on the range of possible claimants who can complain of quality problems. Liability outside contract to third parties (lawyers call this 'tort'—a civil wrong) has no natural limits and so has to be restricted in some way to prevent the courts being flooded with claims: the normal mechanism in tort is to allow losses to be recoverable only where these relate to physical harm to person or property. Pure economic losses are not normally recoverable in tort. Contract law does not make this distinction. Between contracting parties all losses (whether physical or wholly financial) are recoverable as damages so long as they arise naturally, according to the usual course of things, from the breach of contract, or were in the contemplation of both parties when the contract was made.

COLLATERAL WARRANTIES

Even though the courts are placing new restrictions on negligence liabilities of designers and builders, a decade or so of expanded liability has left a raised claims consciousness. Owners and tenants of buildings have become accustomed to holding builders directly responsible (even if they have no contract with them) for mere defects in the buildings which are not otherwise damaging or dangerous. As negligence liability recedes under a new judicial conservatism, owners and tenants are looking for new forms of legal protection. These are being expressed as 'duty of care' letters and deeds, special warranties, and various forms of assignment or novation. They attempt to create either a direct additional responsibility from the builder to the beneficiary, or a transfer of the original clients' rights under the building contract to third party end users.

THE CONSTRUCTION CONTRACT IS NOT THE ONLY SOURCE OF OBLIGATIONS

A party's rights and liabilities (in civil law) in respect of the supply of particular goods and/or services are generally determined by the contractual arrangements governing the supply, but we have seen from the above they may arise otherwise. Apart from the contract, there may, for instance, be a right of payment to a reasonable sum, for example, because the employer has wrongfully prevented performance or because extra work is done outside the contract; or a liability may arise, for example, for misrepresentation or for negligently causing loss or damage to third parties (common law product liability), as well as under the statutory regime of product liability. Common law product liability and the general tort of negligence arises where a person who has suffered loss or damage has legal rights to compensation because the person responsible acted in a way which the law regards as wrong (thereby committing a 'tort'). To succeed in the tort of negligence, the claimant has to establish (1) a duty of care owed to him, (2) breach of that duty, and (3) damage resulting from that breach. Construction industry activities may give rise to other torts, such as nuisance.

COMMON LAW LIABILITY GENERALLY: THE FUNDAMENTAL DIFFERENCES BETWEEN CONTRACT AND TORT LIABILITY

The liabilities likely to arise can best be approached by identifying the duties which the law requires to be observed. As an overview, two groups of these duties may be summarised as follows:

(1) Duties to achieve results.
(2) Duties to avoid particular harm.

This classification of duties is a functional one. It recognises the purposes for which different parts of the law impose obligations on people. This functional analysis also helps to elucidate the reason why the particular forms of liability arise from different legal conceptual classifications; principally contractual liability, and tortious liability for negligence. The analysis also helps to indicate that the remedy available to a claimant will depend very much upon the nature of the duty which is alleged to have been broken and also upon the conceptual source of that duty.

DUTIES TO ACHIEVE RESULTS: FITNESS FOR PURPOSE

The phrase 'duties to achieve results' is intended to connote the legal obligation to achieve a certain level of performance. The person responsible has to meet a performance objective: that the product will perform as required. In the ordinary context of contractors supplying goods or services this performance objective will be in essence a quality or fitness obligation. So the performance will be measured by the extent to which the goods or services supplied achieve the characteristics required. However, it should be noted that the duty of a professional person giving advice is rather different. A professional still has certain duties to achieve results. The law assumes that, in the absence of contrary indications, the result intended is that the professional should take reasonable care and skill in the giving of the advice. Hence the professional person is not normally taken by English law to warrant that the advice will lead to a successful result. The professional's performance obligation is normally limited to the requirement that reasonable care and skill be exercised in rendering the service.

The notion of a 'results-orientated' duty, at least in the context of quality or fitness for purpose obligations, has traditionally in English law been the province of the law of contract. Consistently with that tradition, European product liability (which was implemented in England by the Consumer Protection Act 1987) is an extension of tort, not contract, and it arises only where an unsafe product causes personal injury or damage to other property: the liability does not arise merely because the product itself is defective in terms of quality or fitness for purpose. Indeed, quality and fitness for purpose obligations would unarguably be the exclusive province of contract law were it not for a remarkable expansion in tortious liability for negligence in the decade or so from the mid-1970s to the mid-1980s. For a while, it appeared that the mere failure of a product to perform as well as the user reasonably expected could be redressed by a claim framed in tort. Appellate court decisions in the late 1980s, however, indicate a return to the traditional view that users who want rights to a certain level of quality, fitness for purpose, or freedom from defects in goods and services (which are not otherwise dangerous or damaging) must make their contract to that effect with whomsoever they wish to make responsible. The only significant qualification to this is the contractual context of professional advice: perhaps the reason is precisely that that context bears a marked similarity to the tortious context of negligence. If the professional person's contractual obligation is only to take reasonable care and skill in providing a service, and not to warrant the result, then the obligation in performance terms is hardly distinguishable from tortious liability for negligence.

PROBLEMS OF CONTRACT FORMATION

Letters of intent

The most important legal implication in relation to 'letters of intent' was highlighted by Robert Goff J (as he then was) in *British Steel Corpn v Cleveland Bridge and Engineering Co Ltd* [1984] 1 All ER 504, 24 BLR 94:

> 'There can be no hard and fast answer to the question whether a letter of intent will give rise to a binding agreement: everything must depend on the circumstances of the particular case. In most cases, where work is done pursuant to a request contained in the letter of intent, it will not matter whether a contract did or did not come into existence, because, if the party who has acted on the request is simply claiming payment, his claim will be based on a quantum meruit, and it will make no difference whether this claim is contractual or quasi-contractual . . . But where, as here, one party is seeking to claim damages for breach of contract, the question of whether any contract came into existence is of crucial importance.'

Tenders

Normally, a tender constitutes in law an 'offer' (see eg *Spencer v Harding* (1870) LR 5 CP 561). The party inviting tenders is not usually taken to have intended to accept the highest bid (from purchasers) or the lowest bid (from suppliers). However, such an intention can on appropriate wording be proven. See, for example, dicta in the House of Lords' decision in

Harvela Investments Ltd v Royal Trust Co of Canada [1986] AC 207, [1985] 2 All ER 966 (in which the principal question was the validity of referential bids).

There is an important distinction between discrete firm tenders, and 'standing offer' type tenders (against which goods and services are ordered from time to time). The former may by acceptance give rise to an immediately binding contract. The latter type (standing offers) even if 'accepted' in a commercial sense may not give rise to any binding contract until an order has been placed (and accepted) for a specific supply.

A potential source of dispute lies in the apparent ease of revocability of offers in English law even where these have been relied on. Consider the consequences for assembling tender bids, of the circumstances in the Canadian case of *Northern Construction Co Ltd v Gloge Heating and Plumbing Ltd* (1984) 6 DLR (4th) 450.

Conflicting order documentation: 'the battle of the forms'

Lord Denning offered a forward-looking, practical approach to this problem in the leading case of *Butler Machine Tool Co Ltd v Ex-Cell-O Corpn* [1979] 1 All ER 965, [1979] 1 WLR 401:

> 'In many ... cases our traditional analysis of offer, counter-offer, rejection, acceptance and so-forth is out-of-date ... The better way is to look at all the documents passing between the parties and glean from them, or from the conduct of the parties, whether they have reached agreement on all material points, even though there may be differences between the forms and conditions printed on the back of them ... If they can be reconciled so as to give a harmonious result, all well and good. If differences are irreconcilable, so that they are mutually contradictory, then the conflicting terms may have to be scrapped and replaced by reasonable implication.'

Unfortunately, his remarks were not adopted by his brother judges. Lawton and Bridge LJJ reaffirmed instead the 130-year-old 'set rules' of offer and counter-offer: 'It is a battle more on classical 18th century lines'.

This 'offer and acceptance' approach is well illustrated by *Sauter Automation Ltd v H C Goodman (Mechanical Services) Ltd* (1986) 34 BLR 81.

The PSA accepted a tender from Goodman, the main contractor, for boiler replacement work at Windsor Castle, on the terms of GC/Works/1, ed. 2 with amendment no 4. The PSA approved the use of Sauter as subcontractor to supply controls. Meanwhile Sauter had submitted a quotation to Goodman. It was accepted. Sauter delivered most of the equipment, but had not yet been paid. Goodman fell into financial difficulties, and the PSA determined Goodman's employment but wanted to use the equipment supplied. Sauter claimed still to own the equipment, relying on a retention of title clause in its 'standard conditions of sale' referred to in, and enclosed with, the quotation to Goodman. However, Goodman had accepted the quotation on 'terms and conditions in accordance with the main contract GC/Works/1 edition 2 plus amendment No 4 (see form of contract attached)'.

Sauter argued that the acceptance amounted to an acceptance of Sauter's offer to supply on the terms and conditions mentioned in its quotation, including the retention of title clause.

GC/Works/1 had no provision equivalent to Sauter's clause. On the contrary, GC/Works/1 cl.30(2) provided that every sub-contract should include a provision that from commencement to completion of the sub-contract 'all things for incorporation belonging to [the sub-contractor] which are brought on the site in connection with the sub-contract shall vest in the contractor'.

The judge, Mervyn Davies J, said that Goodman's order was plainly an offer to contract on the GC/Works/1 terms mentioned, and not on Sauter's terms. Goodman was making a counter-offer which killed the Sauter offer. Sauter accepted the counter-offer by proceeding to execute the Goodman order.

However, he also considered the matter on the footing that both sets of conditions were incorporated with GC conditions prevailing in case of inconsistency. Still Sauter's retention of title clause could not stand. Sauter must be taken to have known that PSA and Goodman desired sub-contractor's materials to vest in Goodman once on site.

Contractual obligations: implied terms

Contractual obligations can be express or implied: ie expressed in the terms of the contract agreed between the parties, or regarded by the law as impliedly on one of the parties, even though not spelled out between the parties expressly.

Perhaps the most important illustrative sources of implied terms are the Sale of Goods Act 1979 and the Supply of Goods and Services Act 1982. Subject to what is said below about express contractual provisions seeking to exclude or limit what would otherwise be the obligations between the contracting parties, these statutes impose implied contractual warranties that goods supplied shall correspond with any description by which they are supplied, shall be of merchantable quality, and shall be reasonably fit for any particular purpose made known.

Terms may be implied in contracts as a matter of usual implication at common law, or because a judge regards particular terms as necessarily implied in a particular contract. However, unlike statutory implied terms, common law or 'judge-made' terms will not be implied if they would be inconsistent with the express terms of the contract. Hence the law usually implies that a builder will do his work in a good and workmanlike manner, will supply good and proper materials, and, for example, if building a house it will be reasonably fit for human habitation; but these implications can be excluded by express terms.

The extent of this non-statutory power to imply terms which are not expressed is set out by Lord Wilberforce in the House of Lords in *Liverpool City Council v Irwin* [1977] AC 239, [1976] 2 All ER 39. Where there is an apparent complete contract the courts are sometimes willing to add to terms: this is very common in mercantile contracts where there is an established usage—the courts are spelling out what both parties know and would, if asked, unhesitatingly agree to be part of the bargain. In other cases, where there is an apparently complete bargain, the courts are willing to add a term on the ground that without it the contract will not work. A further category is where the court is simply concerned to establish what the contract is, the parties not having themselves fully stated the terms. The decision of Vinelott J in *Merton London Borough Council v Stanley Hugh Leach Ltd* (1985) 32 BLR 51, 2 Const LJ 189 provides an illustration of judicial flexibility by the use of implied terms, as does *Croudace Ltd v London Borough of Lambeth* (1986) 33 BLR 20, 6 Con LR 70, CA.

On special facts, the law may even go so far as to imply the whole contract, for example directly between a manufacturer and a third party end-user, particularly with regard to collateral warranties of performance or durability of a product.

The courts do not have the power to imply terms into a contract simply because such terms would be reasonable. However, judges have shown themselves able and willing to adapt statutory implied terms (for example as to quality in sales of goods) to new factual contexts by implying analogous terms at common law. An important example of this was the decision of the House of Lords in *Young and Marten Ltd v McManus Childs Ltd* [1969] 1 AC 454, [1968] 2 All ER 1169. But, the courts cannot also adapt by analogy the specific statutory controls on disclaimers or clauses excluding or restricting liability.

IMPLIED TERMS: DESIGN LIABILITY AND FITNESS FOR PURPOSE

In practice the parties often leave unexpressed many matters which later give rise to dispute. The courts therefore are left to fill the gaps by 'implying' (some would say 'imposing') obligations.

In some contexts these implied obligations in contract parallel a concurrent duty in tort (see, for example, the case which established that such concurrent duties could coexist in contract and tort: *Esso Petroleum Co Ltd v Mardon* [1976] QB 801, [1976] 2 All ER 5). It would be wrong, however, to assume that obligations implied in a contract, for example, upon a designer or builder, would only be those which he would otherwise bear in tort.

A contractor may owe, in contract but not in tort, a *strict* liability, by an implied contract term, in respect of fitness for purpose of the building. Whereas, by contrast, consultant designers such as architects and engineers will normally have an implied obligation only to use reasonable care and skill (as in the tort of negligence). Furthermore, contractors exercising design functions (even when employing qualified architects or engineers in house) may still attract the higher strict liability. The development of the law is well summarised by His Honour Judge Newey QC in *Basildon District Council v J E Lesser (Properties) Ltd* [1985] 1 All ER 20 at 27–29:

> 'In *Lynch v Thorne* [1956] 1 All ER 744, [1956] 1 WLR 303 a builder had agreed to complete a partially erected house in accordance with a plan and specification and did so, but a wall then leaked because it was of 9 inches brickwork only. The owner claimed against the builder, but lost in the Court of Appeal. Lord Evershed MR said [1956] 1 All ER 744 at 746, [1956] 1 WLR 303 at 306): "Where there is a written contract expressly setting forth the bargain between the parties, it is, as a general rule . . . well established that terms are to be implied only under the compulsion of some necessity . . . I am, however, prepared to assume for the purposes of this judgment that, whether or not it can be said that any necessity so compels . . . prima facie there is an implied covenant on the . . . builder's part that he will complete the house so as

to make it habitable. Nevertheless, although such a term is prima facie to be implied, it must according to well-established principle always yield to the express letter of the bargain."

In *Hancock v B W Brazier (Anerley) Ltd* [1966] 2 All ER 1, [1966] 1 WLR 1317 the defendants had agreed to erect houses in a proper and workmanlike manner each in accordance with a plan and specification. Two to four years later the floors and walls cracked due to the deleterious effects on concrete of sodium sulphate which unknown to the defendant was in hardcore used by them. The specification had merely referred to "hardcore" without further particularity. Diplock LJ (sitting at first instance) held that since there had been no definite specification concerning the hardcore to be used, as there had been with regard to the brickwork in *Lynch*'s case, there was room for an implied condition that the hardcore should be fit, proper and suitable and that the defendants were in breach of that condition. The Court of Appeal upheld Diplock LJ, Lord Denning MR saying ([1966] 2 All ER 901 at 903, [1966] 1 WLR 1317 at 1332):

> "... when a purchaser buys a house from a builder who contracts to build it, there is a threefold implication; that the builder will do his work in a good and workmanlike manner; that he will supply good and proper materials; and that it will be reasonably fit for human habitation".

In *Young and Marten Ltd v McManus Childs Ltd* [1969] 1 AC 454, [1968] 2 All ER 1169 sub-contractors had agreed with builders that they would roof houses with specified tiles which could only be bought from one manufacturer. They did so and the tiles cracked, because of defects which the sub-contractor could not have discovered. The House of Lords held that the builders' selection of tiles did not prevent there having been an implied warranty as to their quality, so that the sub-contractors were liable. Lord Reid said that it would have made a difference if the manufacturer had only been willing to sell on terms which excluded liability by him (see [1969] 1 AC 454 at 467, [1968] 2 All ER 1169 at 1172).

In *Independent Broadcasting Authority v EMI Electronics Ltd and BICC Construction Ltd* (1978) 11 BLR 29, CA the IBA had employed EMI under the terms of a written contract as main contractors for the design, construction and erection of a television mast, but had insisted that they sub-contract much of the work to BICC. The mast collapsed due to defects in design and IBA sued EMI for breach of contract and negligence and BICC for negligence. At first instance O'Connor J held EMI liable for breach of contract and BICC liable in both contract and negligence.

The Court of Appeal upheld the findings of breach of contract, but decided that BICC had not been negligent. The judgment of the courts was given by Roskill LJ who said (11 BLR 29 at 50–51):

> "... in relation to contracts for work and labour done and materials supplied corresponding obligations have long been implied as to the quality of the workmanship and the materials which would be used".

and, in respect of *Miller v Cannon Hill Estates Ltd* [1931] 2 KB 113 and *Hancock v B W Brazier (Anerley) Ltd* [1966] 2 All ER 1, [1966] 1 WLR 1317 and *Greaves & Co (Contractors) Ltd v Baynham, Meikle & Partners* [1975] 3 All ER 99, [1975] 1 WLR 1095, CA, that:

"It is not easy to see why if, in any of those cases, the builder had been guilty of bad design rather than of the supply of bad materials or bad workmanship, the result should have been different on the ground that, as has been contended, the matter of design should always be regarded as involving no higher duty than that of reasonable care . . ."

Roskill LJ said (11 BLR 29 at 52), giving the basis of the decision:

"We see no good reason . . . for not importing an obligation as to reasonable fitness for the purpose into these contracts or for importing a different obligation in relation to design from the obligation which plainly exists in relation to materials."

The IBA case went to the House of Lords (see (1981) 14 BLR 1). The House of Lords restored O'Connor J's finding that BICC had been negligent and did not find it necessary to decide whether EMI and BICC had each impliedly undertaken to provide a mast which was fit for its purpose, but Viscount Dilhorne (at 26) and Lord Fraser (at 44) each said words to the effect that they probably would have done so.

The implication of a term that a builder should provide a building which is fit for purpose imposes on him a higher duty than is ordinarily implied in a contract for the design of a building by an architect. The latter, like the engineer, solicitor, doctor and other professionally qualified persons, has only to use reasonable care and skill: see *Bolam v Friern Hospital Management Committee* [1957] 2 All ER 118, [1957] 1 WLR 582 and *Greaves & Co (Contractors) Ltd v Baynham, Meikle & Partners* [1974] 3 All ER 666, [1974] 1 WLR1261.

However, it would seem that if the professional person does not merely design, but makes something, it is to be implied that what he has made will be fit for purpose: see *Samuels v Davis* [1943] KB 526, [1943] 2 All ER 3, a case concerning the supply of false teeth by a dentist. Even where the professional man has merely designed, the circumstances may be such as to require that he take out what Lord Denning MR in *Greaves & Co*'s case ([1975] 3 All ER 99 at 105, [1975] 1 WLR 1095 at 1101) described as "special steps . . . in order to fulfil the duty of care". In *Greaves & Co*'s case an engineer had been engaged to design a warehouse, knowing that it was intended for the storage and movement of oil drums, and he was liable when it cracked under the weight of drums.'

So, in several instances, contractors undertaking design responsibilities are unable to take advantage of the lower standard of liability enjoyed by professional designers.

These terms which judges imply into contracts (because they are usual in the industry, or because they are necessary to make the contract work, or because the parties must have impliedly intended such terms) all share the characteristic that they are controllable by the parties. In this respect, such implied terms are very different from a new breed of implied terms by statute. Whereas terms implied by judges are subject to the contrary intention of the parties, terms implied by statute may not be capable of being varied or excluded by the parties.

STATUTORY IMPLIED TERMS

Important sources of implied terms are the Sale of Goods Act 1979 and the Supply of Goods and Services Act 1982. These statutes impose implied contractual warranties:

* that goods supplied shall correspond with any descriptions by which they are supplied;
* that goods supplied shall be of merchantable quality (as reasonably fit for the purpose or purposes for which such a service is commonly bought as it is reasonable to expect having regard to any description applied, the price paid (if relevant) and all other relevant circumstances);
* that goods supplied shall be reasonably fit for any particular purpose made known to the supplier where the purchaser is relying on the skill and expertise of the supplier.

If a transaction involves a supply of goods, then it will attract the implied terms under ss 12–15 of the Sale of Goods Act 1979 or Part I of the Supply of Goods and Services Act 1982. That is, unless the parties are able to provide otherwise, the supplier will warrant his title to supply the goods and the goods shall comply with any description by which they are supplied, be of merchantable quality, be reasonably fit for any particular purpose made known (where the buyer relies on the vendor) and the bulk shall correspond with any sample. Perhaps the most important aspect of these forms of contractual obligation to achieve results is that they are not instances of fault liability. Liability is strict. Reasonable care by the supplier is no defence. The obligations comprise in effect absolute undertakings that these matters shall be fulfilled. It becomes a commercial risk of the supplier, independent of the reason why the goods do not fulfil these obligations on delivery.

A second consequence of treating the transaction as a supply of goods is that the freedom of suppliers to contract out of the obligations just mentioned is significantly curtailed by the Unfair Contract Terms Act 1977. Indeed, users who purchase for private purposes, not in the course of a business, are absolutely entitled to these obligations as to title, quality, fitness for purpose and correspondence with description and sample, and the supplier is unable to contract out of them by contract terms or notices seeking to exclude or restrict such liabilities. Even users who purchase in the course of a business may be able to strike down any such contract terms or notices excluding or restricting these liabilities, as they will not be effective against such a business purchaser unless they are fair and reasonable in the circumstances (according to the way in which those terms are expressed in the Unfair Contract Terms Act 1977).

The implied obligations as to quality and fitness under the Sale of Goods Act 1979 and the Supply of Goods and Services Act 1982 broadly apply only at the time of delivery of the product (or transfer of risk in it) to the buyer/client. There is therefore at present no statutory obligation as to durability. So there is no such thing as a warranty period in law, unless the contract expressly stipulates one. However, if the contract does not provide for specific warranty periods then a kind of durability obligation could be inferred. It would have to be argued that the defect would not have arisen so soon if the design/material/workmanship required had been complied with. That will depend on difficult evidence as to industry standards of quality, use, operating conditions, failure rate, etc. There is another, quite different, way of expressing a period of quality/fitness exposure; that is by reference to the law on limitation of actions which defines within what period a claimant has to commence legal proceedings (see below).

However, what if the transaction is treated only as the supply of a service? It is curious that, by legislation, English law has a highly developed set of obligations which attach end result obligations to the supply of goods; yet, by contrast, the supply of services is not in general regulated to such a degree, even to the extent of an equivalent statutory set of implied terms which the parties could contract out of. Why should English law not similarly expect that a service should be of proper quality (like merchantable quality: as reasonably fit for the purpose or purposes for which such a service is commonly bought as it is reasonable to expect having regard to any description applied, the price paid (if relevant) and all other relevant circumstances) and be reasonably fit for any particular purpose made known to the supplier where the purchaser is relying on the skill and expertise of the supplier? So far, general terms implied by statute in contracts for the supply of services are the rather innocuous set of obligations provided by Part II of the Supply of Goods and Services Act 1982 (in summary, that reasonable skill and care will be exercised in the provision of the services). Even apart from the statute it seems likely that these rather self-evident terms would have been implied into any such contract anyway.

However, the Supply of Goods (Implied Terms) Act 1973 and the Supply of Goods and Services Act 1982 extend to supplies of goods other than by sale, similar obligations as to title, quality, fitness and correspondence with description and sample as would apply in the case of a sale. Furthermore, these obligations will apply if the substance of the transactions does comprise a supply of goods. Section 13 of the Unfair Contract Terms Act could invalidate attempts at exclusion or restriction of the relevant obligation or duty. Even if the statutory implied terms were held not so applicable, because technically the supply was held not to be of goods, the courts could still use their common law powers to imply equivalent terms at common law. But in this latter instance the judges would not have the power also to extend the statutory controls on excluding or restricting such liabilities.

LEGAL CONTROLS ON DISCLAIMERS AND LIMITATIONS OF LIABILITY

At common law, liability may be limited or disclaimed altogether by appropriately clear wording. Obviously this can be by contractual agreement. Duties can also be prevented from arising in tort (but see, eg, *Harris v Wyre District Council* [1989] 2 All ER 514, [1989] 2 WLR 790, HL in relation to s 13 of the Unfair Contract Terms Act 1977).

There are three obstacles which the common law places in the path of the person trying to rely on an exemption or limitation clause to exclude or restrict his liability:

(1) That the clause was not sufficiently notified to the claimant.
(2) That on construction it does not apply to the event which has occurred.

(3) That the doctrine of privity may prevent a contractual clause being used against someone who is not a party to the contract.

These are important obstacles because if a clause fails at any one of these, it is unnecessary to consider the Unfair Contract Terms Act 1977 (UCTA).

Notification

A person relying on an exemption or limitation clause must do what is reasonably sufficient to bring it to the notice of the claimant alleged to be bound by it: *Parker v South Eastern Rly Co* (1978) 2 CPD 416.

> 'In cases in which the contract is contained in a railway ticket or other unsigned document, it is necessary to prove that an alleged party was aware, or ought to have been aware, of its terms and conditions. These cases have no application when the document has been signed. When a document containing contractual terms is signed, then, in the absence of fraud, or, I will add, misrepresentation, the party signing it is bound and it is wholly immaterial whether he has read the document or not.' (Scrutton LJ, *L'Estrange v Graucob* [1934] 2 KB 394).

This requirement of notice is equally applicable where the exempting provision is to be used as a defence to a tort action. However, there are dicta suggesting this may prove a difficult path (see, for example, per Lord Denning MR in *White v Blackmore* [1972] 2 QB 651, [1972] 3 All ER 158, CA).

The degree of notice is also likely to be treated as significant for the purposes of the reasonableness test under UCTA 1977.

Construction

Ambiguities will be construed '*contra proferentem*' (against the party relying on the clause). This approach of the courts is particularly strict in relation to liability for negligence. The classic guidance is found in Lord Morton's judgment in *Canada SS Lines v R* [1952] AC 192 at 208:

> 'Their Lordships think that the duty of a court in approaching the consideration of such clauses may be summarised as follows:
> (1) If the clause contains language which expressly exempts the person in whose favour it is made (hereafter called "the proferens") from the consequence of the negligence of his own servants, effect must be given to that provision. . . .
> (2) If there is no express reference to negligence, the court must consider whether the words used are wide enough, in their ordinary meaning, to cover negligence on the part of the servants of the proferens. If a doubt arises at this point, it must be resolved against the proferens. . . .
> (3) If the words used are wide enough for the above purpose, the courts must then consider whether "the head of damage may be based on some ground other than that of negligence", to quote again Lord Greene in the *Alderslade* case. The "other ground" must not be so fanciful or remote that the proferens cannot be supposed to have desired protection against it; but subject to this qualification, which is no doubt to be implied from Lord Green's words, the existence of a possible head of damage other than that of negligence is fatal to the

proferens even if the words used are prima facie wide enough to cover negligence on the part of his servants.'

However, this has been qualified by the Court of Appeal: *The Raphael* [1982] 2 Lloyds Rep 42. There it was suggested that parallel and co-extensive obligations both in the tort of negligence and contract would not give rise to Lord Morton's third proposition. Also, the third test should be assessed realistically in the light of the parties' intentions.

> 'Thus, if an exemption clause of the kind we are considering excludes liability for negligence expressly, then the courts will give effect to the exemption. If it does not do so expressly, but its wording is clear and wide enough to do so by implication, then the question becomes whether the contracting parties so intended. If the only head of liability upon which the clause can bite in the circumstances of a given cause is negligence, and the parties did or must be deemed to have applied their minds to this eventuality, then clearly it is not difficult for a court to hold that this was what the parties intended—that is its proper construction. Indeed, to hold otherwise would be contrary to commonsense. On the other hand if there is a head of liability upon which the clause could bite in addition to negligence then, because it is more unlikely than not a party will be ready to excuse his other contracting party from the consequences of the latter's negligence, the clause will generally be construed as not covering negligence. If the parties did or must be deemed to have applied their minds to the potential alternative head of liability at the time when the contract was made then, in the absence of any express reference to negligence, the courts can sensibly only conclude that the relevant clause was not intended to cover negligence and will refuse so to construe it. In other words, the court asks itself what in all the relevant circumstances the parties intended the alleged exemption clause to mean.' (May LJ, at 49/50).

In this case, as in others, there are dicta that the passing of UCTA 1977 now enables the courts to take a less strained approach to construction. They are more likely to try to give effect to the parties' intentions, than to defeat the clause applying to negligence. Certainly, the courts seem willing to construe limitation of damages more benevolently than outright exemption clauses: *Ailsa Craig Fishing Co Ltd v Malvern Fishing Co Ltd* [1983] 1 All ER 101, [1983] 1 WLR 964, HL.

Statutory controls

However, certain statutes provide specific obligations and then purport to prevent any contracting out of that obligation. Instances include the Defective Premises Act 1972 and the product liability provisions contained within the Consumer Protection Act 1987. Otherwise, the general legislative interference with freedom of contract in this area, imposing limits on parties' abilities to restrict or limit their legal liabilities, is contained in UCTA 1977.

The title of the Unfair Contract Terms Act 1977 is something of a misnomer. It does not control terms because they are 'unfair'. Rather, it has specific provisions, applying in limited circumstances and mainly to exclusion and limitation of liability clauses. However, it is not limited to contractual obligations and liabilities.

The effects of the provisions of the Act may be summarised as follows (leaving aside certain exceptions from the Act's application such as international supply contracts):

(1) The Act applies, with few exceptions, only to 'business liability'.
(2) Liability in negligence (which includes a contractual duty to exercise reasonable care and skill) causing death or personal injury cannot be excluded or restricted.
(3) Consumers' (ie private persons dealing with businesses) rights against their immediate contractual suppliers, in respect of the description, quality and fitness for purpose of goods supplied, cannot be excluded or restricted.
(4) Otherwise, liabilities for negligence and for misrepresentation and in respect of description, quality and fitness for purpose of goods, can be excluded or restricted but subject to a reasonableness test.
(5) The only control on freedom of contract in respect of more general contractual obligations is to impose a reasonableness test (in favour of a consumer or a person whose contract is on the other party's written standard terms of business) on excluding or restricting liability for breach of contract, or on claiming to be entitled to render no contractual performance or a performance substantially different from that reasonably expected.

There are some guidelines in Sch 2 of the Act for the application of the reasonableness test in supply of goods cases. Otherwise, there is a difficulty of predicting the effect of the reasonableness tests in this Act, in view of the policy of 'minimum guidance by appellate courts' adopted by the House of Lords in *George Mitchell (Chesterhall) Ltd v Finney Lock Seeds* [1983] 2 AC 803, [1983] 2 All ER 737. Lord Bridge expressed the House of Lords' view: that appellate courts should refrain from interference with trial judges' application of what is reasonable in the particular circumstances of a particular case.

The unpredictability of the consequences of this policy is inevitable: see, for example, its application in *Phillips Products v Hyland* [1987] 2 All ER 620, [1987] 1 WLR 659n, CA.

One general factor that has emerged is that clauses are likely to be found reasonable if they are the product of negotiation between interested parties 'on both sides' of the industry concerned. (See the *George Mitchell* case above; *R W Green Ltd v Cade Bros Farms* [1978] 1 Lloyd's Rep 602; and *Walker v Boyle* [1982] 1 All ER 634, [1982] 1 WLR 495.)

Otherwise, illustration may be derived from cases. See by way of general example *Stevenson v Nationwide Building Society* (1984) 272 Estates Gazette 663.

In *Rees Hough v Redland Reinforced Plastics Ltd* (1984) 27 BLR 136, 2 Con LR 109, His Honour Judge Newey balanced the considerations in the following way:

> 'Under Section 11(1) the requirement of reasonableness was that the term should be fair and reasonable having regard to the circumstances when the contract was made.
>
> Considerations which support Redland's contention that their standard conditions were reasonable were: that the contract was between two companies and while Redland was the larger, Rees Hough were capable of looking after themselves; all or most concrete pipe manufacturers contract on the basis of standard terms; Rees Hough had long been aware that Redland had standard terms; Rees Hough had never attempted to negotiate alterations to these terms.
>
> Considerations which were against Redland's contention that their terms were reasonable were that Rees Hough were regular customers of Redland and major purchasers of their jacking pipes; when in the past pipes had been defective, Redland had not relied on the terms but had paid compensation to Rees Hough; Redland did not refer to the terms during the negotiations of the contract; the sums paid by Rees Hough for the pipes were substantial.
>
> Obviously some considerations carried more weight than others; for example that Rees Hough did not lack ability to look after themselves was probably the weightiest in favour of upholding the terms; and, for example, that Redland had never in the past sought to rely on them in their dealings with Rees Hough might well be the weightiest against them. The balance of the considerations was strongly against the terms being reasonable. Therefore Redland could not rely upon the standard terms of sale to invalidate the express and implied terms between themselves and Rees Hough.'

In *Stag Line Ltd v Tyne Shiprepair Group Ltd* [1984] 2 Lloyds Rep 211 Staughton J emphasised that the 'relative bargaining power' test should *not* be applied 'week by week' depending on, for example, how busy the contractor was. However, the capricious effect of a clause requiring defective work to be returned to the contractor's yard for repair was such as to make it unreasonable: it was a capricious allocation of risk because it took no account of the differing circumstances, and costs, of a breakdown.

THE SPECIAL POSITION OF INDEMNITIES

Indemnities, if carefully drawn, have the advantage of not being subject to UCTA 1977 (except as against persons dealing as private consumers, see s 4) and also of enjoying a limitation period which begins only when the primary liability to be indemnified has been ascertained.

But indemnity clauses will be strictly construed:

> 'While an indemnity clause may be regarded as the obverse of an exempting clause, when considering the meaning of such a clause one must, I think, regard it as even more inherently improbable that one party should agree to discharge the liability of the other party for acts for which he is responsible. In my opinion it is the case that the imposition by the proferens on the other party of liability to indemnify him against the consequence of his own negligence must be imposed

by very clear words.' (Viscount Dilhorne, *Smith v South Wales Switchgear Ltd* [1978] 1 WLR 165 at 168.)

THE DOCTRINE OF PRIVITY

A central pillar of English contract law is the doctrine of 'privity': namely, that only the parties to a contract are entitled to the rights it creates, and only the parties to it can be burdened with the obligations it imposes. Third parties who are not privy to the contract, as contracting parties, cannot take advantage of the contractual duties. This doctrine puts a natural limit on the range of possible claimants in respect of quality and fitness for purpose obligations. Only contracting parties can claim. Therefore in contract law there is no particular policy need to restrict the kinds of losses that are recoverable as damages if a duty is broken. Tortious liability to third parties does need to be restricted in some way to prevent the courts being flooded with claims: the normal mechanism is to allow losses to be recoverable only where these relate to physical harm to person or property. We shall see that pure economic losses are not normally recoverable in tort. Contract law does not make this distinction. It allows all losses (whether physical or wholly financial) to be recoverable as damages so long as they may fairly and reasonably be considered either: (a) as arising naturally, according to the usual course of things, from the breach of contract; or (b) such as may reasonably be supposed to be in the contemplation of both parties at the time they made the contract, as the probable result of breach of it. Hence, even unusually remote, purely economic, losses can be recovered in contract if within the contemplation of the parties when they made the contract. (See *Hadley v Baxendale* (1854) 9 Exch 341; *The Heron II* [1969] 1 AC 350, [1967] 3 All ER 686 and *Parsons (Livestock) Ltd v Uttley Ingham & Co Ltd* [1978] QB 791, [1978] 1 All ER 525.)

DISTINGUISHING FEATURES OF CONTRACTUAL LIABILITY

Thus the features of contract law that principally distinguished it from the law of tortious negligence are:

(i) *obligations of 'result'*: performance can be 'guaranteed' in contract. Binding promissory undertakings that a certain state of affairs will be achieved are the hallmark of contractual obligations.
(ii) *strict liability*: contractual obligations can be broken without fault, if they are undertaken in the first place as unqualified promises giving rise to absolute obligations. It would be no defence that the party obliged took all reasonable care.
(iii) *power to limit or exclude liability, or be indemnified*: contracts are just as useful to reduce liabilities (such as, for example, would otherwise arise in tort) as to create them. Contract also offers the power to shift the burden of liability by a matching indemnity agreement.
(iv) *privity*: despite many qualifications, it remains a fundamental rule

that the benefits and burdens of a contract are limited to the parties to the contract.

(v) *basis for compensation*: it follows from (i) above (obligations of result) that the normal basis for assessing contract damages is 'cost of cure', ie the cost of achieving the performance promised under the contract, or the profits lost by its non performance. Technically, these are 'expectation measure' damages. Contract claims are not restricted to reliance losses or wasted expenditure. Also, it follows from (iv) above (privity) that the range of claims is not indeterminate and so contract law has no objection to pure economic losses being recoverable (cf the range of claims in tort, which being indeterminate, need some delimiter like privity: hence 'proximity' or 'reliance' or 'damage').

(vi) *Limitation Acts*: the law treats the wrong as the breach of contract, not the resultant damage. So, time is likely to start running against a contract claimant earlier than against a tort claimant.

LEGAL OBSTACLES TO MOUNTING A SUCCESSFUL CLAIM

There are certain fundamental legal obstacles to be surmounted if any type of claim is to be successful:

— the burden of *proving* the loss
— the need to show that the loss was *caused* by the relevant acts or omissions being relied on
— establishing the legal *quantum* (amount) of the claim
— showing that the loss is not too remote
— and that it could not have been *mitigated* by reasonable conduct.

Proving the loss

The burden of proof is of course normally on the claimant: he who asserts must prove.

Causation

This principle is well illustrated by the judgment of the Court of Appeal in *Lubenham Fidelities and Investments Co Ltd v South Pembrokeshire District Council* (1986) 33 BLR 39.

Lubenhams, as contractors, lost their claim against the architects, Wigley Fox. This was because Lubenhams broke the chain of causation by persisting in the suspension of the works and by disregarding the clause 25 notices. They alone were responsible for what followed and for the termination of the contracts.

Their Lordships reached this conclusion with some reluctance because the negligence of Wigley Fox was undoubtedly the source from which this unfortunate sequence of events began to flow but their negligence was overtaken and, in the court's view, overwhelmed by the serious breach of contract by Lubenhams.

A slight consolation for contractors at least lies in the court's recognition that *some* angry reaction by contractors to improper deductions on a certificate (such as even temporary cessation of work) would have been 'a natural and reasonable consequence of the issue of the certificates'.

Remoteness of damage

The law allows only those losses which are not too 'remote'. The contractual rules are stated in *Hadley v Baxendale* (1854) 9 Exch 341.

> 'Such losses as may fairly and reasonably be considered as either arising—(1st rule) "naturally", ie "according to the usual course of things" from the breach of contract: or
> (2nd rule) "such as may reasonably be supposed to be in the contemplation of both parties at the time they made the contract, as the probable result of breach of it".'

The application of these rules obviously depends upon the particular circumstances of each case, but their importance in relation to the construction industry is increased by two factors:

(a) The recognition of *Minter v Welsh Health Technical Services Organisation* (1980) 13 BLR 1 that similar criteria apply to determine what is recoverable as 'direct loss and/or expense' under the JCT Forms; and,
(b) that even after the House of Lords' decision in *President of India v La Pintada* [1985] AC 104, [1984] 2 All ER 773, financing charges may still be recoverable as damages for non-payment of a sum of money, if the claim can be brought within the contemplation requirements in *Hadley v Baxendale*.

The quantum of damages recoverable

The measure of damages recoverable in a contract claim is as stated in *Robinson v Harman* (1948) 1 Exch 850:

> 'The rule of common law is that where a party sustains a loss by reason of a breach of contract, he is, so far as money can do it, to be placed in the same situation, with respect to damages, as if the contract had been performed.'

However, once again this is qualified by other factors:

- the rules on 'mitigation of damage' by reasonable conduct on the part of the victim
- the possibility of framing the claim on 'wasted expenditure' principle rather than for lost income.

'Wasted expenditure' as a possible basis for damages

There is some controversy over whether a victim of a breach of contract should be free to choose to recover wasted expenditure as damages if that is a more advantageous basis than computing lost profits.

Anglia Television Ltd v Reed [1972] 1 QB 60, [1971] 3 All ER 690 may be explained as turning on the contemplation of the parties that such expenditure would be wasted as a consequence of the breach.

The consequences of such an approach would be that even *pre-contract* expenditure would be recoverable (even though by definition it can hardly have been incurred in reliance on the contract).

The objection to such an approach is that it allows a contractor to an unprofitable contract to cast the burden of the bad bargain back on to the employer even though the unprofitable aspect of the contract is not *caused* by the employer's breach.

Now, however, this issue must be considered in the light of two cases: *C and P Haulage v Middleton* [1983] 3 All ER 94, [1983] 1 WLR 1461 and *CCC Films (London) Ltd v Impact Quadrant Films Ltd* [1985] QB 16, [1984] 3 All ER 298, the implications of which are discussed in [1984] CILL 89.

LESSENING THE LIABILITY BY ALLEGING THAT THE CLAIMANT DID NOT ACT REASONABLY IN RESPONSE

There are various ways of lessening a contracting party's liability for a defect by alleging that the other party did not act reasonably in response to the breach.

In *Basildon District Council v J E Lesser (Properties) Ltd* [1985] QB 839, [1985] 1 All ER 20, Judge Newey held that the concept of blameworthiness as introduced by tort was irrelevant in contract; and so he held the defence of contributory negligence inapplicable in contract.

However, the Court of Appeal in *Forsikringsaktieselskapet Vesta v Butcher* [1988] 2 All ER 43, [1988] 3 WLR 565 held that contributory negligence could be capable of being a good defence covering a limited class of contractual obligations, namely contractual duties of care (ie contractual obligations to exercise reasonable care and skill, analogous to tortious duties of care).

There are other ways of lessening one's own liability by alleging that the claimant asked unreasonably; such as by arguments as to causation, remoteness of damage (see eg *Dodd Properties v Canterbury City Council* [1980] 1 All ER 928, [1980] 1 WLR 433) and the requirement that the claimant mitigate his loss (for example, on the last point, compare *The Solholt* [1983] 1 Lloyds Rep 605 with *Cory & Son Ltd v Wingate Investments (London Colney) Ltd* (1978) 17 BLR 104). In effect, these notions introduce a kind of contributory fault into contract law, without reliance on the Law Reform (Contributory Negligence) Act 1945. However, unlike the 1945 Act, they do not directly enable any percentage apportionment of responsibility to be reflected in the award of damages.

There is also a possibility that the claimant is himself under a duty in the law of negligence, or by an equivalent implied term in contract, to warn of the consequences: see below, *Duty to warn*.

If an employer were claiming for the cost of remedial work done by another contractor, there could also be the argument that the extent of the work was not reasonable (see, for example, *Kaliszewska v John Claque & Partners* (1984) 5 Con LR 62 and *Governors of the Hospitals for Sick Children v McLaughlin & Harvey plc* [1987] CILL 372).

REQUIREMENT TO 'MITIGATE' DAMAGES

Sir John Donaldson MR summed up this principle in *The Solholt* [1983] 1 Lloyds Rep 605 at 608:

'A plaintiff is under no duty to mitigate his loss, despite the habitual use by lawyers of the phrase "duty to mitigate". He is completely free to act as he judges to be in his interests. On the other hand, a defendant is not liable for all loss suffered by the consequence of his so acting. A defendant is only liable for such part of the plantiff's loss as is properly to be regarded as caused by the defendant's breach of duty. As Viscount Haldane LC put it in *British Westinghouse Electric and Manufacturing Co Ltd v Underground Electric Rlys Co of London Ltd* [1912] AC 673 at 689: "The fundamental basis is thus compensation for pecuniary loss naturally flowing from the breach; but this first principal is qualified by a second, which imposes on a plaintiff the duty of taking all reasonable steps to mitigate the loss consequent on the breach, and debars him from claiming any part of the damage which is due to his neglect to take such steps." '

LIQUIDATED DAMAGES

There is a way, apart from 'ascertainment' and 'certification', of avoiding uncertainty of damages claims. If the parties are able to make a genuine pre-estimate, at the time of contracting, of the losses likely to flow from a particular breach, then a *liquidated damages* clause may be used. However, the clause will fail if it is found in law to be a penalty clause.

WHAT IS A PENALTY CLAUSE?

The following guidelines are derived from the classic formulation in Lord Dunedin's judgment in *Dunlop Pneumatic Tyre Co Ltd v New Garage and Motor Co Ltd* [1915] AC 79.

(1) The *words* 'penalty' or 'liquidated damages' even if used are not conclusive.
(2) The essence of a penalty is a payment of money stipulated *in terrorem* of the offending party; the essence of liquidated damages is a genuine covenanted pre-estimate of damage.
(3) The question whether the sum stipulated is penalty or liquidated damages is a question of construction in each particular contract, judged as at the time it was made, not the time of breach.
(4) Aids to construction as a penalty are:
   (a) If the sum is extravagant and unconscionable in amount in comparison with the greatest loss that could be proved to have followed from the breach.
   (b) If the breach is non-payment of money and the sum stipulated is greater than the sum which ought to have been paid.
   (c) There is a presumption (but no more) that it is a penalty when 'a single lump sum is made payable by way of compensation, on the occurrence of one or more or all of several events, some of which may occasion serious and others but trifling damage'.

(d) (On the other hand) a sum may be a genuine pre-estimate even where the consequences of the breach are such as to make precise pre-estimation almost an impossibility.

However, it appears still to be the law, if one can avoid a mere sham, that the rules as to penalties, and the unenforceability of such clauses, do not apply to provisions which exact a sum (even an extravagant one) as the 'price' for the exercise by the other party of a contractual power of termination of the contract other than for breach (see *Bridge v Campbell Discount Co Ltd* [1962] AC 600, [1962] 1 All ER 385).

WHEN LIQUIDATED DAMAGES CLAUSES MAY BE DISPLACED: TIME AT LARGE

The benefits of clarity of definition of the completion date, and its extension, are obvious. However, extension of time clauses are construed strictly and there may therefore be events giving rise to delay which are not provided for by the clause.

If the employer causes such a delay, to which the extension provision does not apply, then time is said to be 'at large'.

The result is that the express completion date ceases to bind and there is an implied obligation to complete *within a reasonable time.* A liquidated clause operable upon failure to complete by the contractual completion date would thus be displaced, though the contractor will be liable at common law for any damages arising through any breach of the substituted completion obligation.

Although this may be advantageous for a contractor's claim, there arises once again the uncertainties inherent in 'reasonableness' based rules of law. The time schedules in the contract would be evidentiary of what was reasonable, but not more than that. However, the burden of proof would be on the employer to show that completion was not within a reasonable time.

OTHER LEGAL BASES FOR CLAIMS

Apart from claims for damages in respect of a breach of contract, in accordance with common law principles, claims may also be made on other bases in law:

(1) On a 'restitutionary' basis for a reasonable sum, for example, by claiming a '*quantum meruit*', rather than in contract.
(2) In accordance with the conditions of a *standard form* contract.
(3) By alleging a breach of duty arising at common law other than in contract: such as in the *tort of negligence* or for *misrepresentation.*

CONTRACT CLAIMS ARISING OUTSIDE STANDARD FORMS ALTOGETHER

These could arise in many ways, including:

(1) 'tailor made' contracts;
(2) an 'implied contract' arising by conduct between parties who do not otherwise record their agreement;
(3) a 'new' contract arising out of continued contractual performance after 'termination' of a standard form contract;

(4) 'collateral' undertakings, for example, to obtain a necessary statutory consent or licence (*Strongman (1945) Ltd v Sincock* [1955] 2 QB 525, [1955] 3 All ER 90).

What principles govern such claims?

The contractor's right to payment may by this route become severely curtailed by the law on 'entire contracts' (see *Hoenig v Isaacs* [1952] 2 All ER 176).

Obviously all matters alleged to be governed by contract will have to be resolved, as best they may, by attempting to infer the contractual intention of the parties, but claims in respect of rights to progress payments, fluctuations, indemnities, etc, will be difficult in the absence of express agreement. Such rights would be hard to imply. Indeed a lack of certainty as to essential terms, at the time of contract formation, will prevent the finding of a contract at all.

The courts look more favourably upon uncertainty arising during performance of an otherwise certain contract, for example because of a provision stating that rates will be fixed only for a period but not then providing for what was to occur thereafter. (Consider *Constable Hart & Co Ltd v Peter Lind & Co Ltd* (1978) 9 BLR 1.)

NON-CONTRACTUAL BASES OF CLAIM

Quantum meruit

Strictly this term applies to a claim in restitution (quasi-contract) for the value of services rendered where there is no contractual entitlement to payment. It could therefore arise in our context, for example:

— where no contract was every concluded;
— where the contract is unenforceable for illegality (though even a restitutionary claim may here be barred) or (rarely) void for mistake;
— where the contract is discharged by frustration (a 'hardly ever' doctrine? *Davis Contractors Ltd v Fareham UDC* [1956] AC 696, [1956] 2 All ER 145), though the contractual regime would apply to rights and liabilities accruing before the time of discharge (subject to the Law Reform (Frustrated Contracts) Act 1943);
— where the contract is 'entire' (complete performance is a condition precedent to the right to payment) and the employer unlawfully prevents completion of performance.

However, the term is also used loosely to describe a contractual claim for a reasonable sum in circumstances where the contract rates cease to be applicable. An instance of rates being fixed only for a certain period has been given above.

Perhaps the most important illustration is that where the contract (standard form or otherwise) has been treated as discharged because of a breach by the employer, or where the employer has, for example, by failure to issue a direction or variation order, rendered performance of the contractor's obligations impossible. (Consider *Holland, Hannen & Cubitts (Northern) Ltd v Welsh Technical Services Organisation* (1981) 18 BLR 80.)

In either circumstances, if the contractor continued with the works (without affirming the contract) he would be entitled to a reasonable sum, rather than contract rates, if that were advantageous to him.

If the contractor decided not to continue, then important differences in the legal assessment of claims could arise as between whether he chooses to exercise an express contractual power of determination or rather regards himself as discharged from the contract by reason of the employer's repudiatory breach. (Consider the implications of *Thomas Feather & Co (Bradford) Ltd v Keighley Corpn* (1953) 52 LGR 30 and of *Lintest Builders v Roberts* (1980) 13 BLR 39.)

Misrepresentation

Rescission of the contract for misrepresentation would rarely be available in building contract cases because the necessary condition of *restitutio in integrum* could not be achieved after commencement of the works.

Nevertheless, there is a valuable right to damages conferred by s 2(1) of the Misrepresentation Act 1967 in respect of a negligent misrepresentation (untrue statement of fact) which induces the making of a contract. The liability might be easier to establish than having to assert a duty of care in negligence, and, more importantly, the burden of proof is reversed. To avoid liability the representor has to prove that 'he had reasonable ground to believe and did believe up to the time the contract was made that the facts represented were true'.

Section 2(2) also confers on the court the power to award damages in lieu of rescission.

Estoppel

The power of modern principles of 'estoppel' should be carefully recognised. They are particularly important in relation to variation and waiver; but they have far reaching significance since words and conduct, particularly in renegotiations, can precipitate binding obligations in circumstances which would not have been sufficient to give rise to contractual liability in the first place.

In the construction industry, there is increasing evidence of estoppel being used to extend the normal periods under the Limitation Acts for time-barring actions (see for example, *Kaliszewska v John Claque & Partners* (1984) 5 Con LR 62; *Low v R J Haddock Ltd* (1985) 6 Con LR 122; and *Billam v Cheltenham Borough Council* (1984) 3 Con LR 99). The principle is no less applicable to defects liability period and any other protection against exposure to liability.

Use of estoppel in respect of employer's promises to pay extra

At present, however, the law still requires evidence of the presence of 'consideration' in order to render binding a new promise (not under seal) to pay more in respect of an existing obligation of a contractor. The limitations of the principle of estoppel, and consequential harshness, can be illustrated by the two Canadian cases: *R C H Enterprises v La Batisse d'Acier Hercule* (1977) 16 NBR (2d) 338; and *Gilbert Steel v University Construction* (1976) 67 DLR (3d) 606. Contrast the English case of *D & C Builders v Rees* [1966] 2 QB 617, [1965] 3 All ER 837.

STANDARD FORMS OF CONSTRUCTION CONTRACT

The standard forms of contract in regular use in the construction industry, such as the JCT 1980 Family of Forms for Building Works and the ICE Conditions 5th Ed for Civil Engineering, can have the advantage of clarifying the contractual obligations, and providing a means of transforming what would otherwise be general liability to be argued over into a debt with the advantages of summary procedure. But, subject to the express terms of any particular contract, the latter does not normally preclude the right to sue for damages for breach of contract.

WHAT ARE THE CONTRACT PROVISIONS?

There are an infinite number of possible forms and variations: all will depend on construction of the contract in the particular case. Great care should be taken to assess the effect of special provisions adopted or drafted for the project, as opposed to standard form conditions.

Generally a building 'contract' may comprise various documents, such as:

- tender documents
- acceptance of tender
- articles of agreement
- conditions of contract
- drawings
- bills of quantities
- specification

and any other document appropriate to the project. Again, generally speaking, the fact that bills of quantities or a specification are used is not conclusive that they form part of the contract documents.

The standard forms, such as JCT and ICE, expressly stipulate what are the contract documents (JCT 80 cl 2.1; ICE 5th Ed article 2). JCT 80 stipulates (cl 2.2) that the contract bills shall not override the articles of agreement, the conditions or appendix. The ICE conditions provide (cl 5) as a general principle that the documents are to be mutually explanatory, and they confer on the engineer power to issue appropriate instructions in the event of ambiguities or discrepancies. This illustrates the wider point, distinctive of ICE, that the engineer has very wide powers indeed.

MAJOR TYPES OF CONTRACT

The major differences between types of construction contract may be illustrated by reference to (a) the provisions for 'pricing' the works and (b) the extent of the obligations undertaken by the contractor.

(a) Different bases for 'pricing' the works

Lump sum contracts

Lump sum contracts, such as JCT 80, with or without quantities, comprise contracts to complete a whole work for a specific sum. It is a matter of construction whether such a contract is *entire*, ie that the complete performace is a condition precedent to the obligation of the employer to pay nothing at all.

Typically, the contract will provide for the right to interim payments as the work proceeds; eg upon certification by the architect or engineer (JCT 80 cl 30; ICE 5th, cl 60). But where retention money is to be held until completion, then the contract may be entire as to the retention, complete performance being a condition precedent to the right to the release of the residue of the retention.

Also, typically, variations and omissions will be ordered during the progress of the works, for which adjustments to the contract sum must be made. The actual sum payable will therefore often be very different from the original lump sum stated. But the principle of payment remains that the lump sum is so adjusted: the actual work is not measured and priced according to contract rates.

'Measure and value', 're-measurement' contracts

Examples of 'measure and value', 're-measurement' contracts are the ICE 5th Ed (consider cl 1(1)(i), 52(2), 55 and 56) and JCT 80 with *Approximate* Quantities. Here the actual work done is measured and valued according to the rates or manner laid down in the contract. So the bills of quantities perform a different function. In a lump sum contract, they define the work for which that sum is payable. Here they provide a schedule of rates and units of measurement.

Once again, by clear words, the contract may on its construction be *entire* as to the whole or part of the sum ascertained to be payable by the employer.

'Cost-plus' contract

An example of a 'cost-plus' contract is the JCT Fixed Fee Form of Prime Cost Contract. Here, the contractor is to be paid the actual cost to him of the work, plus the amounts pr ided in the contract for the contractor's overheads and profit. This method makes the employer particularly dependent on the reliability and efficiency of the contractor, though the contract may be drafted to give some protection to the employer, for example against waste.

As before, whether the parties intend that the completion of the work shall be a condition precedent to the right to payment is a matter of construction.

(b) Contracts differing according to the extent of the contractors' obligation

(i) The degree of prior contractual definition of the works

The contract documents may define the works:

— either *exactly*: as where bills of quantities are used, precisely determining the extent of the works. This enables more accurate pricing in

advance and reduces the potential for disputes as to what is extra work. Provision would still of course be made for variations and omissions;
— or only in *general terms.*

Here, the contractor must do everything impliedly necessary to complete the works as described in the contract documents.

If the contract is a lump sum contract (for example JCT without quantities and with only a widely defined specification) the contractor is at greater risk than if the works had been precisely defined. The sum needs to have provided for the risk. There will be uncertainty whether particular items are to be done within the contract sum, or to be paid for additionally as extras.

If the contract is a 're-measurement' or 'cost-plus' contract, then most of these difficulties do not arise, since the contractor will be paid for the work actually done.

(ii) Responsibility for design: 'employer-designed' contracts vs 'design and build' contracts

The traditional JCT Standard Form and the ICE Conditions assume 'employer-designed' works. So risks associated with defective design or unsuitability for purpose are not borne by the contractor. However, even under these contracts, the contractor could be liable for defects of workmanship or materials; or have to bear the loss or expense associated with discrepancies in the documents which he finds but does not notify to the architect. (JCT 80 cls 2.3, 6.1.2, 26.2.3.)

Also, under such a contract albeit of the traditional kind for employer-designed works, the documents may be drafted expressly to require of the contractor specific design obligations or warranties.

By contrast, under a 'design and build' or 'package-deal' contract, the works are wholly, or partly *contractor-designed*: hence the version of JCT 80 Standard Form 'With Contractor's Design' (or the Contractor's Design Supplement) 1981.

The degree and uncertainty of liability of the contractor increases considerably in proportion to the extent of design responsibility which he undertakes under the contract. The problem that arises is how to make appropriate financial provision for such liability, or to circumscribe it by contractual limitations.

The Standard Form of Building Contract With Contractor's Design 1981 Edition states the contractor's basic 'design and build' obligations in the following words:

> '2.1 The contractor shall upon and subject to the conditions carry out and complete the works . . . and for that purpose shall complete the design for the works including the selection of any specifications for any kinds and standards of the material and goods and workmanship to be used in the construction of the works so far as not described or stated in the employer's requirements or contractor's proposals.
>
> . . .
>
> 2.5.1 Insofar as the design of the works is comprised in the contractor's proposals and in what the contractor is to complete under clause 2 and in accordance with the employer's requirements and the conditions (including any further design which the contractor is to carry

> out as a result of a change in the employer's requirements), the contractor shall have in respect of any defect or insufficiency in such design the like liability to the employer, whether under statute or otherwise, as would an architect or, as the case may be, other appropriate professional designer holding himself out as competent to take on work for such design who, acting independently under a separate contract with the employer, had supplied such design for or in connection with works to be carried out and completed by a building contractor not being the supplier of the design.'

The intent of this latter provision is evident, and it makes the definition of the contractor's *design* obligation depend upon the law governing liability of architects.

GENERAL FEATURES OF STANDARD FORMS OF CONSTRUCTION CONTRACT

The significance of the total of the priced bills of quantities at the time of acceptance of the tender is fundamentally different as between JCT and ICE. Under the JCT Standard Form With Quantities, being a lump sum contract, the total to which the contractor is entitled (subject to adjustments below) is the 'contract sum'. Under ICE, the expressions 'tender total' and 'contract price' have little significance, since the total to which the contractor is entitled becomes ascertained by remeasurement and valuation.

Errors of pricing are in general to be borne by the contractor (which can have a consequential effect on pricing of variations) whereas errors of description and measurement of the works are in general to be borne by the employer (JCT 80 2.2.2.2, and 14.2; ICE cl 55).

Otherwise there are elaborate and extensive provisions under both regimes for adjustments of the total payable to take account of, for example:

- *Variations* of the work whether arising directly from additions instructed by the architect/engineer or because of errors of description in the bills (JCT 80 cl 13, ICE cl 51 and 52).
- *Fluctuations*: but note that under JCT 80 (cf JCT 63) and ICE the contractor is not entitled to additional payment in respect of fluctuations occurring after the contractual date for completion, as extended.
- Sums paid in respect of *insurance*, the premiums for which should under the contract have been paid by the other party.
- The consequences of *hostilities and war damage*.
- Loss and/or damage suffered by the contractor, for example, in relation to prolongation or disruption of the contract programme. Hence JCT 80, cl 26 provides for the ascertainment of additional sums to be payable to the contractor in respect of 'Loss and expense caused by matters materially affecting regular progress of the Works'. The approach under the ICE drafting is rather different. These similar grounds for increases in payments are to be found dispersed in the conditions. Clause 52(4) provides for the allowing of such sums by the Engineer.

The contractor's own obligation *in contract* to the other party to the contract (his client, or the beneficiary of a warranty he has given) to complete the works also embraces elements in the works contributed by others such as domestic sub-contractors and suppliers. However, considerable potential for disputes arises from the limitation of the contractor's responsibility where provision is made for '*nominated*' sub-contractors and suppliers. The relief from certain liabilities in respect of nominated sub-contractors which the main contract grants to the contractor is the price the employer has to pay for the privilege of being able to stipulate for a particular sub-contractor's expertise. The JCT forms, for example, are drafted to protect the employer in respect of this risk by requiring a direct warranty to be given by the nominated sub-contractor to the employer. However, in practice disputes arise either because such a warranty was not secured or because the employer wants the benefits of nomination without allowing the sub-contractor to be formally nominated. In the latter circumstance, the contractor may be at considerable risk of responsibility for what is in law a domestic sub-contractor, whatever label (other than 'nominated') may have been used.

Extremely wide powers to vary the works are given to the architect and engineer by both JCT and ICE. Despite the apparent width of these powers, and the provisions requiring appropriate financial adjustments there must be implied limits to their lawful exercise.

The contractor's obligation is to complete the works by the contractual completion date, unless this is extended (pursuant to the extension of time clauses in the contract, see, for example, JCT 80 cl 25, ICE cl 44) or completion by the due date is prevented by the employer through causes not provided for in the extension of time clauses. In this latter case of prevention, time becomes 'at large': the obligation to complete by the contractual date for completion, is displaced by an obligation to complete within a reasonable time. The liquidated damages clause is also displaced, though the contractor will be liable at common law for any damages arising through any breach of the substituted completion obligation.

Otherwise, under the typical standard forms, the contractor incurs a liability to pay liquidated damages if the contractual date for completion is exceeded without any such entitlement to extension or prevention (see eg, JCT cl 24, ICE cl 47).

COMPATIBILITY BETWEEN MAIN CONTRACT AND SUB-CONTRACT

It is vital that parties ensure that the terms of the main contract and the terms of the sub-contracts are, so far as possible, consistent.

That compatibility is best achieved by using forms designed to be worked in conjunction with one another. But, a common source of misunderstanding arises from references in one of the contracts to another. For example, the main contract (such as JCT 80) will contain provisions the purpose of which is to secure particular sub-contract arrangements, such as those applicable to nominated sub-contracts. However, this does *not* mean that the main contract provisions are legally enforceable by the sub-contractor.

The doctrine of privity of contract has the consequence that the actual legal relations between, for example, main contractor and sub-contractor are governed by the actual sub-contract terms which they enter into, and not

not such terms as may have been intended in the main contract (though compare this general principle with the case of *Sauter Automation v H C Goodman (Mechanical Services)* (1986) 34 BLR 81).

So, careful attention must be given to the right procedures at the time of formation of the main contract and of the sub-contracts, especially where the sub-contract is placed on minimal documentation (such as an order form) and the elaborate standard form conditions are left to be incorporated merely by reference without regard to potential gaps or inconsistencies.

THE USUAL BASES OF SUB-CONTRACT CLAIMS: DELAY, DISRUPTION, LOSS AND EXPENSE

For most purposes, where industry-standard sub-contract forms are used, the principles governing claims for loss and expense arising through the usual causes, such as delay and disruption, are the same as obtain under the main contracts, already considered, subject of course to observance of the particular procedural requirements as to notices, certificates, etc, under each form.

Some of these sub-contract claims can be passed up the contract chain to the employer by the contractor (see, for example, cl 13.1 of the NSC/4 nominated sub-contract form to be operated in conjunction with cl 26.4 of the JCT 80 main contract).

However, other risks are to be borne by the contractor without being able to pass it on. Under cl 13.3 of NSC/4 the main contractor is entitled to claim from the sub-contractor loss and/or expense where the regular progress of the sub-contract works is materially affected by act, omission or default of the sub-contractor. This does not mean that the sub-contractor would become liable for the liquidated and ascertained damages under the main contract. Indeed, on the contrary, 'delay on the part of nominated sub-contractors or nominated suppliers' is a relevant event for an extension of time under cl 25 of the JCT 80 main contract, thereby to that extent removing the liability to such liquidated damages. But the main contractor's claim for such an extension is allowable only if the contractor has taken all practicable steps to avoid or reduce the delay.

(For an illustration of problems associated with the relation of the main contract programme and the sub-contract programme, see *Martin Grant & Co Ltd v Sir Lindsay Parkinson & Co Ltd* (1984) 29 BLR 31, [1984] CILL 137, under JCT 63.)

TORTIOUS LIABILITY FOR NEGLIGENCE

The modern English law on the tort of negligence has been developed almost entirely by judges in case law rather than by legislation. The impetus to the development was the decision of the House of Lords in the famous snail case of *Donoghue v Stevenson* [1932] AC 562. Its major significance was, broadly speaking, that it allowed a short cut for the end user to claim directly against an original manufacturer (if the manufacturer was negligent). This cut out the need to channel claims through the chain of supply contracts from the end user back to the manufacturer. The third quarter of the twentieth century saw the limits of this new principle being explored by litigation. Claimants found the courts increasingly indulgent. People in the business of design, manufacture or supply were held responsible for a wider range of risks, so long as it could be established that they had not taken reasonable care.

It was Lord Denning, in the case of *Dutton v Bognor Regis UDC* [1972] 1 QB 373, [1972] 1 All ER 462, who first articulated the major new proposition that rules of law applicable to goods and products could equally be applied to buildings. For claimants, this arose in the fertile context of litigation against local authorities exercising building control functions. The defendants were particularly attractive targets. They were always there and could afford to pay. It was worth taking cases to the House of Lords, and so as a result of the decision in *Anns v Merton London Borough Council* [1978] AC 728, [1977] 2 All ER 492 the negligence liabilities not only of local authorities, but also of contractors and consultants in the construction industry, were greatly extended. A further extension of negligence liability arose by the courts' willingness to recognise that a contractor could be sued in tort even by his client who had contractual rights against him as well. The allegation of a duty in tort concurrent with obligations in contract between the same parties was normally made by a claimant wanting to take advantage of the longer limitation periods applicable to tort actions under the Limitation Acts. The case of *Batty v Metropolitan Property Realisations Ltd* [1978] QB 554, [1978] 2 All ER 445 illustrated how tort liabilities could arise alongside contractual obligations to the same claimant.

Quality and fitness for purpose obligations had traditionally been the exclusive province of contract law. But, expansion in tortious liability from the mid-1970s to the mid-1980s suggested, for a while, that the mere failure of a product to perform as well as the user reasonably expected could be redressed by a claim framed in tort.

But this extension of liability was quickly restricted again by subsequent appellate decisions (and the wider implications of *Batty* itself have now been disapproved by the House of Lords in *D and F Estates Ltd v Church Comrs for England* [1989] AC 177, [1988] 2 All ER 992 below). In particular, the House of Lords in *Peabody Donation Fund v Sir Lindsay Parkinson & Co Ltd* [1985] AC 210, [1984] 3 All ER 529 placed a restrictive interpretation on the nature of local building control authority's duty. It would not extend to protect developers against pure economic losses. This restrictive approach was further elaborated in the Court of Appeal's five propositions in *Investors in Industry Commercial Properties Ltd v South Bedfordshire District Council* [1986] QB 1034, [1986] 1 All ER 787.

Hence in *Simaan General Contracting Co v Pilkington Glass Ltd (No 2)* [1988] QB 758, [1988] 1 All ER 791 Bingham LJ explained that Lord Wilberforce's two-stage test in *Anns* was treated with some reservation in a series of House of Lords' decisions (see *Yuen Kun Yeu v A-G of Hong Kong* [1987] 3 WLR 776 at 782D) culminating in the conclusion (at 785G) that it was 'not to be regarded as in all the circumstances a suitable guide to the existence of a duty of care'. Increasingly emphasis was placed on the observation of Lord Keith of Kinkel in *Peabody Donation Fund v Sir Lindsay Parkinson & Co Ltd* [1985] AC 210 at 241C (whether just and reasonable that there should be duty). See, for example, *Curran v Northern Ireland Co-ownership Housing Association Ltd* [1987] 2 WLR 1043 at

1052A; *Hill v Chief Constable for West Yorkshire* [1987] 2 WLR 1126 at 1132H.

In *Tate and Lyle Industries Ltd v Greater London Council* [1983] 2 AC 509 at 530H, Lord Templeman said that in the relevant cases 'from *Donoghue v Stevenson* to *Junior Books* the plaintiff suffered personal injury or damage to his property'. The claim in negligence failed because Tate & Lyle were held to have no right to any particular depth of water at their jetties. Both Lord Keith and Lord Roskill agreed with Lord Templeman's speech.

In *Muirhead v Industrial Tank Specialities Ltd* [1986] QB 507, [1985] 3 All ER 705 Robert Goff LJ (as he then was) carefully analysed the speeches of the House of Lords in *Junior Books*. Nourse and O'Connor LJJ agreed, relying in particular on *Spartan Steel and Alloys Ltd v Martin & Co (Contractors) Ltd* [1973] QB 27, [1972] 3 All ER 557 and *Candlewood Navigation Corpn Ltd v Mitsui OSK Lines Ltd* [1986] AC 1, [1985] 2 All ER 935.

The new wave of court decisions suggested a return to the traditional view that users who want rights to a certain level of quality, fitness for purpose, or freedom from defects in goods and services (which are not otherwise dangerous or damaging) must make their contract to that effect with whomsoever they wish to make responsible.

The only significant qualification to this was the case of *Junior Books Ltd v Veitchi Ltd* [1983] 1 AC 520, [1982] 3 All ER 201 where a specialist supplier of goods and services was held to owe a duty to a third party (with whom there was no contract) to take care to avoid the financial losses that would flow from defects in the goods and services provided. This was a special case, on the facts, of a specialist contractor who voluntarily assumed a special responsibility and whose expertise was particularly relied upon by the clients. However, the majority decision in the *Junior Books* case has since been criticised, doubted and apparently disapproved in subsequent decisions. If the case survives at all after the House of Lords' decision in *D and F Estates* [1989] AC 177, [1988] 2 All ER 992, it will only be in the special context of reliance on someone who held themselves out as having a special skill.

Thus the late 1980s heralded new limits on the negligence liabilities of ordinary building contractors and designers. In *D and F Estates*, Wates won before the House of Lords on the important principle that they owed no duty of care to supervise their independent sub-contractors in relation to claims made by third parties with whom they had no contract. The building owners alleged that Wates were negligent in performing their work under the building contract. Wates denied that they were liable and relied on the fact that defective work had been carried out, not by Wates' own labour, but by an independent plastering sub-contractor. That company no longer existed when proceedings were issued against Wates. The House of Lords agreed that Wates could properly discharge their obligations under the building contract by engaging a sub-contractor to carry out all or part of their contractual obligations providing that they took reasonable steps to ensure that the sub-contractor was apparently competent. The approach of the House of Lords is in line with a series of such restrictive decisions. However, the House of Lords went much further!

Contractors gained substantial relief from potential liabilities as a result of this decision, but professional advisers, architects and engineers could still be at risk of wide liability to third parties for economic losses because the decision left undisturbed the liabilities arising from the 'reliance' principle (see the line of cases from *Hedley Byrne & Co Ltd v Heller & Partners Ltd* [1964] AC 465, [1963] 2 All ER 575 through to *Smith v Eric S Bush* [1989] 2 All ER 514, [1989] 2 WLR 790).

There is now explicit recognition that *Anns v Merton LBC* introduced in relation to the construction of buildings an entirely new type of product liability, if not, indeed, an entirely novel concept of the tort of negligence. The English courts seem to have gone even further than the American courts. But, what is not clear is the extent of the liability under this new principle. And the Lords in *D & F* added new criteria for defeating defects claims, but without giving a definitive ruling on what remains from *Anns*.

The *D & F* decision in the House of Lords arguably raises as many questions as it solves. What is the scope of the vital new limiting criterion based on the notion of 'complex structure'? Why do claims for repairs and making good now have to be assessed in a new way? Their Lordships' speeches are not free of inconsistencies. Important potential loopholes can be identified. Lawyers are speculating that the Building Regulations and breach of statutory duty could be an avenue to avoid the strictures of *D & F*.

The crucial distinction to be drawn is between 'dangerous defects' and 'defects of quality'. Indeed it may be misleading to think in terms of 'defects' at all. The 'essential ingredient' is taken from the new orthodoxy of Lord Brandon's dissent in *Junior Books v Veitchi*: there must be danger of physical damage to persons or their property, but *excluding* damage to the very piece of property the defective condition of which gives rise to the danger.

What is a complex structure? Why did the Lords treat walls as independent of foundations, but decorative wallpaper as *not* a different item of property from the plaster to which it was applied? What technical criteria can be formulated to apply this new determinant of defects liability? What is a 'simple product'? Can movable products also be 'complex structures'? What if the damage has yet to occur? Is the cost of *averting* danger recoverable? Does discovery of a defect before it causes injury to person or other property prevent recovery of the costs of making good the defect? Why is the cost of replacing, or making good, defective work now normally irrecoverable?

There also remain questions as to the interaction of the *D & F* decision with previous case law: what are the remaining effects of *Anns v Merton LBC*? Will *Junior Books v Veitchi* and *Batty v Metropolitan Realisations* flourish as cases of 'reliance' on special expertise? Are architects, engineers and other consultants liable in tort for mere defects despite *London Congregational v Harriss*?

Then there is the relationship with statutory provisions: does the *D & F* approach to product liability (with notions of 'complex structure' and 'averting danger') require even the product liability provisions of the Consumer Protection Act 1987 to be re-thought? What is the impact on limitation periods? Why will the *D & F* approach start time running from new points for statute-barring claims?

Essentially, it appears that the clock has been turned back half a century for ordinary negligence claims against contractors and suppliers (assuming they have no liability under the 'reliance' principle from *Hedley Byrne v Heller*). Restored are the principal limitations of Lord Atkins' neighbour principle in *Donoghue v Stevenson* [1932] AC 562:

* there must be personal injury; or
* there must be damage to the plaintiff's property, other than the very part the defective condition of which gives rise to the claim; and
* there must have been no reasonable opportunity for intermediate examination which would have enabled the plaintiff to be aware of and avoid harm before it occurred.

An uncertainty remaining is whether imminent apprehended damage to the plaintiff's person or ('other') property (as opposed to actual damage) would be treated as sufficient to ground a right of suit. It will not, it seems, suffice if the only damage occurring is within property which the defendant had negligently designed or produced and the damage is attributable to that negligence. Difficulties will however arise in determining whether the defendant can be said to have caused damage to 'other' property if one part of the product he supplies causes damage to another he supplies with it (consider, for example, *Aswan Engineering Establishment Co v Lupdine Ltd* [1987] 1 All ER 135, [1987] 1 WLR 1, as well as *D & F*).

The exclusive province of contract is being restated by the judges. In *London Congregation v Harris*, Ralph Gibson LJ said that the ordinary relationship of client and architect, or of client and consulting engineer, was not such that liability for pure economic loss would arise in tort on proof of negligent design or supervision but without proof of damage to property. The concept of negligence was not intended to afford owners of buildings rights equivalent to contract rights.

The new limiting criteria have been articulated by the Court of Appeal, the House of Lords and the Privy Council in a series of decisions in 1987 and 1988. Builders can regard themselves no longer threatened by indeterminate claims by ultimate users of their products for consequential economic losses unrelated to property damage or physical injury. That is quite clear from recent affirmations of the case of the lobsters in Sunderland (*Muirhead v Industrial Tank Specialities Ltd* [1986] QB 507, [1985] 3 All ER 705), as in the case of coloured glass in Abu Dhabi (*Simaan v Pilkington Glass (No 2)* [1988] QB 758, [1988] 1 All ER 791). But there remain difficulties about the precise scope of the criterion requiring damage to property: there are complex implications arising from the case of the buckets on the Kuwaiti quayside (*Aswan Engineering Establishment Co v Lupdine Ltd* [1987] 1 All ER 135, [1987] 1 WLR 1) as well as from *D & F*.

A renewed emphasis is being placed upon the closeness and directness of the relationship (proximity) between the defendant and the claimant, and upon the alternative opportunities for the claimant to have avoided the loss.

Pure economic losses, unrelated to physical damage or personal injury, will be recoverable in tortious actions by third parties only if it can be shown that, in a special relationship of reliance, the defendant voluntarily assumed responsibility for those losses.

DUTY TO WARN

There is, however, a possibility that an ordinary contractor who has not otherwise voluntarily assumed a responsibility or induced reliance, may nevertheless be under a duty in the law of negligence, or by an equivalent implied term in contract, to warn of the consequences of defective work;

see, for example *EDAC v Moss* [1984] CILL 74: however, this latter case must now be reconsidered in the light of its treatment in the *Abbeystead* case at first instance, and more recently in *University of Glasgow v W Whitfield* [1988] CILL 416.

It appeared for a while, as a result of the decisions in *EDAC v Moss* [1984] CILL 74 and *Victoria University, Manchester v Wilson* (1984) 2 Con LR 43 that the courts might impose extensive duties to warn on the various parties to the construction process. Hence, in *EDAC v Moss* it was said that a contractor under an ordinary workmanship contract, who had undertaken no design obligation, could nevertheless owe a duty to warn the building owner and the architects of defects in the latter's design. However, these two decisions have been explained in the case of *University of Glasgow v W Whitfield and John Laing Construction Ltd* [1988] CILL 416 as depending upon a special relationship between the parties. Otherwise, it was said, they could not stand with more recent decisions. Furthermore the reference to a duty to warn the architect was to the architect as agent of the employer.

This latter context is one illustration of many where the ordinary negligence liabilities of a contractor will be extended if the contractor undertakes a special responsibility or induces reliance on his expertise in a special relationship with a particular party.

ARCHITECTS STILL HAVE A DUTY TO WARN OF ENGINEERS' DEFAULT

In *Investors in Industry Commercial Properties Ltd v South Bedfordshire District Council* [1986] QB 1034, [1986] 1 All ER 787, Slade LJ, delivering the judgment of the Court of Appeal, distinguished *Moresk Cleaners v Hicks* [1966] 2 Lloyds Rep 338. He said that it 'was a case very different from the present' and continued:

> 'Clauses 1.20, 1.22 and 1.23 of the RIBA Conditions [of Engagement] clearly contemplate [that] the architect will normally carry no legal responsibility for the work done by [a reputable independent consultant expert] which is beyond the capability of an architect of ordinary competence; in relation to the work allotted to the expert, the architect's legal responsibility will normally be confined to directing and co-ordinating the expert's work in the whole. However, this is subject to one important qualification. If any danger or problem arises in connection with the work allotted to the expert, of which an architect of ordinary competence reasonably ought to be aware and reasonably could be expected to warn the client, despite the employment of the expert, and despite what the expert says or does about it, it is in our judgment, the duty of the architect to warn the client. In such a contingency he is not entitled to rely blindly on the expert, with no mind of his own, on matters which must or should have been apparent to him . . .' (see *Davy-Chiesman v Davy-Chiesman* [1984] Fam 48 at 66A–B).

Further guidance from the Court of Appeal on the potential scope in the construction industry of 'duties to warn', in negligence law, would be most welcome.

The matter was treated pretty robustly by the majority, Lawton and Dillon LJJ, in *Holland Hannen & Cubitts (Northern) Ltd v Welsh Health Technical Services Organisation* (1985) 35 BLR 1. They rejected firmly the suggestion that the structural engineers, AMP, had a duty to warn CED that the visual appearance of the floor might be unacceptable to the architect or building owner. Yet, on the other hand, the argument in favour of imposing such a duty even on structural engineers was cogently put in Goff LJ's dissenting judgment.

WHY WILL TORT LIABILITY BE ASSERTED BY A CLAIMANT?

The simplest reason for framing an action in tort is that the claimant has no contract with the defendant. Of necessity all third party claims have to be grounded in tort. The courts may also continue to find a duty in tort even where there is a contract with the defendant.

The advantages of a tort action are:

* The claim in tort could extend the time limits within which the action could be started (see below).
* The difference in the basis for calculating damages, as between tort and contract, could work to the advantage of the claimant.
* The breach by a defendant of such a duty imposed by law may invite greater judicial disapproval than a mere breach of contract. This might lead not only to judicial sympathy with the claimant but also presumptions that the contract ought not to exclude or restrict that negligence duty imposed by law (see, for example, s 2 of UCTA 1977).

THE IMPORTANCE OF THE NATURE OF THE LOSS SUFFERED BY THE CLAIMANT

Thus, the law does *not* proceed from the assumption that just because a product is defective someone must be legally liable. The law will not necessarily hold a defendant liable even if proved to have been 'negligent'. Liability in tort does not exist without proof of a legally recoverable type of loss. So the claimant relying on an allegation of negligence in tort has to complain not of a 'defect', whether in a product or some professional advice, but of a *loss*; then he must show that *that* defendant owed an obligation to prevent *that* loss arising to *that* party; even if the obligation is owed, it must also be shown to have been broken.

It is vital to distinguish between the different types of losses which the law classifies:

(a) The 'defect' causes personal injury or death.
(b) The 'defect' causes damage to other property.
(c) The 'defect' is such that some part of the product itself is damaged.
(d) The 'defect' is merely such that the product is not as 'good' as it might have been. There is a mere diminution in value or quality compared with that expected.

This 'hierarchy' of losses is very significant in tort law. Liability is progressively more difficult to establish as one moves from category (a) to category (d). The threshold of liability appeared by virtue of *Junior Books v Veitchi* to drop below category (d). The *D & F* decision moved the threshold back up to draw the line between (b) and (c) in ordinary negligence cases (not involving *Hedley Byrne* reliance liability). By contrast, the 'hierarchy' can be irrelevant in contract law. The parties can, by clear drafting of their contract terms, make a designer or builder liable even for the aesthetic defects in category (d), and yet not liable for the apparently more significant losses in categories (a) to (c).

THE CRITERION OF 'DAMAGE TO OTHER PROPERTY'

In *Aswan Engineering Establishment Co v Lupdine Ltd* [1986] 2 Lloyds Rep 347 at 360, Lloyd LJ, with whom Fox LJ agreed, said:

> 'The distinction between a defective product which renders the product itself less valuable, and a defective product which creates a danger to *other* property of the plaintiff, was the corner stone of Lord Brandon's dissenting speech in *Junior Books*. It is a distinction which is well established both in English and American law. Where the defect renders the property less valuable, the plaintiff's remedy (if any) lies in contract. Where it creates a danger to other property of the plaintiff, the remedy (if any) lies in tort, although it may also lie in contract if the manufacturer is also the seller, as in *Grant v Australian Knitting Mills* [1936] AC 85.
>
> *Junior Books* was the first case to cross the line, as it were between tort and contract. That step was justified because the relationship between the parties was such that it could be regarded as equivalent to contract. In the great majority of cases the question whether the danger created is danger to *other* property of the plaintiff admitted of an obvious answer. The peculiarity of the present case is that the position is not so clear.'

The problem was with plastic pails which collapsed when stacked in full sunshine on a Kuwaiti quayside. Their contents, a waterproofing compounding known as 'Lupguard', were a total loss. But Aswan were buying Lupguard in pails; not Lupguard *and* pails. So, was there damage to *other* property? Lloyd LJ speculated on other cases. What if a defective car tyre, part of the original equipment, bursts and the car is damaged? Presumably the car is *other* property of the plaintiff, even though the tyre was a component part of the car. Say a bottle of wine is undrinkable because of a defect in the cork; is the wine other property, so as to enable an action against the cork manufacturer in tort? Suppose the electric motors in *Muirhead* had overheated and damaged the pumps. Would the plaintiff have recovered for physical damage to the pumps as well as to the lobsters? The provisional view was that in all these cases there was damage to other property of the plaintiff, so that the threshold of liability was crossed.

Whether liability would be established in any particular case was another matter. It was clear that much would also depend on the foreseeability of the damage, otherwise the loss would be held too remote anyway.

WHEN ARE ECONOMIC LOSSES RECOVERABLE BY THIRD PARTIES?

To the extent that the courts have come to regard purely economic losses as a form of harm which ought to be remedied and deterred by imposition of duties in tort, then the range of claimants to whom such a duty is owed will also be increased. The reason for this is that physical damage is naturally limited in extent and in a sense self extinguishing (except where, for example, there is a catastrophe with the release of harmful replicating organisms, or of nuclear radiation). By contrast, financial losses are conceptual only, with no necessary relationship to the physical world. Thus there are no natural limits to the extent of the financial losses that could flow from a causative negligent event, so far as tortious negligence liability to third parties is concerned. Contractual liabilities are, by contrast, naturally limited in any event to the parties to the contract (the 'privity' principle). Therefore, contract law does not need to distinguish between physical and financial losses.

The courts thus draw an important distinction between financial losses which are consequent upon physical damage and claims which are for purely economic loss unrelated to physical damage.

Pure economic losses, unrelated to physical damage or personal injury, will be recoverable in tortious actions by third parties only if it can be shown that, in a special relationship of reliance, the defendant voluntarily assumed responsibility for those losses or it is otherwise just and reasonable that he should bear them (see *Smith v Eric S Bush* [1989] 2 All ER 514, [1989] 2 WLR 790).

There is one well established category for the recovery of pure economic loss: that is, cases of professional advice which lead only to financial losses, where it is reasonable for the plaintiff to have relied on the special expertise held out by the adviser: see the case of *Hedley Byrne v Heller & Partners* [1964] AC 465, [1963] 2 All ER 575, HL. Three factors expanded this realm of liability in the 25 years since its first recognition:

(1) The tortious basis of action can be chosen by a victim of negligent professional advice, even though the victim also had a contract with the adviser (see *Esso Petroleum Co v Mardon* [1976] QB 801, [1976] 2 All ER 5 (petrol companies, advice to a potential tenant), *Batty v Metropolitan Property Realisations* [1978] QB 554, [1978] 2 All ER 445, CA (builder/developer's failure to investigate neighbouring ground conditions before building a house) and *Midland Bank Trust Co v Hett, Stubbs and Kemp* [1979] Ch 384, [1978] 3 All ER 571 (solicitors advice to client)). However, there are dicta of the Privy Council in *Tai Hing Cotton Mill Ltd v Liu Chong Hing Bank Ltd* [1986] AC 80, [1985] 2 All ER 947 indicating that their Lordships did not believe there was any advantage for the law's development in searching for liability in tort where the parties were in a contractual relationship. This was said to be particularly so in a commercial relationship. Their Lordships believed it correct in principle and necessary for the avoidance of confusion in the law to adhere to the contractual analysis: on principle because it was a relationship in which the parties had, subject to a few exceptions, the right to determine their obligations to each other, and for the avoidance of confusion because different consequences followed according to whether the liability arose from contract or tort, for example in the limitation of actions.

(2) Liability has been extended to persons other than the immediate client of the adviser (see, for example, the many house surveyor and valuer cases beginning with *Yianni v Edwin Evans & Sons* [1982] QB 438, [1981] 3 All ER 592 (mortgage lenders' valuing surveyor liable to house purchaser)—see also *Smith v Eric S Bush* [1989] 2 All ER 514, [1989] 2 WLR 790, HL, and see *JEB Fasteners v Marks Bloom & Co* [1983] 1 All ER 583, CA (auditing accountants' liability to persons interested in the company)).

(3) Professional advice may be too narrow a definition. Negligent professional acts or omissions, if advisory in nature, may be regarded as breaches of duty leading to recoverable pure economic loss: *Ross v Caunters* [1980] Ch 297, [1979] 3 All ER 580 (liability of solicitor to a beneficiary under the client's will in respect of the drafting of the will). This could always prove a Trojan horse for duties to warn and other generic liabilities.

More recent cases have treated the *Hedley Byrne* principle as depending on a 'voluntary assumption of responsibility', perhaps even 'akin to contract', though in the House of Lords in *D & F* the governing criterion seemed to be 'reliance'.

A remaining problem is whether the *Hedley Byrne* principle extends beyond the category of undoubted professionals acting in advisory capacity (such as lawyers, accountants, surveyors and valuers). There is even doubt as to whether an architect or consulting engineer owes this form of liability when acting in the traditional way as a consultant on a construction project: consider for example, *Pirelli General Cable Works Ltd v Oscar Faber & Partners* [1983] 2 AC 1, [1983] 1 All ER 65, HL; *London Congregational Union Inc v Harriss* [1985] 1 All ER 335, 1 Con LR 96; *Pacific Associates v Baxter* [1988] CILL 460 and *Salliss & Co v Calil* (1988) 4 Const LJ 125. It may be therefore that such liability would not be extended even further to parties who had specialist expertise but were not regarded as consultant professionals in a traditional institutional sense. This last group of potential defendants with specialist expertise would therefore be held liable in the tort of negligence for causing purely economic loss, unrelated to physical damage, only if they could be brought within what remains of the principles articulated by the majority in *Junior Books v Veitchi*. It is very important to note that Lord Roskill actually found for Junior Books on quite precise and detailed reasons on the particular facts: he articulated what has come to be regarded as a checklist of eight factors highlighting the specialist expertise of the defendant sub-contractors in that case who were alone responsible for the product concerned and must have known that the owner of the factory in which they were working was relying on their skill and experience; the relationship between the parties was as close as it could be, short of actual contract. It has since been doubted whether there is any useful purpose in any case citing the majority decision in *Junior Books v Veitchi* (see *Simaan* (CA) and *D & F* (HL)): ie it is to be regarded as a decision entirely dependent upon its own particular facts. Certainly the strict limits on the application of the *Junior Books* majority decision are made very clear by the Court of Appeal in *Muirhead v Industrial Tank Specialities* [1986] QB 507, [1985] 3 All ER 705; *Simaan General Contracting v Pilkington Glass (No 2)* [1988] QB 758, [1988] 1 All ER 791, CA and *Greater Nottingham Co-operative Society Ltd v Cementation Piling and Foundations Ltd* [1989] QB 71, [1988] 2 All ER 971, CA, and the House of Lords in *D & F*.

The resolution of some of these difficulties may come from a more explicit recognition that the true distinguishing feature is between cases where a product (ie a thing, an artefact) is supplied or physical work is carried out, on the one hand, and, on the other hand, those cases where only advice is given. This would go a long way to explaining why professional advisers can owe duties to third parties in tort to avoid purely economic losses, whereas for all other categories of defendant only the victims of actual (or, perhaps, apprehended) physical damage can recover. The tort duty cannot be viewed in isolation from the contractual obligations that normally attach to the relevant category of defendant. In all those cases where a product is supplied or physical work is carried out, the normal form of contractual obligation will be one to achieve results: a performance obligation warranting quality or fitness for purpose. Those, however, who merely give advice will, even in contract (and in the absence of terms to the contrary), owe an obligation only to take reasonable care in the formulation and giving of the advice; they do not implicitly warrant that the advice will lead to successful results by action in reliance thereon. The adviser category therefore enjoys a reduced form of contractual liability which, by being framed as a duty to take care, is analogous to a tortious duty in negligence. Thus, third party victims of negligent professional advice will find it relatively easy to assert the view that a duty of care which the professional already owes to his client ought also to be owed to foreseeable categories of third party who might also rely on the advice. This is especially so because the form of the advice will often be a report which foreseeably can be passed on to third parties in circumstances where it must have been known to the original professional adviser that third parties would receive and act on its content. Contrast the position of a third party who is complaining of loss resulting from a product supplied to another or from physical work carried out for another. Here the essence of the complaint is likely to be that the product or the work has not met the performance objective expected (for example it is defective). Even if the third party victim can show reliance on the person responsible for the product or work by asserting that the victim purchased from another the property comprising or incorporating the product or work on the strength of the reputation or representations of the person responsible, there will be the answer that the original purchaser of the product or work had the contractual opportunity to bargain for performance obligations. Therefore the third party victim should have similarly sought contractual protection from his immediate vendor when taking over the product or work. There is no justification for his having rights in tort direct against the person responsible.

The dilemma in respect of economic loss claims arises from a conflict of social policies. In a market economy, there are countless opportunities to profit lawfully and yet thereby foreseeably inflict economic loss on others. On the other hand, there is social unease (which appears to have influenced judges more in post-War Britain) that the wrongdoer should not be permitted to escape responsibility for foreseeable harm inflicted by want of reasonable care.

Another factor is the pragmatic problem of the need to control the unacceptable proliferation of claims. Hence the need for control mechanisms stretches back to the workers' wages claim in *Cattle v Stockton Waterworks Co* (1875) LR 10 QB 453.

However, it has to be recognised in the context of litigation that all loss is ultimately economic (see per Oliver LJ, *Leigh and Sillivan Ltd v Aliakmon Shipping Co Ltd* [1985] QB 350, [1985] 2 All ER 44 in the Court of Appeal). Much of the difficulty that has beset this area of law in recent years has flowed from a failure to discern different classes of economic loss. Instead, the notion of 'economic loss' suffers agglomeration, and consequent confusion.

A starting point is to seek to identify the proper provinces of tort and contract. What is tort for? What do we mean by 'contract'? Should not lawyers address more the purposes of these conventional categorisations? For, it is not just the law of tort that has been the vehicle for judicial expansion of responsibilities. In other periods, the law of contract was also a cloak for judges' instrumental decision-making in expanding liabilities. Consider *Dick Bentley Productions Ltd v Harold Smith (Motors) Ltd* [1965] 2 All ER 65, [1965] 1 WLR 623, CA and *Esso Petroleum Co Ltd v Mardon* [1976] QB 801, [1976] 2 All ER 5, CA, and compare the development of *Hedley Byrne v Heller* [1964] AC 465, [1963] 2 All ER 575 from *Donoghue v Stevenson* [1932] AC 562. An acute way of focusing this question of the boundaries of contract and tort is to consider the justification, if any, for the development of parallel duties in contract and tort between the same parties: *Midland Bank v Hett Stubbs* [1979] Ch 384, [1978] 3 All ER 571. Here we have not a principled result but distortion from the law on limitation of actions.

It will be seen that at root the courts have, over two decades, created a problem of social policy still requiring resolution. What are the proper limits for imposing obligations in the law of tort? How should these relate to the parties' autonomy in agreeing their own contractual responsibilities? Much of this century has seen a drift in the law away from 'caveat emptor' (let the buyer beware) to a desire to lay responsibility on those regarded as 'at fault'. But in relation to goods that was mainly achieved by legislative policy. Yet the abandoning of 'caveat emptor' in relation to buildings and land has been by judicial intervention. Legislation should be the appropriate, and proper, vehicle for policy change: it is informed by consultation, it can distinguish policies for consumers from those for business. The present law on negligence liability in the construction industry is the product of haphazard, accidental occurrences of litigation. Indeed many of these changes in the law were retrospective in effect: an intolerable constitutional anomaly. Parties proceeded, for example, in repairing buildings, on what the law of negligence appeared to be, only to find years later when in an appellate court that the judges had decided to change the policy again.

WHAT DEGREE OF CARE IS REQUIRED TO AVOID BEING FOUND NEGLIGENT?

The normal criterion of negligence liability is pitched by the law at a level of reasonableness consonant with the average competence of the defendant concerned. Furthermore, that competence is to be judged by the standards prevailing at the time of the alleged negligence and not with the benefit of hindsight. In other words, defendants are entitled to the benefit of the 'state of the art' defence. With regard to professional services, such as design, there are abundant dicta from the courts defining the standard of care required. It has been particularly well explained by Bingham LJ in the Court of Appeal in the Abbeystead case (*Eckersley v Binnie & Partners* [1988] CILL 388). Though he was dissenting, and would himself have allowed the engineers' appeal, nevertheless his observations are of general application:

> 'The law requires of a professional man that he live up in practice to the standard of the ordinary skilled man exercising and professing to have his special professional skills. He need not possess the highest expert skill; it is enough if he exercises the ordinary skill of an ordinary competent man exercising his particular art. So much is established by *Bolam v Friern Hospital Management Committee* [1957] 2 All ER 118, [1957] 1 WLR 582 which has been applied and approved time without number. "No matter what profession it may be, the common law does not impose on those who practise it any liability for damage resulting from what in the result turn out to have been errors of judgment, unless the error was such as no reasonably well-informed and competent member of that profession could have made" (*Saif Ali v Sydney Mitchell & Co* [1980] AC 198 at 220D, per Lord Diplock).
>
> From these general statements it follows that a professional man should command the corpus of knowledge which forms part of the professional equipment of the ordinary member of his profession. He should not lag behind other ordinarily assiduous and intelligent members of his profession in knowledge of new advances, discoveries and developments in his field. He should have such awareness as an ordinarily competent practitioner would have of the deficiencies in his knowledge and the limitations on his skill. He should be alert to the hazards and risks inherent in any professional task he undertakes to the extent that other ordinarily competent members of his profession would be alert. He must bring to any professional task he undertakes no less expertise, skill and care than any other ordinarily competent members of his profession would bring, but need bring no more. The standard is that of reasonable average. The law does not require of a professional man that he be a paragon, combining the qualities of polymath and prophet.
>
> In deciding whether a professional man has fallen short of the standards observed by ordinarily skilled and competent members of his profession, it is the standards prevailing at the time of acts or omissions which provide the relevant yardstick. He is not . . . to be judged by the wisdom of hindsight. This of course means that knowledge of an event which happened later should not be applied when judging acts and/or omissions which took place before that event . . . ; . . . it is necessary, if the defendant's conduct is to be fairly judged, that the making of [any] retrospective assessment should not of itself have the effect of magnifying the significance of the . . . risk as it appeared or should reasonably have appeared to an ordinarily competent practical man with a job to do at the time.'

However, contractors must recognise that this relatively low standard of care of the ordinarily competent practitioner applies only to obligations involving reasonable skill and care, such as the ordinary negligence responsibility (whether in contract or in tort) of a consulting architect or engineer in respect of design. If a contractor undertakes design along with his building obligations, it does not follow that in respect of that design a contractor will enjoy this low care-based form of liability. It is clear from the case law that such a design and build contractor may be held impliedly to have warranted the fitness for purpose of the design.

Two consequences follow:

(a) Contractual documentation must be reviewed very carefully to ensure that there is not a mismatch of obligation as between the contractual obligations of the contractor to his client employer on the one hand and that contractor's rights on the other hand against outside designers who are commissioned for part of the design. Without proper contractual drafting the latter may be held only to owe a duty of reasonable skill and care, yet the contractor may have a more onerous responsibility to the client.

(b) There are also implications for professional indemnity cover in relations to design activities. The case of *Wimpey Construction UK Ltd v Poole* (1984) 27 BLR 58 witnessed the spectacle of a contractor seeking to persuade the court that it had been negligent because it ought to be required to owe a higher standard of care than that of the ordinarily competent. Why should a contractor be arguing for a higher degree of responsibility on itself? The reason was that they were suing their own insurers on their professional indemnity (PI) cover, having already carried out remedial works for the client. If, however, the defects which were remedied were not the result of care below that of the reasonable average, then it would not constitute negligence within the meaning of the PI policy.

The application of the principles governing the required standard of care obviously depends on the particular facts of each case. Two points should, however, be emphasised, and they are well illustrated by *Wimpey Construction v Poole* [1984] 2 Lloyds Rep 499 and *Rimmer v Liverpool City Council* [1985] QB 1, [1984] 1 All ER 930:

(i) Codes of practice and British standards are of immense importance as indicators of the appropriate standard (cf *Kaliszewska v John Claque & Partners* [1984] CILL 131); but new methods are not in themselves wrong so long as appropriate warnings are given (*Victoria University, Manchester v H Wilson* [1984] CILL 126).

(ii) One must be careful not to judge the standard with the benefit of hindsight, whether arising from revised CPs and BSs or from the consequences of the 'defect'.

VARIATIONS IN THE STANDARD OF CARE

The issue was fully discussed in *Wimpey Construction v Poole* [1984] 2 Lloyds Rep 499 where Wimpey had carried out remedial works in respect of a project designed and built by them and were seeking to recover the cost from their insurer. Wimpey were arguing that they had been negligent in their design systems, but the insurer denied this. The *Bolam* test was regarded as applicable, but Wimpey argued three qualifications to it in order to produce a higher duty and so make it easier to establish their own 'negligence' (so as to bring the remedial work within the terms of the policy):

(1) The first qualification argued for, but rejected by the judge, was that the *Bolam* test ('the standard of the ordinary skilled man exercising and professing to have that special skill') was not applicable if the client obtains and pays for someone with specially high skills. The issue had been considered, but not decided, by Megarry J in *Duchess of Argyll v Beuselinck* [1972] 2 Lloyds Rep 172 at 183/4: 'If the client engages an expert, and doubtless expects to pay commensurate fees, is he not entitled to expect something more than the standard of the reasonably competent?'

Megarry J's question appears not to have been further considered. But, Webster J in *Wimpey v Poole* rejected the qualification, holding himself bound by the clear words of the *Bolam* test, as approved without qualification by the Privy Council in *Chin Keow v Government of Malaysia* [1967] 1 WLR 813 and the House of Lords in *Whitehouse v Jordan* [1981] 1 All ER 267, [1981] 1 WLR 246.

(2) Webster J accepted the second qualification; that it is the duty of the professional man to exercise reasonable care in the light of his knowledge and that the question whether he exercised reasonable care cannot be answered by reference to a lesser degree of knowledge than he had, on the grounds that the ordinarily competent practitioner would only have had that lesser degree of knowledge. This was treated by the judge as flowing naturally from Lord Atkin's formulation in *Donoghue v Stevenson* [1932] AC 562 at 580; but it seems analogous to the Court of Appeal's approach in *Greaves & Co (Contractors) Ltd v Baynham, Meikle & Partners* [1975] 3 All ER 99, [1975] 1 WLR 1095.

(3) The third qualification would have rendered the *Bolam* test in effect inapplicable. It was that the test was to be applied to Wimpey's most experienced designer, or to Wimpey as a company, assuming it employs the most experienced designers and at least one designer of exceptionally high qualifications. In the event, it was unnecessary to decide whether this was the appropriate test since, in Webster J's judgment, even on this test Wimpey was not negligent.

The extent of likely liability depends upon the relationship between the nature and magnitude of the loss, the *actual* level of knowledge of the defendant, and the consequent standard of care required.

Another focus of the question was the case of *Kimbell v Hart District Council* (1987) 9 Con LR 118, before His Honour Judge David Smout QC.

There, the suspect soil did not prove to be unsuitable until the extreme weather conditions made it so. Its vulnerability lay principally in its organic content. His Honour looked to see what warning was available in the early sixties which put or should have put a local authority on notice of possible danger of construction on subsoil of this nature, and to what extent if at all construction founded in such subsoil contravened the byelaws.

However, the 'state of the art' defence may be unavailable in respect of untried designs if the client is not warned. This is made clear by Judge Newey's decision in *Victoria University, Manchester v H Wilson* [1984] CILL 126:

> 'For the architects to use untried or relatively untried materials or techniques could not in itself be wrong, as otherwise the construction industry could never make any progress. However, architects ventur-

ing into the untried or little tried were wise to warn their clients specifically of what they were doing and to obtain their express approval. When the architects mentioned their intention to tile to the plaintiffs, anxiety was displayed which made it all the more incumbent on the architects to be careful. The university wanted a low maintenance building and the architects wrote saying the tiles should last the life of the building. Any doubts about the reliability of the tiles should have been resolved by not using them. Although not obliged to follow the recommendation contained in literature on the subject, the architects should certainly have taken the information into account as opposed to disregarding it. They designed the centre without features to protect from the rain; they used fondu No 1 without waterproof additive and failed to bring about necessary changes in design when the staining began. It also would seem that on no occasion did they discover that the sub-contractors were not doing their work properly. Consequently it was to be inferred that the architects did not inspect properly. Accordingly, the architects acted in breach of contract and were negligent in their design for both phases, in their supervision and failure to review the design.'

BREACH OF STATUTORY DUTY: CIVIL LIABILITY FOR BREACH OF THE BUILDING REGULATIONS

In *Perry v Tendring District Council* (1984) 3 Con LR 74, His Honour Judge Newey QC summarised the law on liability for breach of statutory duty as follows:

'The question of whether a statute, which is silent as to civil liability, nonetheless creates it has been considered by the courts on many occasions, most notably by the House of Lords in *Cutler v Wandsworth Stadium Ltd* [1949] AC 398, [1949] 1 All ER 544, by the Court of Appeal in *Monk v Warbey* [1935] 1 KB 75; *Square v Model Farm Dairies (Bournemouth) Ltd* [1939] 2 KB 365, [1939] 1 All ER 259 and *McCall v Abelesz* [1976] QB 585, [1976] 1 All ER 727 and by Lord Goddard CJ, sitting at first instance, in *Solomons v Gertzenstein Ltd* [1954] 1 QB 565 at 576. Mr Gibson provided me with a long schedule of appellate and first instance cases in some of which the decision went one way and in some the other.

I think that the effect of the cases is clear. The question of whether an Act creates liability in damages must be decided principally by reference to its wording, but regard may be had to consideration such as the pre-existing law. If an Act makes no provision for penalties or other means of enforcement, the assumption is that an action may be brought for breach of it. If the Act provides sanctions for breach of it, the assumption is that no action will lie. Where, however, the Act is plainly intended to protect an ascertainable class of persons and there are no common law rights upon which they may rely, it may be construed as creating a cause of action for breach of statutory duty.

In *Anns'* case the parties were the lessees of a block of flats and a local authority; no builders were involved. Lord Wilberforce said at 758:

"The position of the builder. I agree with the majority in the Court of Appeal in thinking that it would be unreasonable to impose liability in respect of defective foundations upon the council, if the builder, whose primary fault it was, should be immune from liability. So it is necessary to consider this point, although it does not directly arise in the present appeal."

Lord Wilberforce next considered whether the builder could be liable for negligence in respect of defective premises and after deciding that he could be, continued:

In the alternative, since it is the duty of the builder (owner or not) to comply with byelaws, I would be of the opinion that an action could be brought against him, in effect, for breach of statutory duty by any person for whose benefit or protection the byelaw was made."

Lord Wilberforce's words were, as he himself indicated obiter and they included 'in effect', but coming from such a source they obviously carry considerable weight.

In *Eames London Estates Ltd v North Hertfordshire District Council* (1980) 18 BLR 50 Judge Fay QC, Official Referee, after quoting Lord Wilberforce, held builders to be liable for breach of byelaws irrespective of negligence. He went on to say that he also held them liable in negligence. In *Worlock v SAWS* (1981) 20 BLR 94 Woolf J said obiter that he was satisfied that it would be wrong to regard the Building Regulations (which in 1966 took the place of building byelaws) as giving rise to a statutory duty creating an absolute liability. He said at 109:

"In my view, when the speeches in the case of *Anns* are considered, which deal in part with the position of the builder, they are inconsistent with any conclusion . . . It seems to me very difficult to accept that a person in the position of the plaintiff could establish an absolute duty against a builder by virtue of statute when the contract under which the building work was performed was one which created no such obligation".

In *Taylor Woodrow Construction (Midlands) Ltd v Charcon Structures Ltd* (1962) unreported Waller LJ in the Court of Appeal said:

"Whether or not a breach of [a Building Regulation] would by itself give rise to an action for damages without proof of negligence is to say the least doubtful . . . I say that the question of proof of negligence is doubtful because the only expression of view which gives any support to any other view was contained in the speech of Lord Wilberforce in *Anns* . . . Woolf J in *Worlock* came to the conclusion that it was not an absolute statutory duty but a duty which was a duty of care, and without expressing a concluded opinion about it, it seems to me . . . that a regulation of this kind is very difficult to construe as a regulation imposing an absolute duty in an action for damages."

In view of Waller LJ's and Woolf J's views I feel able not to follow Lord Wilberforce's dictum and Judge Fay's judgment which was based upon it.

In my view the Public Health Act 1936 does not contain any indication that it is intended that byelaws made under powers delegated by it should give rises to claims for damages. The Act provided effective means of enforcement, including injunction.

The Act was plainly intended to protect owners and occupiers of buildings, but they were not without remedies at common law, as in respect of almost all matters covered by the byelaws they could bring actions for negligence. Possibly the only exceptions are byelaws dealing with size of windows and space about buildings.

The local authority's liability in *Anns* was not for breach of statutory duty, but for negligence in the exercise of statutory powers. The builders in that case would probably have been liable in negligence.

In my opinion building byelaws did not give rise to liability in damages, but I trust that before long there will be a specific decision of the Court of Appeal on the subject.'

In *Kimbell v Hart DC and Comben & Wakeling* [1986] CILL 302, a breach of statutory duty, under s 64 of the Public Health Act 1936 was also relied on. However, applying the reasoning of His Honour Judge Newey QC in *Perry v Tendring District Council* (1984) 3 Con LR 74 at 89–91 [1985] CILL 145 to a breach of s 64, Judge Smout did not construe s 64 as imposing an absolute duty. Any breach of that statutory duty without proof of negligence did not of itself give rise to a claim in damages. The plaintiffs' claim could lie only in negligence.

The building byelaws in force in this case dated back to 1953. Byelaw 16, on clearing turf and other vegetable matter, was not to be read as requiring removal of all organic matter of vegetable origin from the subsoil. Byelaw 18, on foundations, was directed at such a degree of settlement as impaired stability of any part of the building. Here the stability of the floor was impaired, and the slab was a foundation: see *Worlock v SAWS* (1981) 20 BLR 94 (Woolf J); on appeal (1983) 22 BLR 26, CA. There had thus been on the face of it a breach of the byelaw. But as that did not of itself render the local authority negligent, one came back again to the state of the art in 1962.

Were the local authority negligent in failing at that time to reject plans which, as it transpired, did show that the work proposed contravened the byelaw? Applying the standard of care of an ordinary competent local authority possessed of the skill and knowledge that such an authority ought to have had at that time, His Honour did not find negligence. Even if the local authority had carried out detailed site investigations which had revealed up to 7 per cent organic content in the subsoil, the local authority would not have been negligent in passing the plans. They were not put on notice at that time that subsoil with such content would be vulnerable. The plaintiffs' claim against the defendants accordingly failed.

A SOLUTION, BUT NOT YET IN FORCE: CIVIL LIABILITY FOR BREACH OF THE BUILDING REGULATIONS

There is therefore considerable uncertainty now as to whether builders are liable at all, let alone without proof of fault, for breach of statutory duty for non-compliance with the building regulations. The *D & F Estates* decision in the House of Lords could be read as assuming that Lord Wilberforce was right in *Anns* to regard the builder as under such a duty.

It is extraordinary therefore that the matter has already been legislated on by Parliament, yet the relevant provision of the Building Act has yet to be brought into force. Section 38 does not yet apply, even though it states:

> 'breach of a duty imposed by building regulations, so far as it causes damages, is actionable, except in so far as the regulations provide otherwise, and
>
> . . . as regards such a duty, building regulations may provide for a prescribed defence to be available in an action for breach of that duty'.

NON-COMPLIANCE WITH APPROVED DOCUMENTS

The status of approved documents, in liability terms, is made plain by s 7 of the Building Act 1984, and this section of the 1984 Act has been brought into force:

> '7. (1) A failure on the part of a person to comply with an approved document does not of itself render him liable to any civil or criminal proceedings; but if, in any proceedings whether civil or criminal, it is alleged that a person has at any time contravened a provision of building regulations—
>
> (a) a failure to comply with a document that at that time was approved for the purposes of that provision may be relied upon as tending to establish liability, and
>
> (b) proof of compliance with such a document may be relied on as tending to negative liability.'

BURDEN OF PROOF: WHO HAS TO SHOW COMPLIANCE?

In *Rickards v Kerrier District Council* [1987] CILL 345, the High Court had to consider for the first time an important practical point arising in respect of the new 1985 Building Regulations. It concerned the situation where a local authority had served a notice under s 36 of the Building Act 1984 (the Act under which the Regulations were made).

The judge held that the burden of proving non-compliance with the Regulations was on the authority, but if the latter showed that the works did not comply with the approved document (under s 6 of the Act) then the burden shifted. The appellant against the notice would then have to show compliance with the Regulations.

LIABILITY OF LOCAL AUTHORITIES

The principles are stated in the House of Lords judgment in *Peabody Donation Fund v Sir Lindsay Parkinson* [1985] AC 210, [1984] 3 All ER 529. Not only does that decision restrict the local authority's duty to a very limited range of loss (threat to health or safety), but it also lends weight to two limitations of general application in relation to finding a duty in tort:

(i) that it depends on the 'power/instruction' under which the defendant was acting; and

(ii) that it depends on the nature of the loss for which the claim is made.

The following extracts from Lord Keith's judgment demonstrate the approach that must be taken:

> 'The true question in each case is whether the particular defendant owed to the particular plaintiff a duty of care having the scope which is contended for, and whether he was in breach of that duty with consequent loss to the plaintiff. A relationship must exist before any duty of care can arise, but the scope of the duty must depend on all the circumstances of the case . . .
>
> So in determining whether or not a duty of care of particular scope was incumbent upon a defendant it is material to take into consideration whether it is just and reasonable that it should be so.
>
> The purpose for which the powers contained in paragraph 15 of Part III of Schedule 9 have been conferred on Lambeth is not to safeguard building developers against economic loss resulting from their failure to comply with approved plans. It is in my opinion to safeguard the occupiers of houses built in the local authority's area, and also members of the public generally, against dangers to their health which may arise from defective drainage installations.'

Furthermore, the House held that *Acrecrest v W S Hattrell & Partners* [1983] QB 260, [1983] 1 All ER 17, CA was wrongly decided and was overruled. *Dennis v Charnwood Borough Council* [1983] QB 409, [1982] 3 All ER 486 was treated as justified on the basis that the plaintiffs, as owners who were the intended occupiers of the house, were within the ambit of the duty of care laid down in *Anns*, because their health and safety might be injured if the foundations were inadequate.

The Court of Appeal's judgment in *Investors in Industry Commercial Properties v South Bedfordshire District Council* [1986] QB 1034, [1986] 1 All ER 787, CA is of considerable importance. It held, inter alia, that on the basis of *Peabody* a local authority in exercising supervisory powers, will normally owe no duty to an original building owner, because it is normally incumbent on the building owner itself to ensure that the building is erected in accordance with the relevant building regulations. A fortiori (again on the basis of *Peabody*) a local authority, in exercising these powers, will normally owe no duty to an original building owner who has had the benefit of the advice of architects, engineers and contractors and has relied upon it.

A vital element in *Anns v Merton LBC*, however, which remains unaffected by these more modern restrictive decisions, is that a public authority has a potential immunity from suit as a result of public law principles. Unlike a private defendant, a public body may rely on a defence that it exercised its discretion reasonably in the allocation of scarce resources, even though some loss resulted to the particular plaintiff. This is the distinction in *Anns* between decisions taken at the 'policy' level and those taken at the 'operational' level. It is relevant only where the activity in question is the exercise of discretionary powers rather than statutory duties.

The aspect of the *Anns v Merton* decision that has changed is the extent of losses recoverable from local authorities. In *Dutton* the council was liable to the owner occupier for the estimated cost of repairs; and in *Anns* damages could include damage to the dwelling-house itself, so that what was recoverable was the expenditure necessary to restore the dwelling to a condition in which it was no longer a danger to the health or safety of occupiers. In *Ketteman v Hansel Properties Ltd* [1984] 1 WLR 1274 at 1290, Lawton LJ explained the meaning of 'present or imminent danger to health or safety' (a point not taken further on appeal to the House of Lords in that case).

In the light of these authorities the duty of an authority exercising powers under the building regulations, or the like, differs substantially from the duty of private persons, such as contractors, under the ordinary law of negligence under *D & F Estates*. The council's duty is owed only to owner occupiers and, unless perhaps the circumstances are special, not even to them if they are 'first builders', in the sense of having caused the buildings to be erected. The duty is limited to not causing danger to health or safety, which was either actual or likely to arise soon. A plaintiff's cause of action is complete when the authority's lack of reasonable care had resulted in such danger or imminent danger, even though at that stage the plaintiff had not suffered any loss.

The special nature of this duty therefore flows from the statutory definition of the local authority's building control powers.

It does not mean that all local authority activity is similarly restricted in terms of liability. For example, there have been cases on the responsibility of local authorities for damage (which could be latent) caused by trees. See, for example, *Low v R J Haddock Ltd* [1985] CILL 162, and *Solloway v Hampshire County Council* (1981) 79 LGR 449. These will turn not only on the statutory duties of highway authorities, but also on the ordinary common law of negligence.

WHY ARE APPROVED INSPECTORS' LIABILITIES DIFFERENT?

By virtue of the provisions in the Building Act 1984, building control functions can now be carried out by Approved Inspectors. But, their liabilities are governed by private law and not by the public law considerations which affect local authorities. Hence the Approved Inspector has a contract with the builder or developer whereas the local authority does not, even though it receives fees for building control activities. Having a contract with the Approved Inspector gives some measure of control to the contractor and facilitates clarity as to the allocation of risk. Like local authorities, the Approved Inspector's liability is, by implication from the Building Regulations themselves, limited to what is necessary to secure reasonable standards of health and safety for persons in or about the building and others who may be affected by the failure to comply. However, under the Approved Inspector Regulations an Approved Inspector is required to be satisfied 'within the limits of professional skill and care'. This links the liability to the concept of professional skill and care already well defined by the courts. It implies a potentially more onerous liability for Approved Inspectors than for local authorities, precisely because local authorities have the benefit of the elasticity of discretion available by public law considerations described above.

THE DEFECTIVE PREMISES ACT 1972

The legal liabilities of those involved in design and construction began to increase dramatically in the early 1970s. There was the passing by Parliament of the Defective Premises Act 1972. However, its principal provisions concerning dwellings were for many years of little significance since they did not apply to houses covered by the NHBC's predecessor schemes to the Buildmark. However, houses covered by the NHBC scheme are now governed by the 1972 Act. Furthermore, the restrictive approach to contractors' liability adopted in *D and F Estates v Church Comrs* [1989] AC 177, [1988] 2 All ER 992 adds significance to what has thereby become the potentially wider liabilities arising under the Act. The purpose of the Defective Premises Act 1972 is stated in its long title:

> 'An act to impose duties in connection with the provision of dwellings and otherwise to amend the law of England and Wales as to liability for injury or damage caused to persons through defects in the state of premises.'

The Act came into force on 1 January 1974. Section 1 substantially implements the Law Commission's recommendations in its Report No 40 'Civil Liability of Vendors and Lessors for Defective Premises'.

Section 1 imposes a duty to build dwellings properly. A person taking on work for or in connection with the provision of a dwelling (whether the dwelling is provided by the erection or by the conversion or enlargement of a building) owes a duty (if the dwelling is provided to the order of any person) to that person; and to every person who acquires an interest (whether legal or equitable) in the dwelling.

The duty is to see that the work which he takes on is done in a workmanlike or, as the case may be, professional manner, with proper materials and so that, as regards that work, the dwelling will be fit for habitation when completed.

However, a person who takes on such work for another on terms that he is to do it in accordance with instructions given by or on behalf of that other shall, to the extent to which he does it properly in accordance with those instructions, be treated as discharging the duty (set out above) except where he owes a duty to that other to warn him of any defects in the instructions and fails to discharge that duty. But a person shall not be treated as having given instructions for the doing of work merely because he has agreed to the work being done in a specified manner, with specified materials or to a specified design.

A person who in the course of a business of providing dwellings or installations in dwellings (or in the exercise of a statutory power of making such provision) arranges for another to take on work for it in connection with the provision of a dwelling shall be treated as included among the persons who have taken the work.

The cause of action for breach of the duty is deemed to have accrued at the time when the dwelling was completed, but if after that time a person who has done work for or in connection with the provision of the dwelling does further work to rectify the work he has already done, the cause of action in respect of that further work is deemed to have accrued at the time when the further work was finished.

The duties imposed by the Act are in addition to any duty a person may owe otherwise. Furthermore, any term of an agreement which purports to exclude or restrict, or has the effect of excluding or restricting, the operation of any of the provisions of this Act, or any liability arising by virtue of any such provisions, shall be void.

Section 2 of the Act then specifically excludes from the application of s 1 dwellings to which an 'approved scheme' applies conferring rights in respect of defects when they are first let or sold for habitation. This limitation upon the new statutory duty does not follow directly from any specific recommendation in the Law Commission's report, although the report discussed the scheme operated by the (then) National House-Builders Registration Council and it was presumably such schemes as this that Parliament contemplated might receive the approval of the Secretary of State under s 2 conferring exemption from liability for breach of statutory duty under s 1.

LIMITATION OF ACTIONS

The principle of the English law of limitation which therefore applied to latent damage cases until the coming into force of the Latent Damage Act 1986, is that a plaintiff must commence his action within a particular period beginning with the date of the accrual of his cause of action. So, the period for actions resulting from tortious negligence not involving personal injury or death is six years; and the cause of action accrues in such cases when the actual damage occurs whether or not it is yet discoverable.

The difficulty that arises from this normal rule is how, in law, to identify when the actionable form of damage occurred. The implication of cases in the late 1980s restricting contractors' negligence liability to third parties is that what constitutes sufficient harm to be actionable damage in tort must (in the light of those cases) be more than mere defects in the building itself. So, under a restrictive judicial attitude to tortious negligence liability, a cause of action would not accrue normally until there is actual (or perhaps apprehended) physical damage to person or other property.

The result of the courts' narrowing liability in tort is the renewed importance of contractual lines of claims. It appears that the Latent Damage Act 1986 applies only to tortious negligence, and that it therefore leaves unaffected contractual limitation periods (even though breach of contract can cause latent damage). For the reasons justifying this view see Phillip Capper's *Latent Damage Act 1986: the Impact upon the Profession and the Construction Industry*. So, in contract cases where the parties have not agreed any particular limitation period, the usual periods in the Limitation Act 1980 will continue to apply:

* 12 years from the relevant breach of contract, in cases of contracts under seal;
* six years from breach for simple contracts (ie not under seal).

Although the principle is that contractual causes of action accrue at the time of the breach of contract, a breach of a contractual duty would often be regarded as continuing at least until completion of the contract and in some cases even later.

A warranty as to fitness for purpose, however, is presumably not broken (depending on its terms) until it first becomes unfulfilled: the breach of contract would then be regarded as occurring at the date of the failure of the warranty, not at the time of any particular act or omission which may (for example during construction) have been the reason for the eventual failure of the warranty. On this view there is no conflict between normal statutory limitation periods and the periods of, for example, 60-year or building lifetime warranties. Rather, the limitation periods applicable to accrual of causes of action arising from breaches of contract operate in the normal way from the date of the breach upon the eventual first failure of the warranty. The same would apply to 'duty of care' warranties, though the breach in those cases would, as in tort, arise at the time of the act or omission complained of, such as the failure to take reasonable care.

Parties to a contract have the freedom (subject to the Unfair Contract Terms Act 1977) to provide expressly for their own limitation period and so cut down the period of exposure that would otherwise apply under the 1980 Act. Also limitation periods can be extended beyond the statutory periods as they operate as defences which the defendant can agree not to plead.

Alternatively matching protection can be sought by a potential defendant from another by requiring an indemnity from that other. However, it should be noted that the way in which indemnities operate can give rise to very long periods of protection or exposure (depending on whether you are giving or receiving the indemnity). The call on an indemnity could extend well beyond the 15 year long stop period which, under the Latent Damage Act 1986, would bar the third party tort claim. This is because the right to sue on an indemnity accrues only when the loss indemnified has itself been established. Therefore, if a contracting party were successfully sued in tort 14 years after a breach of duty and the claim were the subject of an indemnity under seal the party granting the indemnity could be sued up to 26 years after the relevant breach of duty.

So far as negligence actions on the law of tort is concerned, the new time limits are laid down by the Latent Damage Act 1986. The new limitation timetable in the Act is:

* 15 years from breach of duty, if this expires first (the 'long stop');
* otherwise, whichever is the later of six years from accrual of the cause of action (occurrence of the damage) or three years from its discoverability.

These new limits apply only to negligence actions and negligence appears to mean for this purpose only tortious negligence. Certainly, they do not apply to claims including damages for personal injuries, nor to cases of deliberate concealment. The point must be emphasised that all these periods start from different times and that the purpose of the 15 year long stop is that it may expire before the six year or three year period.

The 1986 Act also confers new rights on successive owners. A problem had arisen because in *Perry v Tendring District Council* (1984) 30 BLR 118 it had been held, following *Pirelli*, that a successive owner of property already latently damaged on disposition to him had no right of action because he had no interest in the property when the damage occurred. The purpose of s 3 of the 1986 Act is to cure this gap in the law. Despite the extremely convoluted drafting of s 3, which does give rise to some legal difficulties, the intended effect in the end seems to be relatively simple: broadly speaking, a person acquiring an interest in property after the damage occurs but before knowledge of it has arisen is given a fresh cause of action which is treated by the statute as accruing to that new person as from the date of the original damage. So the new person is put broadly into the same position as the person who owned the property at the time the damage occurred, with an extension period running for three years from discovery, subject to the long stop.

The most novel aspect of the Act is its introduction of the so called 'long stop'. However, a complicating feature is that the 15 year period is timed as from the date of the breach of duty. There is complex case law showing that some breaches of duty can be regarded as continuing or revived by later conduct (such as remedial works). A further difficulty is that past case law concerned with establishing a breach of duty is focused more on the point that it had happened rather than when it happened. There are four important cases where the defendant's period of exposure to liability may extend beyond 15 years from breach of duty, because the long stop does not apply:

* Deliberate concealment
* Rights of contribution
* Claims under contractual indemnities
* Property claims involving damages for personal injuries

There was controversy in Parliament because the long stop would not protect builders in deliberate concealment cases. Deliberate concealment includes deliberate commission of a breach of duty in circumstances in which it is unlikely to be discovered for some time. In such a case, the limitation period will not even begin to run until the plaintiff has discovered the deliberate concealment (or could reasonably do so). There is some suggestion in recent case law that the courts may more readily impute 'deliberate concealment' to a contractor than they would under the previous statutory wording of 'fraudulent concealment'.

COMMON LAW PRODUCT LIABILITY

The House of Lords in *D and F Estates v Church Comrs* [1989] AC 177, [1988] 2 All ER 992, said that *Anns v Merton London Borough Council* [1978] AC 728, [1977] 2 All ER 492 had introduced an entirely new type of product liability, if not, indeed, an entirely novel concept of the tort of negligence. In doing so, the English courts seemed to have gone even further than the American courts.

It seems, however, clear that for ordinary negligence claims, the *D & F* decision firmly stopped common law negligence becoming a vehicle for general product liability. We have seen above that it restored the principal limitations from the famous snail case *Donoghue v Stevenson* [1932] AC 562: there must be personal injury; or, there must be damage to the plaintiff's 'other' property (ie other than the very part the defective condition of which gives rise to the claim); and, there must have been no reasonable opportunity for intermediate examination which would have enabled the plaintiff to be aware of the potential for harm before it occurred. Difficulties remain about the requirement of damage to 'other property'; see *Aswan Engineering Establishment Co v Lupdine Ltd* [1987] 1 All ER 135, [1987] 1

WLR 1, CA, as well as *D & F* (what *is* a 'complex' product; how is one part of a complex product to be distinguished from another?).

The crucial distinction thus now to be drawn is between 'dangerous defects' and 'defects of quality'. But, what if the injury or damage has yet to occur? Is the cost of *averting* danger recoverable? Does discovery of a defect before it causes injury to person or other property prevent recovery of the costs of making good the defect? Or, did the Lords intend that the costs of averting danger would be recoverable only in *Anns* type actions (and thus perhaps only in breach of statutory duty cases)?

EUROPEAN PRODUCT LIABILITY

Against this new common law background, it is instructive to recognise the limits of the new statutory regime of product liability. The policy behind *D & F* mirrors much of the statute. Equally, uncertainties raised by *D & F* as to 'other property' and the costs of 'averting danger' could cause problems under the statute.

The European Directive and the Consumer Protection Act 1987

The European Community Directive on Product Liability has been implemented in the UK by the Consumer Protection Act 1987, Part I, which came into force on 1 March 1988. Despite some of the fanfare when it was implemented in the UK, the liabilities which are there imposed are by no means absolute. Careful attention to the provisions of the legislation reveals a good many grounds on which any potential defendant can limit the risk of liability. Inevitably, with complex legal matters, the particular wording used in the legislation has to be interpreted. However, in this case there is from the outset a complicating factor. The UK Act implements the European Directive. But it does so in very different words. There is a potential for a conflict of meaning here. The Act seeks to get round that difficulty by the interpretation provision in s 1(1) of the Act:

> '1. (1) This part shall have effect for the purpose of making such provision as is necessary in order to comply with the product liability Directive and shall be construed accordingly.'

Broadly, the Directive, implemented by the 1987 Act, imposes a liability without fault—'strict liability'. It is no defence to say that all reasonable care had been taken. It does not displace ordinary negligent liability to third parties but merely adds an alternative, easier access to compensation for the victim.

The claimant must still prove the damage, the defect and the causal relationship between them. Rights of contribution between defendants who have caused the same damage are preserved, as is the principle of contributory negligence (which reduces damages payable in proportion to any blame on the part of the victim).

What is a product?

The definition itself is contained in s 1(2) and is as follows:

> ' "product" means any goods or electricity and (subject to subsection (3) below) includes a product which is comprised in another product, whether by virtue of being a component part or raw material or otherwise.'

Further definitions are found in s 45 of the Act:

> ' "goods" includes substances, growing crops and things comprised in land by virtue of being attached to it and any ship, aircraft or vehicle;
> "substance" means any natural or artificial substance, whether in solid, liquid or gaseous form or in the form of a vapour, and includes substances that are comprised in or mixed with other goods;'.

Limits on liability: 'producers' and 'suppliers'

'Producers' are defined as manufacturers, importers, and any person who by using his name or mark in relation to the product holds himself out to be the producer. There is a subsidiary liability on any 'supplier' of a product if the supplier does not identify the person who supplied it to him.

Who is a supplier?

A fundamental notion common to both Part I of the 1987 Act (on product liability) and Part II (on criminal liability in respect of safety requirements) is the meaning of 'supply'. This is a central question in relation to the application of the statutory product liability provisions to the construction industry. All turns on the rather peculiar provisions tucked away in s 46 of the Act:

> '46 (1) Subject to the following provisions of this section, references in this Act to supplying goods shall be construed as references to doing any of the following, whether as principal or agent, that is to say—
> (a) selling, hiring out or lending the goods;
> . . . ;
> (c) the performance of any contract for work and materials to furnish the goods;
> . . .
> [(2) . . .]
> (3) Subject to subsection (4) below, the performance of any contract by the erection of any building or structure on any land or by the carrying out of any other building works shall be treated for the purposes of this Act as a supply of goods in so far as, but only in so far as, it involves the provision of any goods to any person by means of their incorporation into the building, structure or works.
> (4) Except for the purposes of, and in relation to, notices to warn or any provision made by or under Part III of this Act to supplying goods shall not include references to supplying goods comprised in land where the supply is effected by the creation or disposal of an interest in the land.'

It is not apparent from the European Directive why ss 46(3) and (4) were necessary in the UK legislation. Indeed, it may be that the UK was wrong to introduce this immunity for builders who build on their own land and then sell the building with the land. The question arises whether the interpretation provision in s 1(1) would allow an English court to ignore s 46(4) in order to give effect to the Directive.

Limits on liability: 'defect'

There has to be a defect in the product. But, this does not mean simply a lack of quality or fitness for purpose. There is a 'defect' only if the product is not safe as persons generally are entitled to expect. Safety includes risk of damage to products *within* the product, and to other property.

Limits on liability: 'damage'

The liability arises only if a narrowly defined form of damage is suffered: death or personal injuries; or, damage to any item of property other than the defective product itself (subject to a lower threshold of value of the damage to the property (£275), to discourage small claims; and, a requirement that the property was in use by a private consumer). By contrast with *D & F*, 'other property' here also excludes any other product in which the defective product is comprised and which was supplied with the defective product.

So, the liability will not arise simply because a user has found quality defects in the product itself.

Limits on liability: defences

The Act forbids contracting out, or other simple avoidance of the liability, by conventional disclaimers (see s 7). The emphasis here is on limiting or excluding the liability by terms, notices and other provisions. However, careful attention to the legal implications of this Act can lead to useful devices for controlling the extent to which any product can be said to be defective.

The Act provides certain limited defences. These are set out in s 4(1):

(a) that the defect is attributable to compliance with any requirement imposed by or under any enactment or with any Community obligation; or
(b) that the person proceeded against did not at any time supply the product to another; or
(c) that the supply was not in the course of a business; or
(d) that the defect did not exist in the product at the time it was first supplied by the producer to another; or
(e) that the state of scientific and technical knowledge at the relevant time was not such that a producer of products of the same description as the product in question might be expected to have discovered the defects if it had existed in his products while they were under his control; or
(f) that the defect—
  (i) constituted a defect in a product ('the subsequent product') in which the product in question had been comprised; and
  (ii) was wholly attributable to the design of the subsequent product or to compliance with instructions given by the producer of the subsequent product.

The last three of these defences (1) (d), (e) and (f) are likely to prove much more significant in practice than the first three (1) (a), (b) and (c).

An important advantage for any potential defendant is the scope for reasonable argument as to the extent of any alleged liability. To that extent, the question whether the defect existed in the product 'at the relevant time' (which broadly means the time of original supply) will leave considerable scope for argument.

The 'development risk' defence was framed very narrowly in the European Community Directive: 'That the state of scientific and technical knowledge at the time when [the producer] put the product into circulation was not such as to enable the existence of the defect to be discovered'. This reference in effect to *all* scientific and technical knowledge makes the defence narrower than the normal 'state of the art' defence in ordinary negligence liability actions.

However, the implementation of the 'development risk' defence in the UK Act has arguably been framed too liberally for producers. The 1987 Act provides that it shall be a defence 'that the state of scientific and technical knowledge at the relevant time was not such that a producer of products of the same description as the product in question might be expected to have discovered the defect if it had existed in his products while they were under his control'. This seems much closer to the common law negligence test of 'reasonable competence having regard to the scientific and technical knowledge available to the defendant at the relevant time'. The UK Act has therefore been challenged by consumer organisations as failing to implement faithfully the European Directive.

For the construction industry in particular the final defence set out in (f) is a very significant line of defence indeed. Here it is clear that careful attention to contractual and other documentation (with a legal eye) could create some solid defences. All will depend on when a product is being supplied within a product. This makes crucial the extent to which a building can itself be said to be a product. If this defensive provision is applicable to construction, the vital need will be to secure clear definition of the specification.

How long can statutory product liability exposure last?

Victims will be able to start an action within three years from the damage, or from its discoverability if later. This is directly analogous to the provisions of the Latent Damage Act 1986. However, there will also be a long stop period applicable to product liability claims. This is different to that introduced by the Latent Damage Act 1986 for ordinary negligence claims in three respects: the long stop period is only ten years; it does not start from breach of duty, but rather from the time the product was supplied; and it extinguishes the right, rather than merely barring the remedy (this is significant in relation to rights of contribution between defendants).

CHAPTER 2

The nature of expert evidence

Anthony Thornton QC, Assistant Recorder, MA, BCL (Oxon)
Kim Franklin LLB, ACIArb, Barrister

WHAT IS EVIDENCE?

Introduction

There are invariably many matters upon which parties to a law suit disagree: from the suitability of the other to operate in the business world, their choice of chairman or marketing strategy through to any want of skill demonstrated by them in, for example, the design of a building or its construction.

For the guidance of the court and the parties, their lawyers ascertain and isolate by the process of exchange of pleadings those disputed facts which are material to the particular case. Once the material facts in issue have been identified the parties and their lawyers aim to prove (or disprove) those facts to the satisfaction of the court.

Information relied upon to establish a disputed fact is known as evidence. Whether such information can be presented to the court and, if so, in what way is determined by the law of evidence. The quest for proof is regulated and restricted by a plethora of legal rules, a full discussion of which is beyond the scope of this work. There are, however, some fundamentals upon which the complex framework of the law of evidence is based.

The facts to be proved

In any legal proceedings the facts that need to be proved are governed by the substantive law. If a plaintiff alleges negligence he must show that the defendant owed him a duty of care, that the defendant was in breach of that duty and that as a result, the plaintiff suffered damage. Knowledge of the substantive law is necessary to identify the legal issues of a particular case. Only facts which are relevant to the legal issues need to be proved. Irrelevant facts are otiose and therefore not admissible as evidence.

This can be illustrated by way of example. Polly alleges that David drove negligently and caused an accident in which she was injured. The information available to Polly includes the following facts:

(1) David has an extensive criminal record for vehicle theft.
(2) An eyewitness saw that David was driving on the wrong side of the road when the accident happened.

(3) A passenger in David's car told Polly that this was the fifth accident David had been involved in that month.

Clearly only the eyewitness's statement is relevant to the issue of whether David's carelessness caused the accident. The other matters are irrelevant and Polly would not be able to rely upon them at trial.

The obligation to prove

As a general rule the party who makes an allegation has to prove it: in civil cases it is usually the plaintiff. It is said in legal jargon that the plaintiff bears the burden of proof. In fact the plaintiff's onus is twofold; firstly, he must produce enough evidence to get his case off the ground or to make it a reasonable possibility at least that the court will find in his favour and then he must prove his case to the satisfaction of the court. The two hurdles are known respectively as the evidential burden and legal burden of proof.

The amount of proof required

The burden of proof would be onerous indeed if the plaintiff had to satisfy the court to the point of certainty that his version of the disputed matters was correct. In civil cases the standard of proof is the balance of probabilities. The court must therefore be satisfied that the plaintiff's version is more likely than the defendant's. Should the plaintiff fail to discharge the burden to this standard then the court will find against him.

The regulation of proof at law

Only relevant information can be used to prove facts in dispute but not all the available relevant information can be used. The rules of evidence dictate what information is admissible at trial. Evidence can be inadmissible because certain methods of giving evidence are prohibited or because the evidence by its nature is inadmissible. It is far from easy to detect an underlying justification for the extensive and complex rules. As a generalisation, however, it could be said that the rules have developed because either the evidence itself or the method by which it is given is considered unreliable or contrary to public policy.

Types of evidence

Evidence can be classified according to the way in which it is presented to the court; namely, oral, documentary or real. Oral evidence is information by way of spoken statement given by a witness usually under oath from the witness box. It is by far the most common form of evidence. Documentary evidence is information obtained from reading documents or sometimes listening to tape recordings. Real evidence is information obtained by inspection of locations, animals or other material objects.

WHAT IS EXPERT EVIDENCE?

As a general rule a witness may not express his opinion when giving evidence. A witness must limit his evidence to the facts which he personally perceived and not draw inferences from them. The rule is based on the notion that it is the function of the judge to draw inferences and form opinions from the evidence whilst witnesses state the facts from which such inferences can be drawn.

It was soon recognised, however, that there are certain matters upon which the judge lacks the necessary knowledge required to draw the right inferences from the facts stated by witnesses. Thus where matters calling for specialist skill, knowledge or expertise are concerned a witness is allowed to state his opinion provided he is an expert.

As long ago as 1553 Sauders J said:

> '... if matters arise in our law which concern other sciences or faculties, we commonly apply for the aid of that science or faculty which it concerns. Which is an honourable and commendable thing in our law. For thereby it appears that we don't dispute all other sciences but our own, but we approve of them and encourage them as things worthy of commendation.'
> (*Buckley v Rice-Thomas* (1554) 1 Plowd 118 at 124)

The role of the modern expert witness developed during the eighteenth century. In *Folkes v Chadd* (1782) 3 Doug KB 157 the well-known engineer Mr Smeaton was called upon to give his opinion upon the effect of the erection of an artificial bank upon the choking up of a harbour since he

> 'understands the construction of harbours, the causes of their destruction and how remedied'.

Similarly in *Beckwith v Sydebotham* (1807) 1 Camp 116 shipwrights testified as to the seaworthiness of a ship. The judge considered that the jury might be assisted by the opinion of those peculiarly acquainted with it in their professions or pursuits.

The duties of an expert witness were set out in *Davie v Edinburgh Magistrates* 1953 SC 34, 1953 SLT 54:

> 'Their duty is to furnish the judge or jury with the necessary scientific criteria for testing the accuracy of their conclusions, so as to enable the judge or jury to form their own independent judgment of the application of these critieria to the facts proved in evidence.'

Subjects upon which expert evidence is admissible

The field of subjects which the courts have treated as requiring a sufficient degree of specialised knowledge to render expert evidence admissible is large, diverse and ever expanding. Whether a particular aspect of a case requires explanation by an expert is a question for the judge. Some areas obviously call for expert opinion, such as medicine, science, engineering, accident investigation and the genuineness of works of art.

In other areas, however, the issue is not so clear cut. In *R v Turner* [1975] QB 834, [1975] 1 All ER 70 the accused who was charged with murdering his girlfriend pleaded provocation. He sought to call a psychiatrist to give evidence to the effect that he had a deep relationship with the girl and was vulnerable to an explosive outburst of rage upon her confession of infidelity. It was held that the expert should not be called since the jury did not need to be told how normal men behave when their women admit to infidelity. As Lawton LJ said (at 481):

> 'An expert's opinion is admissible to furnish the court with scientific information which is likely to be outside the experience and knowledge of a judge or jury. If on the proven facts a judge or jury can form their own conclusions without help, then the opinion of an expert is unnecessary ... The fact that an expert witness has impressive scientific qualifications does not by that fact alone make his opinion on matters of human nature and behaviour within the limits of normality any more helpful than that of the jurors themselves; but there is a danger that they may think it does.'

The qualifications of an expert

It is for the judge to decide whether the proposed witness has enough experience or training to render him an expert in any particular field. It is not, however, merely a question of professional qualification. Unqualified medical students have been allowed to give evidence as medical experts and an amateur student of handwriting (who was by profession a solicitor) was permitted to give evidence as an expert (*R v Silverlock* [1894] 2 QB 766).

Specialisation is a matter of degree: a police officer who has extensive experience in investigating road traffic accidents may be an expert for the purposes of reconstructing a particular motor accident but an experienced driver does not have expertise on the subject of the abilities of someone charged with dangerous driving.

The extent of expert evidence

It is a general rule of common law that an expert should not be asked to state his opinion upon the very issue the judge is asked to determine—the ultimate issue. The rationale is this: the parties are entitled to have their case decided by a judge. The exchange of the views of eminent experts upon the issues can lead to a balancing of opinions and may shift the responsibility from the bench to the witness box. The problem was summarised thus*:

> 'If a cardinal of the Roman Catholic church is testifying before a jury mainly composed of Catholics, and states that, in his opinion, the defendant was driving negligently, it can hardly be supposed that the verdict would be other than for the plaintiff.'

In civil cases this rule has been relaxed by s 3 of the Civil Evidence Act 1972 which provides that an expert witness may give evidence upon any issue in the proceedings.

THE COURSE OF EVIDENCE—IN COURT

A witness gives evidence in court by way of examination. He is questioned by the legal representatives of the parties to the proceedings and sometimes by the judge. The witness is first questioned by the party at whose instance he has been called. This is known as examination-in-chief. He is then cross-examined by the other parties in the case. Finally he can be re-examined by the original questioner.

*King & Pillinger 'Opinion Evidence in Illinois' 60 LQR 202

Examination-in-chief

During examination-in-chief the witness should not be asked leading questions, that is, those that suggest the desired answer. The rule is aimed at preventing the witness from becoming a mere mouthpiece for the party calling him. By way of example, a witness should not be asked, 'Is it your view that the contractor's operatives were at fault for failing to clear wall ties of mortar droppings?' but instead should be asked, 'What are your views on the question of wall ties and mortar droppings?'

Examination-in-chief can be substantially reduced or avoided by the exchange, in advance of the hearing, of the witness's evidence submitted in written form and known as a proof of evidence. This has the advantage of reducing the amount of court time spent recording the witness's evidence-in-chief. The parties can concentrate immediately upon the aspects of the witness's evidence which are disputed which will be the focus of cross-examination. Proceeding straight to cross-examination has the disadvantage that the witness is not given the opportunity to settle into the witness box and become confident in giving evidence before his evidence is attacked in cross-examination.

As a general rule experts are not called as witnesses unless the substance of their evidence has been disclosed in the form of a written report. This fact has encouraged the practice with regard to experts of not giving them the opportunity to give their evidence-in-chief but immediately tendering them for cross-examination.

Cross-examination

Any witness who is not called by a party can be cross-examined by that party. If a witness gives evidence of a fact in examination-in-chief and he is not cross-examined on that fact, it is assumed that the fact is not in dispute. The aim of cross-examination is twofold: to obtain relevant information that is favourable to the case of the party carrying out the cross-examination and to undermine the accuracy of unfavourable evidence given in chief.

The pursuit of these aims is relatively unrestricted and the cross-examiner may ask leading questions and make a general attack on the witness's credit and character. Cross-examination is subject to the ordinary rules of admissibility of evidence and will not be allowed, for example, on matters that are irrelevant to the issues. Also the judge has a discretion to disallow any question which appears vexatious or offensive.

Re-examination

After cross-examination, the witness may be re-examined by the party calling him. Re-examination is confined, however, to matters that were raised in cross-examination. Questions can not be asked that should have been asked in examination-in-chief since new matters may only be introduced with the leave of the judge. The object of re-examination is to clarify any false impressions that may have been created by cross-examination and to rehabilitate a witness who has been shaken by cross-examination. Leading questions are not permitted in re-examination any more than in examination-in-chief.

THE HEARSAY RULE

Introduction

Witnesses giving evidence swear or affirm that their statement will be true. A person can only pledge the truth of facts which are within his own knowledge. Thus if the witness has been told by the contractor's chief surveyor, for example, that the clerk of works was always drunk, the witness can not swear that it is true that the man had a drinking problem. Statements made by persons other than the witness testifying, in this example, the chief surveyor, are hearsay and sometimes called strict hearsay. It is a general rule of the law of evidence that assertions by persons other than the witness who is testifying are inadmissible as evidence of the facts asserted. It should be emphasised at this point that hearsay statements are not invariably inadmissible, they are inadmissible *to prove the truth of the facts contained in the statement*.

This point can best be illustrated by an example of a criminal case *Subramaniam v Public Prosecutor* [1956] 1 WLR 965. Subramaniam was charged with acts of terrorism. His defence was duress in that he had been threatened by the terrorists to co-operate. At trial, the judge said he could not relate the threats that had been made as they were hearsay. On appeal it was held that the judge had been wrong. The fact that the statements were made was relevant to the question of duress irrespective of whether they were true. Thus had a terrorist threatened Subramaniam that he was going to kill his mother, that statement would be inadmissible if Subramaniam were seeking to prove that the terrorist intended murder. In that case, however, Subramaniam sought to prove that threats of whatever nature had been made. His evidence was therefore admissible.

Previous inconsistent statements

It is also a general rule that previous assertions of the witness who is testifying are inadmissible. If the assertion is consistent with the evidence he is giving then it would be a waste of the court's time to repeat it when he gave the statement first hand. If, however, the previous statement is inconsistent with the evidence he is giving then he may be asked in cross-examination whether he made the previous statement. Even if the witness admits to it this will not prove that the statement was true but merely cast doubt on the veracity of the witness's evidence. Thus if a witness swears that he met the architect on site on 1 April and it can be shown that he previously maintained that he never met him in April at all, that previous assertion is inadmissible as evidence of the fact that no meeting took place. It is admissible, however, to show that it would be unsafe to believe the witness's statement that a meeting did take place.

These two rules fuse together and are generally known as the rule against hearsay. The rule is subject to many exceptions. The exceptions in civil cases are far wider in effect than those in criminal cases with the result that the rule has its most startling effect in criminal cases. This work is concerned primarily with the position in civil cases.

THE CIVIL EVIDENCE ACT 1968

The Civil Evidence Act made significant inroads as to the effect of the hearsay rule in civil cases. Section 2 concerning the admissibility of out-of-court statements, s 4 relating to the admissibility of records and statements contained in documents and s 5 which deals with statements produced by computers, together cover most kinds of strict hearsay statements. Section 3 deals with the second limb of the hearsay rule relating to previous inconsistent statements.

Section 2—Admissibility of out-of-court statements as evidence of the facts stated

By virtue of s 2 first-hand hearsay statements are admissible in civil cases. If the original speaker had direct personal knowledge of the facts with which his statement dealt then that statement can be proved in court by anyone who heard the statement or (if it was written) read it. Thus considering our previous example of the drunk clerk of works, provided that the chief surveyor had personal knowledge of the clerk of works' alcoholism when he told the witness the unfortunate facts, then the witness could give evidence of the conversation to prove that the clerk of works' mind was seldom on the job.

If, however, the witness's evidence is to the effect that the architect told him that the chief surveyor constantly complained that the clerk of works drank to excess then he can not rely upon s 2 since the chain between the surveyor's observation and its repetition in court has two links, namely the architect and the witness. This is sometimes known as 'double-hearsay' and is inadmissible.

Section 3—Witness's previous statement—evidence of facts stated

Section 3 provides that previous statements made by witnesses giving evidence are admissible as evidence of any fact stated in the previous statement. Section 3 has therefore removed the difficulties created by the second limb of the hearsay rule as to whether previous consistent or inconsistent statements can be put to a witness and if so the effect of so doing. Before this enactment the judge could not rely upon previous inconsistent statements of witnesses even if it were proved that they had been made. At best a previous inconsistency would show that the witness was unreliable.

Returning to our example of the April Fool's Day meeting, by virtue of s 3 if it can be proved, for example, by another witness's statement or a document, that the witness had previously maintained that he did not meet the architect in April then that statement can be relied upon to show that no meeting took place on 1 April despite the fact that the witness is swearing to the contrary in court. Section 3 does not alter the position that proof of a previous inconsistent statement undermines the credibility of the witness giving contrary evidence.

Section 4—Admissibility of records as evidence of facts stated

Section 4 renders admissible, hearsay statements even second, third or fourth hand provided that they are:

(1) contained in a document with it or form part of a record; and

(2) that the record is compiled by a person acting under a duty and who relays the statement from either an eyewitness or another intermediary acting under a duty.

'Record' is interpreted widely and it need not be in any special form but can be a single document setting out the fact of a transaction (*R v Jones (Benjamin)* [1978] 2 All ER 718, [1978] 1 WLR 195). The phrase 'acting under a duty' is defined by the section to include acting in the course of trade, profession or employment whether paid or unpaid. It is evident therefore that provided each intermediary link between the eyewitness and the compiler of the record was acting under a duty it does not matter how long the chain of hearsay is between the two.

Section 5—Statements produced by computer

Section 5 runs in tandem with s 4 but deals with records produced by computers. A computer is defined as any device for the storing and processing of information.

Procedure under the Civil Evidence Act

If a party wishes to rely upon the exceptions to the hearsay rule provided by the Act certain procedural requirements must be complied with. The Act is usually implemented by a party who does not intend to call an eyewitness and needs to rely upon the exceptions in order to prove his case. In such a case notice should be given to the other side of the intention to rely upon the exceptions within 21 days of the hearing. The notice should specify the statement, who made it and to whom it was made.

Sometimes there are special reasons why the eyewitness cannot be called. These are specified by s 8(2)(b) of the Act, namely that the witness is

(1) dead; or
(2) beyond the seas; or
(4) unfit; or
(5) cannot with due diligence be found; or
(6) cannot be expected to have any recollection of the matters in question.

If notice is given that the eyewitness is not to be called for a special reason as specified by the Act, the other side can only object to the party relying upon the statutory exceptions to the hearsay rule if they dispute the special reason.

For example Conwright Contractors want to rely in court upon the statement made by Sydney, their site foreman, to their lawyers when legal proceedings were first brought against them, four years ago. Sydney has now left Conwright and the last they heard of him he was on a contract in the Middle East. They give the other side notice that they intend to rely upon his statement and that he cannot be called because he is beyond the seas and cannot with due diligence be found. The other side object roundly, they want Sidney called so that they can cross-examine him. They challenge the special reason and say that Conwright have not used due diligence to find Sydney and that had they done so they would have discovered that he set up his own window fixing concern in Penge. They ask that Sydney be called and Conwright are not allowed to rely upon the statutory exception.

If, however, no special reason is mentioned then the other side can serve a counter notice requiring the eyewitness to be called. If the witness's evidence is particularly contentious then he will be required so that he can be cross-examined. If his evidence is largely accepted then the other side will not object to his statement being proved under the exceptions and will not serve a counter notice.

The Act goes on to provide certain safeguards to prevent the statement being accepted as gospel truth by the judge. When deciding how much credit or weight he should give to such a statement, the judge must bear in mind whether the witness made the statement when the facts were observed and whether either he or any intermediary would have a motive to misrepresent the facts. Equally, if the eyewitness is not called then evidence which would have been tendered to discredit that witness can still be included.

COMMON LAW EXCEPTIONS TO THE HEARSAY RULE

The Civil Evidence Act 1968 abolished all common law exceptions in civil cases but went on to preserve certain exceptions under s 9.

Informal admissions

An admission is a statement made by a person against his interests. Informal admissions differ from formal admissions in that formal admissions are made openly and notified to the other side; informal admissions are made and later denied at trial.

If a person is not prepared to repeat his admission in the witness box then it can only be proved at trial under an exception to the hearsay rule. The admission can be proved but only if it were made by a party to the proceedings. This includes the parties' agents and employees provided that it can be shown that the admission was made with the party's authority and was made voluntarily. Section 9 of the Act provides that an informal admission can be proved in a civil case on the basis that a party to the proceedings is unlikely to have made the admission were it not true.

Statements in the public domain

If a document has been prepared for the use of the public by a person acting under a duty to do so then it is admissible without calling a witness with first-hand knowledge to prove the facts to which it refers. This exception is justified on the basis it would be impractical to prove such facts in documents of this kind. It is not enough, however, for the document to be available for public inspection: it must have been prepared for that purpose.

The exception includes the official register of births, deaths and marriages, the findings of public inquiries, and official maps and histories and has been extended to include companies' registers and accounts.

Other common law exceptions

Other exceptions to the hearsay rule at common law are more obscure and need not be dwelt upon. An admission can be made by implication by a defendant if an allegation is put to him and his general demeanour and conduct is such as to justify the inference that he admits the allegation.

In civil proceedings statements as to public rights or general rights can be admissible if they are not otherwise admissible under the Act. Public rights are those of the whole population, such as the right to use the pavement; general rights affect limited sections of the community, such as the right to use certain common land. A statement made before the dispute between the parties and made directly on the point is admissible.

Statements made by deceased relatives are admissible to prove matters of relationship by blood or marriage between two or more persons.

EXPERT EVIDENCE AND HEARSAY

Although the general rule is that for a witness to give evidence he must be able to say that he has both seen and heard that to which he deposes; that he is both an 'oyant' and a 'voyant' (see Thayer *Preliminary Treatise on Evidence at the Common Law* 523–4), it is clear that the statutory and common law exceptions have made significant inroads to that rule. Were that not the case, expert witnesses would be a rare breed indeed, since the chance of an expert on accident reconstruction witnessing a road traffic accident or an expert on chimney failure seeing the chimney collapse are slim.

By virtue of the Civil Evidence Act, opinions of experts based upon facts related to them by third parties who had observed them are admissible. But in *Henthorn v Fisk* [1981] CLY (unreported) 76, CA a case involving personal injury, Lawton LJ said:

> 'A medical report which sets out what the doctor has been told does not carry any evidential weight unless the person doing the telling is called as a witness or the parties have agreed that what the doctors were told should be accepted as true.'

Further, opinions based on expertise in part derived from generic hearsay material, which may in fact be incorporated into the expert's evidence, even though he has no personal knowledge of its factual basis, which, for example, may be in the form of information gleaned from others during a professional career. Works of reference or specific studies, are admissible.

Opinions based on more specific hearsay material, such as, for example, opinion survey evidence in a trademark case, are not admissible (*Mobil Oil Corpn v Registrar of Trademarks* (1983) 51 ALR 735). If, however, the opinion is not based solely upon inadmissible hearsay, then the statements may be proved as an additional basis for the opinion rather than as evidence of their truth (*R v Abbey* (1982) 138 DLR (3d) 202); *H v Schering Chemicals Ltd* [1983] 1 All ER 849, [1983] 1 WLR 143).

PRIVILEGE

Introduction

When a party claims legal privilege he is claiming a right not to disclose a known fact even though it may be relevant to the determination of an issue in the proceedings. Because legal privilege deprives the judge of relevant evidence, strong arguments are required in support of the party's right to refuse to answer a question or supply information.

Although there are several heads of privilege including the privilege against self incrimination and privilege attaching to marital communications, only two heads will be discussed here, namely legal professional privilege and that relating to statements made in the course of negotiations towards a settlement of an action.

Legal professional privilege

All communications passing between a client and his lawyer in the course of their professional relationship are privileged from production whether in connection with a specific dispute or not. Communications passing between either a lawyer or his client and a third party are privileged but only if litigation is pending and the communication is made predominantly for that purpose. The two limbs of this rule can be considered separately.

Client and lawyer communications

The rationale for this head of privilege is that, in the public interest, clients should receive proper legal advice without their advisors being concerned that their advice may be disclosed to all and sundry. The privilege is the client's and cannot be waived by his lawyer. If, however, the client wishes to waive privilege generally or with regard to specific communications only he should do so unequivocally (*Doland Ltd v Blackburn Robson, Coates & Co* [1972] 3 All ER 959, [1972] 1 WLR 1338). Communications are only privileged if they pass between lawyer and client in the course of their professional relationship. If therefore the communication is made prior to the commencement of the relationship or after it ceased, it will not be privileged and similarly if the communication is made in a personal capacity. Lawyers include practising barristers, solicitors and legal staff of a government department or company.

Litigation as a predominant purpose

If a communication is made between either a lawyer or his client and a third party it is privileged from production to the court only if it were made predominantly for the purpose of pending or contemplated litigation (*Waugh v British Railways Board* [1980] AC 521, [1979] 2 All ER 1169). It is clear that a mere possibility of litigation is not sufficient to bring the communication within this head of privilege and that it must be a definite prospect. For example, a surveyor's report on a property made at the request of a solicitor for the information of his client who intended to lend money on the property was not privileged (*Wheeler v Le Marchant* (1881) 17 Ch D 675).

If litigation is contemplated, the communication must be shown to have been produced for use in the litigation. This rule has given rise to problems since when it is discovered that, for example, a building is suffering damage, or there has been an accident at work, the usual reaction of the parties is to ascertain what has gone wrong so as to remedy it or prevent it from happening again. Very often the lawyers are involved at this stage but litigation could not be said to be a definite prospect. Reports are commissioned and the defects investigated or the cause of the accident established. When litigation is underway the question arises as to the standing of these reports. In *Longhorn v British Transport Commission* [1959] 2 All ER 32, [1959] 1 WLR 530 it was held that a report prepared by a third party in order to discover the cause of the accident and to prevent its recurrence does not attract privilege.

Thus experts' reports prepared for the purpose of pending or contemplated civil proceedings or in connection with the obtaining or giving of legal advice are privileged from disclosure. Further, s 2 of the Civil Evidence Act can not be relied upon to undermine this basic rule of substantive law (see *Worrall v Reich* [1955] 1 QB 296, [1955] 1 All ER 363 and *Causton v Mann Egerton (Johnsons) Ltd* [1974] 1 All ER 453, [1974] 1 WLR 162, CA). Thus one party cannot compel the disclosure of such reports by the other party unless the privilege is waived.

Once a document is privileged it remains so. Thus a report prepared for use in particular litigation and therefore privileged can not be disclosed in any subsequent litigation even if the parties or their lawyers have changed.

If privilege attaches to certain facts they can still be proved if they can be proved independently, for example, by evidence independent of the lawyer, client or third party. If copies of a privileged document fall into wrong hands it can still be proved (*Calcraft v Guest* [1898] 1 QB 759). Also, in a criminal case, it was held that the prosecution were entitled to make use of an incriminating note from the accused to his counsel found on the floor of the court (*R v Tompkins* (1977) 67 Cr App Rep 181). If, however, the evidence had been stolen, the position is not so clear. Illegally obtained evidence is generally admissible (*R v Sang* [1980] AC 402, [1979] 2 All ER 46, CA). If, however, confidential information is stolen then an injunction may be ordered to prevent its disclosure. Confidentiality is not, itself, a strong enough argument to protect information from disclosure in legal proceedings.

Statements made in the course of negotiations

As it is in the public interest that litigation should be avoided wherever possible, concessions made by a party in the course of negotiations with a view to settlement are privileged from disclosure. Were it otherwise then parties would be reluctant to make concessions or negotiate at all.

Negotiations and the statements made in the course of them are described as being 'without prejudice'. A statement is not privileged, however, merely because it is described as being 'without prejudice'; the statement must form part of a bona fide attempt to compromise the proceedings. The head of privilege does not only apply when negotiations are conducted by the parties' lawyers. Whenever parties attempt to settle their differences out of court and by whatever means, their negotiations are privileged.

Once the parties have reached an agreement the privilege attached to the 'without prejudice' negotiations no longer applies. The court can examine the 'without prejudice' correspondence to determine whether an agreement was reached and to enforce the same if a party seeks to avoid his obligations under the agreement (*Tomlin v Standard Telephones and Cables Ltd* [1969] 3 All ER 201, [1969] 1 WLR 1378). In *Rush & Tompkins Ltd v Greater London Council* [1988] 3 All ER 737, 43 BLR 1 the House of Lords held that correspondence conducted on a without prejudice basis with a view to reaching settlement in one piece of litigation was inadmissible in subsequent litigation whether or not an agreement was reached.

SIMILAR FACT EVIDENCE

As discussed earlier, information is admissible as evidence if it is relevant and if it can be proved in a manner which is allowed by the rules.

Considerations of public policy, however, render some categories of evidence inadmissible. There is a general rule which is applicable in both civil and criminal cases that it is not permissible to call evidence which shows that a person has acted on previous occasions in a way similar to that to be considered by the court.

The rule is known as the rule against similar fact evidence. The rationale behind it is that although it is natural to draw inferences from people's previous conduct when considering allegations as to their present conduct it is in fact unsafe to do so. Just because he has done it in the past doesn't mean that he did it this time. Given the natural human tendency to assume that he did, however, similar fact evidence is considered to be misleading or prejudicial and is usually inadmissible.

It is in criminal cases that the rule against similar fact evidence has its greatest effect since there is an obvious danger of prejudice to an accused with a criminal record. In civil cases there has been some debate as to whether the rule applies at all.

In *Brown v Eastern and Midlands Rly Co* (1889) 22 QBD 391, for example, Stephen J said:

> 'when the question is whether a particular act is a public nuisance, it is difficult to see how it can be proved to be so except by shewing cases in which it has interfered with a public right'.

Thus in *Moore v Ransome's Dock* (1898) 14 TLR 539, CA evidence of previous complaints about accidents was admitted to show that the owners of the dock knew that it was in a dangerous condition and in *Hales v Kerr* [1908] 2 KB 601 evidence of previous outbreaks of a skin disorder among the defendant barber's customers was allowed to show that he was negligent in his practices.

More recently in *Mood Music Publishing Co Ltd v De Wolfe Ltd* [1976] Ch 119, [1976] 1 All ER 763 the plaintiffs claimed breach of copyright in that the defendants had deliberately copied a musical work produced by the plaintiffs. The defence was that the similarity between the works was coincidental. The plaintiffs for their part sought to rely upon evidence of previous infringements of copyright by the defendants. The Court of Appeal dealt with the exclusionary rule in this way:

> 'The criminal courts have been very careful not to admit such evidence unless its probative value is so strong that it should be received in the interests of justice, and its admissions will not operate unfairly to the accused. In civil cases the courts will admit evidence of similar facts if it is logically probative, that is if it is logically relevant in determining the matter which is in issue; provided that it is not oppressive or unfair

to the other side; and also that the other side has fair notice of it and is able to deal with it.'

It is clear that the rule is applied less rigidly in the civil courts. It is apparent, however, that a balancing approach is called for similar to that used in criminal cases. In *Berger v Raymond & Son Ltd* [1984] 1 WLR 625 Warner J held that the discretion to exclude operated on a basis different from criminal cases. The case raised the question of the forgery of various share transfers by the defendant. The plaintiffs relied upon evidence of other transfers which it was alleged had been forged by the defendant. The judge held that factors other than prejudice to the defendant were relevant, such as the lengthening of the trial, the undesirability of relitigating issues disposed of in previous proceedings and the burden on the defendant in adducing evidence.

It seems therefore that similar fact evidence is not excluded in civil cases by the discretion of the judge but by rule. The rule is, however, based on somewhat imprecise elements and not applied as rigidly as in the criminal courts.

THE COURSE OF EXPERT EVIDENCE—PROCEDURE

Introduction

The rules of civil procedure govern how proceedings are prepared and brought to trial and conducted at trial. Pre-trial procedure and hearings are described as 'interlocutory'. One of the objectives of the rules is to avoid the situation where the other side is confronted at trial with evidence upon which they have not had the opportunity to take advice or form a view or call evidence to meet.

Although, superficially, such an approach may seem to undermine the very object of litigating—if you tell the other parties what you are going to say then you have given your case away—the procedure is adopted to ensure that the trial is spent determining those issues in dispute only thereby avoiding expensive time wasting and overlong trials.

This objective is all the more worthwhile in the case of expert evidence since the parties are unlikely to be in a position to digest and deal with detailed expert opinions on technical or other complicated matters if they are expressed for the first time at the actual hearing. If they were expected to, it can be seen that injustice may result since points would be missed, opinions hastily formed and evidence hurriedly presented. In order to avoid rushed presentation of their case, the other party may apply for an adjournment which, if granted, would waste more time.

The rules governing experts, reports and the giving of oral expert evidence in civil proceedings are set out in RSC Order 38 Part IV. The rules restrict the right of parties to adduce expert evidence in civil proceedings as a matter of course, and they provide the machinery for the pre-trial disclosure by each party to the other of the expert evidence intended to be relied upon at the trial.

The objects intended to be achieved by the rules may be said to include the assisting of the parties to reach a fair settlement, the avoidance of surprise at trial, the securing of agreed experts' reports thereby shortening the evidence and freeing experts from attendance at trial and enabling experts to prepare their evidence upon the matters that are in dispute only.

RSC Order 38

Order 38, rule 36 sets out the basic limitations to the calling of expert evidence by a party. The rule has the effect of precluding every party from adducing any expert evidence at the trial save in the following circumstances:

(1) with the leave of the court;
(2) where all parties agree;
(3) where the evidence is given by affidavit;
(4) where the party seeking to adduce such evidence has first applied to the court to determine whether or not he must disclose the contents of his expert evidence and if so required has done so;
(5) where automatic directions concerning the disclosure of experts' reports have been complied with.

It is clear therefore that no party to an action will be allowed to call and rely upon expert evidence of whatever nature at the trial unless they have applied to the court for one of the relevant directions for disclosure or the evidence is agreed. If the party fails to obtain a direction from the court or to agree the substance of their expert evidence then such evidence will be excluded at the trial.

Order 38, rule 38 provides for the compulsory disclosure and exchange of experts' reports. When deciding whether to make such an order, the court has regard to the following circumstances :

> '(a) that the expert evidence is based on a version of the facts in dispute between the parties
> (b) that the expert evidence is based upon facts which are neither
> (i) ascertainable by the expert by the exercise of his own powers of observation, nor
> (ii) within his general professional knowledge or experience'.

Order 38, rule 38 also provides for without prejudice meetings of experts before or after disclosure of their reports with a view to identifying those parts of their evidence which are in issue.

Application to the court for leave

The interlocutory procedure varies depending on whether the case is to be tried in the Queen's Bench Division, by Judges who hear a wide variety of civil disputes or as official referee's business by judges who specialise in cases with a high technical content, usually building disputes.

In the Queen's Bench Division an application for a direction giving leave to adduce expert evidence is made to a Queen's Bench Master. Masters deal with the great majority of interlocutory matters in the High Court. The application can be made at any stage but usually when directions are sought as to the hearing of the matter generally. In the Queen's Bench Division, cases are not put into the list of cases to be heard by a judge until they have been 'set down for trial'. Cases are set down for trial when all interlocutory stages are complete and the case is ready for a full hearing. Thus if the case is to be heard in the Queen's Bench Division an application can be made for leave to call expert evidence even after the action has been set down for trial. Such an application should obviously be made in good time before the trial for the very reasons discussed above.

Actions started as official referee's business follow a slightly different path. When the writ instigating the action is issued the case is allocated to one of the judges who tries official referees' business. Shortly after service of the statement of claim, which sets out the plaintiff's case, an application can be made to the judge for directions as to the future conduct of the case right up to the trial date. Directions would be given at that stage as to the calling of expert evidence. Upon an application for directions before the official referee, a typical order would be as follows:

(1) Defence to be served within 14 days.
(2) Reply, if so advised, 14 days thereafter.
(3) Discovery of relevant documents in the power or possession of the parties by exchange of lists of documents 28 days thereafter.
(4) Inspection of such documents on seven days' notice.
(5) Experts limited to two per party.
(6) Experts of like disciplines to meet without prejudice to agree facts and narrow issues 28 days thereafter.
(7) Experts' reports to be exchanged 42 days thereafter.
(8) Signed statements of witnesses of fact to be served two weeks before trial.
(9) Trial date 1 April time estimate: two weeks.

Some of these directions relate to the exchange of pleadings and preparation of the documents to be used at trial. Some, however, deal specifically with the preparation and calling of expert evidence and should be looked at in more detail.

The number of expert witnesses

The court has the power to limit the number of experts to be called by each party (Order 38, rule 4). The order tends not to specify the disciplines in which such witnesses should be expert. Each side is limited to the same number of experts. Thus if one party desires to call two witnesses and the other desires to call one the order will limit experts to two on each side. It should be borne in mind that because the parties feel at this interlocutory stage that two experts will be necessary and the judge makes an order in those terms such an order is not conclusive on the question of whether two experts were in fact necessary. This becomes of some importance when costs incurred in the litigation are investigated by the taxing master to determine how much the losing side should pay.

Further, although the Court can limit the number it can not determine at an interlocutory stage whether the evidence of experts of specific disciplines would be admissible (*Sullivan v West Yorkshire Passenger Transport Executive* [1985] 2 All ER 134, CA).

Exchanges of experts' reports

The court is empowered to make this order by Order 38, rule 38. The purpose of the order is to save expense by dispensing with the calling of experts where there is in reality no dispute and if there is a dispute by avoiding parties being taken by surprise as to the true nature of the dispute and seeking to amend their pleadings or adjourn the case.

Thus the court will usually make an order for exchange of reports (*Ollett v Bristol Aerojet Ltd* [1979] 3 All ER 544n, [1979] 1 WLR 1197n). The court will not make such an order, however, if it is satisfied that there is sufficient reason for not giving such a direction. The party seeking an order for disclosure has the burden of satisfying the court that such an order should be made. The burden is not, however, a heavy one. The matters to which the court should have regard are specified in the rule.

If the court declines to make such an order then the party does not have to disclose the report of his expert but relies upon oral evidence given at trial. The situation differs from that where no application has been made for leave to call expert evidence in which case such evidence cannot be called.

If, however, the court declines to make an order requiring a party to disclose the substance of their expert evidence then the court will ordinarily decline to order that the other side disclose their expert's report. It is in exceptional circumstances only that the court will order that one party disclose their expert report whilst at the same time declining to order that the other party disclose theirs.

The requirement that experts' reports be exchanged is not limited to independent experts. Thus 'in-house experts', the parties themselves and their employees who will give expert evidence at trial are required to reduce the substance of their evidence to writing and disclose it to the other side. In *Shell Pensions Trust Ltd v Pell Frischmann & Partners* (1986) 3 Const LJ 57 Judge Newey said:

> 'The rules in Order 38 refer to "expert evidence" and not to "evidence given by independent experts". They apply generally—to independent experts, to so called "in-house" experts and to the parties themselves. I think the court has power in this case to direct that the substance of any expert evidence which the defendant consulting engineers intend to give themselves or call their employees or former employees to give on their behalf should be disclosed in the form of written reports.'

The expert's written report should set out both the substance of the factual description of, for example, the machine or the circumstances of the accident and his expert opinion in relation to its failure or the accident since that is the very justification for calling him (*Ollett v Bristol Aerojet* above).

Meeting of experts without prejudice

The court has power to order that experts meet without prejudice with a view to identifying those parts of the evidence which are in issue.

Order 38, rule 38 (3) provides:

> 'In any cause or matter the court may, if it thinks fit, direct that there be a meeting "without prejudice" of such experts within such periods before or after the disclosure of their reports as the court may specify, for the purpose of identifying those parts of their evidence which are in issue. Where such a meeting takes place the experts may prepare a joint statement indicating those parts of their evidence on which they are, and those on which they are not, in agreement.'

This important step towards the open system of trial is implemented by the official referees as standard practice. Although the question of whether such a meeting should take place before the exchange of reports is a matter for the judge, practitioners differ in their views as to which approach is preferable. Some feel that a meeting after exchange of reports is of little value because the experts have researched the matter thoroughly, considered their views at length and committed them to writing and are unlikely to change their minds significantly. If there was not much common ground between the experts in the first place then little further agreement is likely to be reached.

Other practitioners feel that a meeting before exchange of reports is of limited use since the experts, not having researched their views thoroughly are unlikely to know what they are and certainly are not sufficiently familiar with the issues to record any agreement.

In any event experts should seek proper briefing before they attend such a meeting. They should also be quite clear as to what it is they are agreeing before it is recorded in the written statement.

In *Richard Roberts Holdings v Douglas Smith Stimson Partnership* (31 July 1989, unreported) Judge Newey held that an expert does not have authority to bind the parties instructing them and that a joint written statement made at the conclusion of a 'without prejudice' meeting does not automatically become 'open', unless it is subsequently ratified by the instructing party. He went on to find, however, that different considerations might apply to any meetings between experts during the course of the trial and that the experts may be held out by the parties or their representatives as having authority to reach a binding agreement depending upon the facts of the particular case. It is, however, difficult to see any distinction between meetings held before trial and those held in the course of the trial.

Joint written statement

For the meeting of experts an agenda is usually prepared setting out the issues for discussion and upon which it is hoped agreement will be reached. It will be of some help to the experts if the lawyers in the case prepare a list of issues that are in dispute as disclosed in the pleadings. The experts should also consider the matter to determine whether there are any technical issues in the case that have not been identified by the lawyers.

The rule then envisages that each issue will be discussed by the experts with a view to reaching agreement or at least narrowing the field of dispute. If the case concerns particularly complicated technical evidence and involves a number of parties a lot of time should be spent drawing up the list of issues for discussion and provision should be made to record the agreement or disagreement of each expert.

Should agreement be reached this can be indicated by way of a joint written statement. Equally, however, it is envisaged by the rule that the experts may not agree anything, leaving all the issues in dispute. In such a case they should prepare a joint statement to this effect.

CHAPTER 3

View from a solicitor

Andrea Burns LLB (Hons), CMA

The role of the solicitor in construction disputes is initially one of investigation and evaluation. The solicitor's duty is to discover the facts and advise the client. A solicitor, however, is rarely qualified to give an opinion upon technical matters which arise in construction disputes and therefore will require the assistance of one or more experts who are technically qualified to express an opinion in relation to the matters in dispute. Frequently the outcome of the whole case can depend upon the judge's view of conflicting expert opinion.

Expert evidence is not a new concept. From an early stage in the development of the common law witnesses were required to state facts and were not allowed to intrude on the role of judges or juries by expressing opinions. To this, however, soon rose an exception namely when a court required assistance in order to understand the facts in *Buckley v Rice Thomas* (1554) 1 Plowd 118. The value of expert opinion evidence was established in the sixteenth century.

The case of *Folkes v Chadd* (1782) 3 Doug KB 157 is often regarded as the principal case upon the admissibility of matters of opinion. Lord Mansfield at 159 said:

> '. . . in matters of science, the reasonings of men of science can only be answered by men of science'.

This case involved an action for trespass. A bank had been erected for the purpose of preventing the overflowing of the sea. It was alleged that the bank had caused damage to the harbour which suffered from decay. An engineer, Mr Smeaton, was called to give expert evidence and his testimony showed that in his opinion the bank was not the cause of the problem, and that its removal would not provide a solution. The other party objected upon the basis that Mr Smeaton was going to speak not as to fact but as to opinion. Lord Mansfield said that the opinion, however, is deduced from facts which were not disputed—the situation of banks, the course of tides and of winds and the shifting sands. He said:

> 'I cannot believe that where the question is whether a defect arises from a natural or an artificial cause the opinions of men of science are not to be received'.

The nature of expert evidence

Expert evidence is essentially evidence of opinion. The opinion will be deduced from facts. An expert is able to give an opinion because he has particular experience in relation to the question upon which he is required to give an opinion.

The nature of expert evidence was illustrated in the case of *Reckitt & Colman Products Ltd v Borden Inc (No 2)* [1987] FSR 407. In this case objection was taken to evidence being given by a witness on the basis that it was expert evidence for which provision had not been made by order. The witness was a market researcher who had carried out tests upon matters such as brand awareness among the general public. The studies had not been commissioned for the purpose of legal proceedings. Walton J said that the witness was not giving any evidence whatsoever which was a matter of opinion in the slightest; he was simply reporting the results of a survey. The judge said that he did not think that this could be fairly described as expert evidence. The market researcher did not require any expertise to say what was the result of the enquiries. He would not at the end of the day say a single sentence which would start off with the words 'In my opinion . . .' and it seemed to the learned judge that this was really the essence of expert evidence. Someone comes in and says 'In my opinion, for example, this lemon juice is not as good as that lemon juice'.

Walton J said that as the witness was not going to be asked what his opinion on anything was, merely as to what the summation of the results were, this was not strictly opinion evidence, and therefore he did not propose to give effect to the objection.

An expert is entitled to express his opinion upon matters within his field of competence. In expressing his opinion, he will be relying on facts. A question arose in the case of *English Exporters (London) Ltd v Eldonwall Ltd* [1973] Ch 415, [1973] 1 All ER 726 as to whether valuers were entitled to give hearsay evidence on comparables. It was held in this case valuers, in building up their opinions about values, would no doubt have learned much from transactions in which they themselves had been engaged and of which they could give first hand evidence. Megarry J also said, however, that a valuer will have learned much from many other sources including much of which he could give no first hand evidence. Textbooks, journals, reports of auctions and other dealings and information obtained from his professional brethren and others, some related to particular transactions and some more general and indefinite will all have contributed their share. Megarry J said that much or most of this would be accurate although some would not, and even what is accurate so far as it goes may be incomplete in that nothing may have been said of some special element which affects value. Nevertheless, His Honour said that the opinion that the expert expresses is none the worse because it is in part derived from matters on which he could give no direct evidence. He said that even if some of the extraneous information which he acquires in this way is inaccurate or incomplete the errors and omissions would often tend to cancel each other out. His Honour said no question of giving hearsay evidence arose in such cases; the witness stated his opinion from his general experience. His Honour, however, went on to say that it was one thing to state 'From my general experience of recent transactions comparable with this one, I think the proper rent should be £x': it was another thing to say 'Because I have been told by someone else that the premises next door have an area of x sq ft and were recently let on such and such terms for £y a year, I say the rent of these premises should be £z a year.' The latter was hearsay evidence. His Honour said that he knew of no special rule giving expert valuation witness the right to give hearsay evidence of facts.

In summary, His Honour was saying that although an expert valuer may in evidence express his opinion on values even though substantial contributions to the formation of those opinions have been made by hearsay, he cannot give hearsay evidence as to the facts of transactions which lie outside his personal knowledge. This ruling, it is submitted, is applicable to other types of expert evidence in that most professionals will acquire a great deal of their knowledge other than by first hand direct experience.

In the case of *R v Abadom* [1983] 1 All ER 364, [1983] 1 WLR 126 a Mr Cook was an expert, being a principal scientific officer at the Home Office Forensic Laboratories. He was giving evidence on the likelihood or otherwise of fragments of glass having come from a sample being a broken window. Kerr LJ said that as an expert in this field Mr Cook was entitled to express an opinion on this question subject to laying the foundation for his opinion and subject of course to his evidence being tested by cross-examination for evaluation by the jury. He said that in the context of evidence given by experts it was no more than a statement of the obvious that, in reaching their conclusion, they must be entitled to draw upon material produced by others in the field in which their expertise lay. It was their duty to consider any material available in their field and not to draw conclusions merely on the basis of their own experience which was inevitably likely to be more limited than the general body of information which might be available to them. His Lordship said that where the expert relies on the existence or non-existence of some fact which is basic to the question on which he is asked to express his opinion, that fact must be proved by admissible evidence. Once the primary facts on which their opinion is based have been proved by admissible evidence, experts are entitled to draw on the work of others as part of the process of arriving at their conclusion. Where they have done so his Lordship said that experts should refer to this material in their evidence so that the cogency and probity of value of their conclusion can be tested and evaluated by reference to it.

Kerr LJ said that it did not seem to him, in relation to the reliability of opinion evidence given by experts that they must necessarily limit themselves to drawing on material which had been published in some form. Part of their experience and expertise might well lie in their knowledge of unpublished material and in their evaluation of it. He said that the only rule in this regard was that they should refer to such material in their evidence so that it could be tested and evaluated. The Court of Appeal said that Mr Cook's reliance on the Home Office statistics did not infringe the rule against hearsay.

It seems an obvious statement that the expert must be competent within the particular field in question. However, in the Privy Council case of *US Shipping Board v The St Albans* [1931] AC 632 there was a dispute concerning the cause of a collision of two ships, the *Crown City* and *St Albans*. There were in evidence three photographs taken from a third moving ship showing the colliding ships just before, during and after the collision. At first instance, the judge found the *St Albans* to blame. The

Supreme Court of New South Wales, however, on appeal, reversed the decision as new evidence was adduced as to the cause of the collision. The new evidence was that of three land surveyors who made calculations which they claimed showed that the *St Albans* was not to blame.

On appeal to the Privy Council the question of the admissibility of this evidence was considered. Lord Merrivale, who delivered the judgment in the Privy Council, said that some of the issues in the case were as follows:

> '... the difference of scale in the picture obtainable by a single lens of objects in the direct line of view and objects in the margins of the field; the effect in photography of the extent of the focal angle; the results due to development on a plane surface of pictures obtained in photographic perspective; the means of neutralising the effect of the curve of the field of the lens. Counsel purported to discuss the topics in question in the light of personal experience, as matters of common knowledge.'

However, such evidence is usually required to be established by experts. It was held that the skill or science needed to produce an accurate result by the process adopted was not that of a land surveyor and that in the absence of expert evidence the reversal of the decision of the trial judge was not warranted.

It is a question of judgment as to whether expert evidence is required. In the *US Shipping Board v The St Albans* (above) the evidence was not of the correct type, in that the expert did not have the skill and knowledge required. In some cases expert evidence is inappropriate altogether. For example, in *Halvanon Insurance v Jewett Duchesne (International)* [1987] 1 FTLR 503 there was a dispute as to whether a person had authority to sign a reinsurance form. This was a document which to some extent gave authority but it had endorsed upon it 'Excluding USA'. The defendant produced expert evidence to prove that the authority did not permit the signatory to sign contracts which did not contain words 'Excluding USA'. Staughton J held that no expert evidence was required to say that and no custom or practice was alleged. It was simply the ordinary meaning of the English language. No allowance would be given for the costs of the expert witness. He said that too often unnecessary expert evidence was adduced which simply caused prolongation of trials and unnecessary expense.

CHOOSING AN EXPERT

The solicitor will normally be responsible for recommending to his client, appointing and instructing an expert. It is comparatively unusual for clients to approach an expert themselves. There are a number of factors to be taken into account in making the choice. Perhaps the most important is the qualification of the person or persons to give evidence on the client's behalf.

CONFLICT OF INTERESTS

A conflict of interests can arise if an expert is asked to act for a party opposing one of his clients or someone with whom he has a particular relationship. In those circumstances it would not be proper for him to act, and he should decline the instructions. It has been known for an expert to unwittingly give advice to both parties. In the case of *Harmony Shipping Co SA v Saudi Europe Line Ltd* [1979] 1 WLR 1380 the plaintiffs sought an injunction restraining a handwriting expert, Derek Davis, from giving evidence in a trial upon the basis that he had also advised the defendants.

Lord Denning MR gave judgment in this Court of Appeal case and said:

> 'Mr Davis is an expert in handwriting. He finds himself in an embarrassing position. He has been consulted by both sides in an action. The question is whether he should give evidence for one side without the consent of the other.'

Mr Davis tried to avoid accepting instructions from more than one side in any particular case. Solicitors approached him to give evidence, but he happened to be engaged in another case and was waiting to be called as a witness. Therefore, he saw the solicitor concerned outside Court 26 at the Royal Courts of Justice in the Strand. He expressed his opinion as to the genuineness and authenticity of the documents. At the same time there was some discussion about his fee and Mr Davis said that it was not his practice to accept instructions from one side once he had been instructed by the other side. Lord Denning said that something was said to the effect that Mr Davis would give his usual undertaking that he would not accept instructions from the other side. Lord Denning said that he thought it could be inferred that Mr Davis said that in his opinion the letters were not genuine. His evidence would therefore not help the plaintiffs and the solicitor told Mr Davis that they would not be wanting his assistance again, but if they did, they would let him know. That was in February 1979.

In April 1979 Mr Davis was consulted by another set of solicitors about the case. He examined the documents and gave his opinion of them. Something was said in the conversation with the solicitor of the defendants, as a result of which for the first time it occurred to Mr Davis that he had already been consulted by the other side. He referred to his file and realised it might be the same matter. He immediately told the solicitor 'I cannot accept any further instructions in the matter, since I have already been consulted by the other side'.

Lord Denning said that there was a question of principle. If an expert witness has been consulted by one side and has given his opinion to that side, can he thereafter be consulted and subpoenaed by the other side to give his opinion on the facts of the case?

Lord Denning said that so far as witnesses of fact were concerned, the law was as plain as can be. There is no property in a witness. The reason being that the court has a right to every man's evidence. Its primary duty was to ascertain the truth. The question was whether this applied to expert witnesses. They may have been told the substance of the parties' case. They may have been given a great deal of confidential information on it. They may have given advice to the parties. Communications between the solicitor and expert will normally be protected by legal professional privilege and cannot be communicated to the court except with the consent of the party concerned. Lord Denning said that subject to disallowing any questions which infringed the rule about legal professional privilege it seemed to him that an expert witness fell into the same position as a witness of fact. It was right and proper for Mr Davis to have been subpoenaed by the defendant.

The plaintiff further alleged that Mr Davis had contracted with them that he would not give evidence for the other side. Lord Denning, however, said that a contract by which a witness bound himself not to give evidence before the court on a matter which a judge said he ought to give evidence would be contrary to public policy and would not be enforced by the court. Lord Denning said that if an expert could have his hands tied by being instructed by one side, it would be very easy for a rich client to consult each of the acknowledged experts in the field. Each expert might give an opinion adverse to the rich man, yet the rich man could say to each 'Your mouth is closed and you cannot give evidence in court against me'. This would not be permitted as it was contrary to public policy.

Qualifications

It is not necessary for the expert to be formally qualified. In the case of *James Longley & Co Ltd v South West Thames Regional Health Authority* (1983) 25 BLR 56 there was a review of a taxation of costs in a claim brought by James Longley & Co Ltd against the South West Thames Regional Health Authority. There was only one item in dispute, namely the fees paid to an expert witness. Mr Short was the witness and he carried on a business of a claims consultant in building arbitrations and similar cases. The respondents objected having to pay Mr Short's fees and one of the points they raised was that Mr Short was not professionally qualified as an architect or quantity surveyor and was therefore not qualified to give expert evidence. Lloyd J, however, said that an expert may be qualified by skill and experience as well as by professional qualification. There could be no reasonable doubt as to Mr Short's skill and experience.

This case endorsed the rule which had been formulated as long ago as 1894 in the case of *R v Silverlock* [1894] 2 QB 766 where expert evidence had been challenged. In that case a solicitor gave evidence upon the handwriting of the defendant. It was objected that the solicitor was not an expert and could not give evidence as to his opinion. The solicitor said, however, that he had since 1884, quite apart from his professional work, given considerable study and attention to handwriting, and especially to old parish registers and wills, and had on several occasions professionally compared evidence in handwriting but had never before given evidence as to handwriting. He also said that he had formed an opinion that the defendant was guilty before he had begun to compare the handwriting. The objection was overruled and the evidence was admitted. The jury convicted the defendant.

On appeal, one of the questions raised was whether it was necessary for a witness to be professionally qualified. Lord Russell CJ said:

> 'It is true that the witness who is called upon to give evidence founded on a comparison of handwritings must be peritus; he must be skilled in doing so; but we cannot say that he must have become peritus in the way of his business or in any definite way. The question is, is he peritus? Is he skilled? Has he an adequate knowledge?'

Formal qualification therefore was not necessary.

It is necessary to choose an expert from the correct discipline. For example, it would be pointless instructing a handwriting expert to give evidence upon whether an architect had been negligent or not in his design of a building. This is an extreme example. Insofar as it is practicable it would be wise when criticising the architect's design to employ another architect to give his opinion as to what would be the standard of the ordinarily competent architect using reasonable skill and care—the Bolam test. The evidence should normally come from someone who is of equal experience or standing to the professional person in question although evidence from a person who is acquainted with standards may also suffice. Regard must be made to the judgment of Slade LJ in *Investors in Industry v South Bedfordshire District Council* [1986] QB 1034, [1986] 1 All ER 787, CA where he said:

> 'The expert evidence before the judge consisted of evidence from three engineers and one architect. . . . The questions put to the engineers and answered by them included questions relating to the nature and extent of the professional duties owed by [the architects] to [the property developers]. However, we think that little reliance can be placed on their answers to these particular questions which related to a profession other than their own.'

The expertise of an engineer is completely different from an architect. The question remains whether a professional carrying out similar duties but of a different discipline to another party can give credible evidence as to the nature and extent of the professional duties owed by that other party. An example would be a building surveyor giving expert evidence on the duties of care owed by an architect.

In the case of *Worboys v Acme Investments* (1969) 4 BLR 133 there were allegations that an architect had been negligent in preparing plans. Acme Investments Ltd had not, however, produced any expert evidence as to a breach of professional duty by the architect. Their counsel urged that this was a class of case in which the court could find a breach of such duty without having before it the standard type of evidence as to what constituted lack of care on the part of a professional man in the relevant circumstances. Sachs LJ said that there may well be cases in which it would not be necessary to adduce such evidence as, for instance, if an architect omitted to provide a front door to the premises. He said it would be grossly unfair to architects if the courts could without the normal evidence condemn a professional man. The complaint was that there were no downstairs WCs in some of the houses in the particular development in question. Sachs LJ said how particularly unfair it would be if the architect were held to be negligent without any evidence of the usual type being adduced. Mr Berry of Acme Investments was a man of no less than 25 years' experience of development schemes and Sachs LJ said who of all people would be likely to know best whether houses of this type were saleable in that area without any downstairs WCs. He added that even if the architect were blameworthy Mr Berry had approved the plans which was sufficient to break the chain of causation.

Experience

It is important for the expert to be experienced in his field. An expert will often have spent many years in practice and will often only towards the latter end of his career be involved in giving evidence. It is likely that the more experienced and the more senior the expert the more weight will be given to his evidence. It is likely that in cases where there are defects in a building, that the expert in question will have a hand in the design and specification of remedial works. Great emphasis has been placed by the court on the benefit of experience.

Personality

An expert witness, although independent, will assist a team in prosecuting or defending a claim. He will usually be involved in meetings with clients and counsel and perhaps other experts. There is therefore an element of 'horses for courses' here in that a personality clash can impede the smoothrunning of the case. It is necessary to consider the expert's abilities in relation to negotiations since it is likely that he will be involved in 'without prejudice' meetings with an expert of like discipline representing the other party or parties to the action. If the case goes to court or to arbitration then he will be required to give evidence in the witness box. Has he had experience in giving evidence and is he likely to be able to do so with confidence? These matters must be weighed up by the person selecting the expert witness.

Independence

An expert is not called as an advocate of his client's case. Garland J in *University of Warwick v Sir Robert McAlpine* (1988) 42 BLR 1 at 22 said:

> 'First, the role of the expert. It appeared to me that some (but by no means all) of the experts in this case tended to enter into the arena in order to advocate their client's case. This led to perfectly proper cross-examination on the basis: "You have assembled evidence and advanced explanations which you consider most likely to assist your client's case".
>
> It is much regretted that this had to be so. In their closing speeches counsel felt it necessary to challenge not only the reliability but also the credibility of experts with unadorned attacks on their veracity. This simply should not happen where the court is called upon to decide complex scientific or technical issues. To a large extent this excessively adversarial approach to expert evidence could have been avoided if experts who had at various times expressed contrary or inconsistent views had dealt with this in their reports giving any necessary explanations.'

His Honour went on to say that experts who change their minds at a late stage or introduce a new theory or interpretation should commit their views to writing and furnish reports to the other parties at the earliest opportunity. His Honour quoted Lord Wilberforce in *Whitehouse v Jordan* [1981] 1 WLR 246 at 256:

> 'It is necessary that expert evidence presented to the court should be, and should be seen to be, the independent product of the expert, uninfluenced as to form or content by the exigencies of litigation. To the extent that it is not, the evidence is likely to be not only incorrect but self-defeating.'

Instructing the expert witness

The first approach

Once a solicitor has met with the client and has ascertained the nature of the problem and the issues involved, the next step will be for him to collect together all necessary documentation in order to assess the case and decide what action should be taken. At that stage he may say to the client that it would be a good idea for one or more experts to be involved. This is particularly so in relation to building defect claims. It is vital to have an expert inspect the premises, take photographs and any necessary samples and other evidence prior to remedial works being carried out. It is a plaintiff's duty to permit a defendant access for such inspection and to allow him facilities for so doing. If acting for a potential plaintiff it would be important to consider with the client the necessity for remedial works and the proposed programme in conjunction with the appointment of the expert or experts. When acting for a defendant, it is obviously important to obtain from the plaintiff or his solicitors details of their complaints and allegations and copies of any reports and programme of remedial works.

When acting for a plaintiff it would usually be prudent to send a letter before action outlining the claim and inviting the defendant to admit liability. When acting for a defendant it will be necessary for the solicitor to notify the plaintiff's solicitors of his interest and to make arrangements for the inspection of the alleged defects. If the solicitor's client is insured then consideration ought to be given as to whether notification should be made pursuant to the terms of the policy.

Terms of engagement

It is likely that the first approach by a solicitor to the proposed expert will be made by telephone when he will outline his client's case, giving the proposed expert some idea of the sums in dispute and the questions which will arise in the proceedings. If the expert agrees to act he should be asked for details of his terms; for example, an hourly rate, and as to whether disbursements are included in his fee structure. The solicitor will then arrange for papers to be sent to the expert and for a meeting to take place, probably on site with the client present. If a solicitor instructs an expert that solicitor will usually be directly and personally responsible for that expert's fees, with reimbursement by the client. Some solicitors may prefer the expert to be instructed and paid by the client direct. This should be clarified at the outset. If it is more convenient for the solicitor to engage the expert directly, he should consider requesting a sum on account of costs and disbursements from the client.

Terms of reference

An expert will only be as good as his instructions permit. His terms of reference should be clear and concise. Lloyd J said in *James Longley & Co Ltd v South West Thames Regional Health Authority* (1983) 25 BLR 56 at 63:

> 'There is no doubt that the calling of unnecessary expert evidence has done much to lengthen trials, and should for that reason be discouraged. But in some cases expert evidence may have the opposite effect;

> in complex building disputes, for instance, it may tend to simplify the issues which the judge has to decide, and thereby shorten rather than lengthen the trial.'

Solicitors should instruct the expert to set out his report so that the issues are identified and there is no doubt as to the expert's terms of reference. Reports will then be able to be compared and contrasted. It will also be far easier for the parties to identify upon which issues they are in agreement and upon which matters they are in dispute.

Site inspection

It is important for a solicitor to get to grips with the technical issues and there is no better way of so doing than visiting the site with the client and experts. This can transform a purely academic set of facts into reality. He or she will be able to appreciate much better the issues involved in the case. It is also often very helpful for counsel to visit the site although at an early stage this may not be a practical proposition bearing in mind the costs involved in this exercise and the demands upon counsel's diary. Solicitors should encourage the client and expert to collect all the evidence they can. This is particularly the case in relation to defects claims.

(a) Photographs It is almost impossible to take too many photographs. If the dispute goes to trial or to arbitration then a choice can be made as to what photographs will be used. Sometimes the judge or arbitrator will not have the opportunity of a view and great reliance will be placed on photographs. Where remedial works are carried out much of the evidence will be destroyed and therefore photographic and other such evidence is the only record of the defects. The expert ought to be encouraged to take the photographs and as soon as they are developed they should be dated and sufficiently labelled to identify the particular point which they illustrate. Unless otherwise agreed between the parties, the taker of the photographs, ie the photographer, will have to prove them in the witness box. Photographs not only provide a record but if properly used can make what would otherwise be a very turgid subject much more interesting.

(b) Samples In some circumstances it is important to take samples, for example where the mortar mix varies from the specification and is too weak, thereby causing building failure. Samples may have to be analysed by a laboratory, thus entailing the involvement of a further expert. In construction disputes it is quite difficult to make a great deal of use of samples. For example, if a roof is leaking this may be due to a number of factors, such as thermal movement or faulty workmanship. It will rarely be possible to take a sample which will illustrate the problems which have been encountered.

Order 38, rule 5 states:

> 'Unless, at or before the trial, the Court for special reasons otherwise orders, no plan, photograph or model shall be receivable in evidence at the trial of an action unless at least 10 days before the commencement of the trial the parties, other than the party producing it, have been given an opportunity to inspect it and to agree to the admission thereof without further proof.'

The expert will usually include photographs in his report which will be exchanged at least ten days before the commencement of the trial. If there are other photographs, plans or models which are not revealed to the other party at least ten days before trial, then a judge allowing the admission of such evidence must include a note of so doing in the certificate for the information of the taxing master who will consider the question when the costs of the successful party are taxed. A successful litigant can enforce against his opponent only the taxed bill which, despite changes to the taxation rules, may be considerably less than his actual costs. The range of recoverable costs is somewhere between half and three-quarters of his actual costs, dependent upon the nature and conduct of the case.

(c) Video The use of video cameras and machines is not widespread at the present time. It is, however, conceivable that this might prove to be a very useful way of illustrating the problems in building failure by, for example, the filming of a building being opened up, and such a film may be of great visual impact. There are facilities in the official referee's courts for the showing of videos and if such facilities are required then the solicitor in charge of the case should make arrangements with the clerk to the official referee to whom the case has been designated. Arrangements should be made shortly before the trial.

In defects cases, it will be useful to have a video of the site prior to remedial works being carried out, during the course of the remedial works and also after they have been completed.

Models

Solicitors may consider making use of a display or model. Arrangements should again be made with the official referee's clerk for facilities to be made available.

Counsel

In major disputes counsel will often be instructed at an early stage in the proceedings. The expert will often be required to provide a preliminary report having perused documentation supplied to him by instructing solicitors and having visited the site in question.

Defects claims

In cases relating to defects this report can perform two functions. The first is to identify the defects and if acting for a plaintiff make recommendations as to the remedial works. The second is to give an opinion upon whether the defects are due to defective workmanship or faulty design or perhaps both. The report will often prove to be an invaluable guide as to whether a plaintiff should pursue his action and if so whether to do so by arbitration or in the courts. If the expert is acting for a defendant he may be able to indicate whether an offer in settlement should be made at an early stage, or whether in the expert's opinion there is a defence. For example, he may be an architect advising another architect or his insurers whether there has been a breach of duty. He may say that the building has failed due to the poor standard of workmanship which might not have been appreciated by a competent architect acting within the normal purview of supervisory duties. He may say on the other hand that a design fault caused the failure of the building for which the architect is wholly responsible. However, rarely is it possible for an expert to be categoric at the outset. In defects cases much depends upon what is discovered during the opening up of the building when remedial works are carried out.

Money claims

Where the claims or defence is essentially in relation to monetary issues, it may not be necessary to involve the expert at such an early stage. The solicitor, counsel and client may simply be meeting in conference to discuss the formulation of the claim with the expert acting in a more periphery manner in the early stages. He may, for example, spend a good deal of time in his client's office going through files and either formulating a claim for loss and expense due to disruption, or perhaps may compile a claim for extension of time. These cases tend to be much more straightforward in terms of liability in contrast to a claim for defects which involves often much more complex issues concerning building failure. In monetary claims and claims for extension of time records of the contractor or employer are of the utmost importance. If a contractor is making a claim and has not served the requisite notices and has not kept records, he will be faced with grave problems in making a claim against the employer for loss and expense.

The first conference with counsel will therefore be an opportunity for all parties to meet—counsel, solicitor, client and expert—and to discuss the merits of the case and the way forward. Counsel will hopefully glean sufficient information for him to formulate a statement of claim, points of claim or a defence and any counterclaim.

The proceedings

Arbitration v litigation

At a very early stage consideration will usually be given to the question of the method of resolving the dispute. It will be necessary to turn to the contract to see whether there is an arbitration clause. The court has a discretion pursuant to s 4 of the Arbitration Act 1950 as to whether to stay proceedings where there is an agreement to arbitrate. Section 4 states as follows:

> '(1) If any party to an arbitration agreement, or any person claiming through or under him, commences any legal proceedings in any court against any other party to the agreement, or any person claiming through or under him, in respect of any matter agreed to be referred, any party to those legal proceedings may at any time after appearance, and before delivering any pleadings or taking any other steps in the proceedings, apply to that court to stay the proceedings, and that court or a judge thereof, if satisfied that there is no sufficient reason why the matter should not be referred in accordance with the agreement, and that the applicant was, at the time when the proceedings were commenced, and still remains, ready and willing to do all things necessary to the proper conduct of the arbitration, may make an order staying the proceedings.'

There are certain advantages and disadvantages to proceeding by way of arbitration. The traditional advantages are said to be that the procedure is simple, quick and less cumbersome than that of the courts. It, however, is fair to say that this is not the case in many arbitrations which tend to mirror court proceedings. Confidentiality is, however, maintained and the arbitrator can be chosen by the parties who are at liberty to choose an arbitrator who is technically qualified in relation to the matters in dispute. Rights of appeal are very severely restricted and the arbitration will usually settle the dispute once and for all.

Critics of the arbitration procedure will point to corresponding disadvantages. Their comments would be as follows:

Speed It is possible for one party to delay matters with no readily available sanction. If a party delays then the sanction for the other party is to make an application to the High Court pursuant to s 5 of the Arbitration Act 1979 for the powers of the arbitrator to be extended. This section provides:

> '5–(1) If any party to a reference under an arbitration agreement fails within the time specified in the order or, if no time is so specified, within a reasonable time to comply with an order made by the arbitrator or umpire in the course of the reference, then, on the application of the arbitrator or umpire or of any party to the reference, the High Court may make an order extending the powers of the arbitrator or umpire as mentioned in sub-section (2) below.
> (2) If an order is made by the High Court under this section, the arbitrator or umpire shall have power, to the extent and subject to any conditions specified in that order, to continue with the reference in default of appearance or of any other act by one of the parties in like manner as a judge of the High Court might continue with proceedings in that court where a party fails to comply with an order of that court or a requirement of rules of court.'

If a party wishes to make application for security for costs in the arbitration that application must be made to the High Court pursuant to s 12(6)(a) of the Arbitration Act 1950. An arbitrator has no power to order security for costs unless the arbitration agreement or the rules pursuant to which the arbitration is governed expressly confers upon him such power and this is quite rare.

Flexibility It is often said to be an advantage that arbitration is the flexible option enabling the parties to choose their own representation. However, it is quite common for an arbitration to be conducted in exactly the same manner as High Court proceedings with representation of the parties by solicitors and counsel.

Costs Arbitration can be conducted economically. Alternatively, if solicitors and counsel are engaged then it can be even more expensive since the arbitrator's fee and hire of the room must be borne by the parties whereas court fees are minimal.

Final decision The advantage is that arbitration will often provide a final decision but of course the corresponding disadvantage is that there are severely restricted rights of appeal. The parties may by choice make an exclusion agreement, ie an agreement excluding the right of appeal. If there is no such exclusion agreement an appeal can only be made to the court on a question of law arising out of an arbitration award. No appeal may be brought even on a question of law unless either the other party consents or the court grants leave. The court will not grant leave unless it considers that, having regard to all the circumstances, the determination of the question raised could substantially affect the rights of one of the parties. These restrictions are contained within s 1 of the Arbitration Act 1979.

The House of Lords in a case known as *The Nema* [1982] AC 724, [1981] 2 All ER 1030 had to consider inter alia the principles upon which leave to appeal should be given.

Uncomplicated An advantage is often said to be that the amount of documents can be restricted and the procedures can be simplified—this is rarely the case, especially if a large amount of money is at stake.

Choice of arbitrator/location

The parties can agree upon the person appointed to be arbitrator. They can also agree on the location of the arbitration hearing.

Arbitration on documents alone

Because of the number of construction cases where there are multifarious disputes on fact, this is not often a viable proposition. The Arbitration Rules now contained in JCT 80 provide for three procedures for the conduct of an arbitration which are set out in

Rule 5: Procedure without hearing
Rule 6: Full procedure with hearing
Rule 7: Short procedure with hearing

The Rules give the parties themselves an opportunity to choose which of the three procedures shall apply. But if the parties neither agree to the procedure of rule 7 nor jointly decide between the other two, then the arbitrator is required to direct which of the other two shall apply. A direction that rule 6 shall apply instead of rule 5 must be made having regard to information the parties have supplied and/or any representations they have made to him.

As indicated above, there are certain negative factors with regard to arbitration but if the parties are able to adopt a somewhat streamlined approach in restricting the amount of evidence and narrowing the issues, arbitration can be a satisfactory mode of resolving a dispute. Richard Hawkins and Norman Royce in their chapters have dealt comprehensively with the subject of arbitration so that this chapter is henceforth confined to a view from the solicitor pursuing an action in the High Court.

OFFICIAL REFEREE'S COURTS

As His Honour Judge John Newey QC has explained in his chapter—'An Official Referee's View'—the official referee's courts were created in 1876 to deal with technical matters. They deal with the majority of construction disputes in the High Court. There is a special procedure adopted in that the official referee will usually deal with the interlocutory applications throughout the action and then try the case himself. He will have a particular interest therefore in the action as it progresses.

A plaintiff can either issue a writ or originating summons with the words 'Official Referee's Business' upon it at the outset of the case, or proceedings can be transferred to the official referee's court which often occurs at the summons for directions stage. Official referee's business is allocated by the rota clerk of the High Court to official referees in rotation.

OFFICIAL REFEREE'S BUSINESS INCLUDES CLASSES OF ACTIONS WHICH ARE CONCERNED WITH THE FOLLOWING MATTERS:

(a) civil or mechanical engineering;
(b) building and other construction work generally;
(c) claims by and against engineers, architects, surveyors, accountants and other such specialised professional persons or bodies;
(d) claims by and against local authorities relating to their statutory duties concerning the development of land or the construction of buildings;
(e) claims between neighbouring owners and occupiers of land in trespass, nuisance and liability under *Rylands v Fletcher* (1868) LR 3 HL 330;
(f) claims between landlord and tenant for breaches of repairing covenants;
(g) claims relating the quality of goods sold or hired;
(h) claims relating to work done and materials supplied or services rendered; and
(i) claims involving the taking of accounts especially where these are complicated.

A practice direction of 1968 states that:

> 'At the first summons for directions the solicitor should be in a position to state the nature of the claim and defence.'

The official referee will hope to obtain an appreciation of what are the issues in the case and of the sums in dispute. It is not uncommon for him to enquire of the parties as to whether there will be any further defendants or third parties joined in the action. He will ascertain whether any preliminary issues could be tried separately and whether the case should be tried by virtue of a Scott Schedule (see later) and whether expert evidence will be required. He will deal with the service of pleadings, discovery by way of list of documents and inspection of documents. Order 36, rule 6 was amended in October 1982 to include a specific requirement that the application for directions should include an application for a fixed date for a hearing. Thus the parties know from the outset what is the timetable for the conduct of the action and what will be the trial date.

Directions

Order 36, rule 6 of the Rules of the Supreme Court states as follows:

> '6–(1) An application for directions (including an application for a fixed date of hearing) shall be made by the plaintiff to the official referee to whom the business has been allocated within 14 days of—

(a) the giving by a defendant of notice of intention to defend, or
(b) the date of the order transferring the cause or matter, whichever is the later.'

If the plaintiff does not make an application for the directions then any other party may do so. The summons does not need to be particularised and the form in general use merely asks for 'Such directions as may be appropriate' or for 'General directions'. Pleadings must be lodged at the time of the issue of the summons for directions. On further applications or summonses before the court then again all pleadings and affidavits must be lodged at least 48 hours prior to the summons taking place. The official referee will usually acquaint himself with the facts of the case prior to the hearing of the summons.

Representation

It is not uncommon for solicitors to brief counsel to appear upon the first summons for directions. However, it is usually somewhat unnecessary, since the directions in general will be in the usual form and it is merely necessary for the solicitor representing the client to explain to the official referee the general nature of the case and to ask for the directions he requires. If in doubt, he should confer with counsel, who may have already advised in conference and/or settled pleadings.

A typical order of the official referee on a summons for directions is included in the chapter on evidence by Anthony Thornton QC and Kim Franklin. Interlocutory proceedings are conducted by the official referee in his chambers. Solicitors will draw up the orders and have them sealed by the rota clerk. Summonses and applications are usually heard at 10 am. The official referee assigned to the case will normally deal with all interlocutory applications and proceedings relating to it. The exception is of course an application for an interim payment under Order 29, rules 9–18 which has to be taken by another official referee. In the absence of an official referee, or with his consent, any interlocutory application may be made to or dealt with by another official referee. It is possible to transfer the action to another official referee who perhaps has conduct of a related action.

Open system of pre-trial procedure: witnesses of fact

A distinction is drawn between witnesses of fact and expert witnesses.

The official referee will usually order pre-trial disclosure of expert evidence by exchange of reports and he might order an exchange of witness statements pursuant to Order 38, rule 2A. This rule states as follows:

'38/2A–(1) This rule applies to any cause or matter which is proceeding in the Chancery Division, the Commercial Court, the Admiralty Court or as official referees' business, and in this rule "the Court" includes an official referee.

(2) At any stage in any cause or matter to which this rule applies, the Court may, if it thinks fit for the purpose of disposing fairly and expeditiously of the cause or matter and saving costs, direct any party to serve on the other parties, on such terms as the Court shall think just, written statements of the oral evidence which the party intends to lead on any issues of fact to be decided at the trial.

(3) Directions given under paragraph (2) may—
(a) make different provision with regard to different issues of fact or different witnesses;
(b) require any written statement served to be signed by the intended witness;
(c) require that statements be filed with the Court.

(4) Subject to paragraph (6), where the party serving a statement under paragraph (2) does not call the witness to whose evidence it relates no other party may put the statement in evidence at the trial.

(5) Subject to paragraph (6) and unless the Court otherwise orders, where the party serving the statement does call such a witness at the trial—
(a) the party may not without the consent of the other parties or the leave of the Court lead evidence from that witness the substance of which is not included in the statement served, except in relation to new matters which have arisen in the course of the trial;
(b) the Court may, on such terms as it thinks fit, direct that the statement served, or part of it, shall stand as the evidence in chief of the witness or part of such evidence;
(c) whether or not the statement or any part of it is referred to during the evidence in chief of the witness, any party may put the statement or any part of it in cross-examination of that witness.

(6) Where any statement served is one to which the Civil Evidence Acts 1968 and 1972 apply, paragraphs (4) and (5) shall take effect subject to the provisions of those Acts and Parts (III) and (IV) of this Order. The service of a statement pursuant to a direction given under paragraph (2) shall not, unless expressly so stated by the party serving the same, be treated as a notice under the said Acts.

(7) Where a party fails to comply with a direction given under paragraph (2) he shall not be entitled to adduce evidence to which such direction related without the leave of the Court.

(8) Nothing in this rule shall deprive any party of his right to treat any communication as privileged or make admissible evidence otherwise inadmissible.'

Order 38, rule 2A is designed for the following beneficial purposes:

(1) The fair and expeditious disposal of proceedings and savings of costs.
(2) The elimination of any element of 'surprise' before or at trial as to the witnesses each party intends to call at the trial or as to the substance of their evidence.

(3) The promotion of a fair settlement between the parties. The parties will be able to make an assessment of the strengths and weaknesses of their cases.
(4) The avoidance of a trial.
(5) The identification of the real issues and the elimination of unnecessary issues.
(6) The encouragement of the parties to make admissions of fact, which they are often reluctant to do.
(7) The reduction in the number of pre-trial applications, such as for further and better particulars or further discovery of documents or for interrogatories.
(8) The possible elimination of giving long drawn out evidence in chief.
(9) The improvement of the process of cross-examination.
(10) The concentration of the parties and the trial judge on the real matters in controversy between the parties.

The written statement served must be full and complete. It must be 'the truth, the whole truth, and nothing but the truth'. The party serving the witness statement may not lead evidence from his witness, the substance of which is not included in the statement served except as to a new matter, or with the consent of the other parties or with the leave of the court. It is therefore essential that very great care is taken over the preparation of the witness statements. The party serving the statement may apply to the court to amend the statement to correct any error or mistake or other misstatement. The opposite party may apply to the court to amend the statement by striking out such material as they say is irrelevant or hearsay evidence of expression of opinion or other inadmissible evidence.

EXPERT EVIDENCE

The court will normally make an order for expert evidence where necessary. Order 38, rule 4 states:

> 'The Court may, at or before the trial of any action, order that the number of medical or other expert witnesses who may be called at the trial shall be limited as specified by the order.'

As Judge Newey has said in his chapter the official referee will have to be persuaded of the need before he will agree to more than one witness of the same discipline being called by a party. This is in order to save costs and time.

The exchange of experts' reports is governed by Part IV of Order 38 which was added by RSC (Amendment) 1974 (SI 1974/295). The rules restrict the right of the parties to adduce expert evidence in civil proceedings as a matter of course and provide the machinery for the pre-trial disclosure by each party to the other of expert evidence. The rules are intended to make an advance in the direction of a more open system of pre-trial proceedings so that the parties can prepare their case on the basis of material evidence known to them as opposed to doing so in the dark. The intention is to:

a) assist the parties to reach a fair settlement;
b) avoid surprise at the trial;
c) secure agreed experts' reports and narrow the issues, obviating the need for attendance of experts at the trial;
d) shorten the evidence at the trial;
e) enable experts to prepare their evidence more thoroughly and helpfully.

Exchange will usually be simultaneous. The *Practice Direction* [1974] 2 All ER 966 states that if the parties have agreed as to adducing expert evidence or disclosure of reports, this fact will be recorded on the summons for directions.

If both parties have instructed or are likely to instruct experts, the question of disclosure of reports will be dealt with at the summons for directions; any order for disclosure will normally be by way of exchange. In other cases, disclosure of one party's report may only be ordered in exceptional circumstances or the parties may be given leave to call expert witnesses without disclosure of reports; liberty to apply subsequently for disclosure may be given.

In the case of *Kirkup v British Rail Engineering Ltd* [1983] 3 All ER 147, [1983] 1 WLR 1165 the Court of Appeal held that a sequential exchange of reports was fair in the circumstances. This was a personal injury case where the area of inquiry going back to 1952 involved investigation of the plaintiff's various working conditions and the states of knowledge about the consequences of excessive noise, making it difficult for the defendants to prepare their expert evidence without details of the plaintiff's case in relation to those matters.

The disclosure of experts' reports is governed by Order 38, rule 38. Sub-paragraph 3 of that rule provides as follows:

> '(3) In any cause or matter the Court may, if it thinks fit, direct that there be a meeting "without prejudice" of such experts within such periods before or after the disclosure of their reports as the Court may specify, for the purpose of identifying those parts of their evidence which are in issue. Where such a meeting takes place the experts may prepare a joint statement indicating those parts of their evidence on which they are, and those on which they are not, in agreement.'

The effect of this rule is to provide for compulsory disclosure and ordinarily for the compulsory exchange of experts' reports before the trial. Sub-paragraph (3) empowers the court to direct that the experts of the parties must meet 'without prejudice' and at such a meeting they can prepare a joint statement indicating those parts of their evidence on which they are and those on which they are not in agreement. The power under the rule may be exercised without the prior consent of the parties. The intention is that the parties will know before the trial the rationale and the extent of the agreement or disagreement between these experts and this may well promote a settlement between them. The process of the trial itself should be made more smooth and its length significantly shortened.

Very often clients have experts within their own organisation. They then query the reason for appointing an independent expert. There are several advantages in so doing:

The first is that the independent expert will look at the case dispassionately and will be better able to give advice to the client. Secondly, an independent expert will be used to preparing experts' reports, attending experts' meetings and giving evidence.

In some cases, however, evidence is given by a member of a client's firm. In *Shell Pensions Trust Ltd v Pell Frischmann & Partners* [1986] 2 All ER 911, Shell Pensions Trust Ltd claimed damages against the defendants, Pell Frischmann & Partners, for negligence. By a summons the plaintiffs applied for an order that unless the defendants disclosed to the plaintiffs the expert evidence on which they intended to rely, they should be debarred from relying on expert evidence. Pell Frischmann & Partners are consulting engineers.

On 24 December 1984 His Honour Judge Hawser QC, sitting as an official referee, gave leave to both parties to call expert evidence and ordered that expert witnesses' reports be exchanged by 31 October 1985 and that the witnesses should meet by 30 November 1985. On 25 November 1985 Judge Hawser extended the time for the exchange of the experts' reports until 16 December 1985, the plaintiffs duly disclosed a report, but the defendants did not. The defendants' solicitors wrote to the plaintiffs' solicitors, saying that their understanding was that exchange of experts' reports was limited to persons who were not witnesses of fact, and that their clients would contend at the trial that the buildings were structurally sound and had adequate fire resistance as had been 'proved' by load tests and fires. They asserted that a defendant is entitled to give evidence on his own behalf to rebutt allegations made against him without disclosure of his evidence in advance. They gave notice that they would be adducing evidence from the defendants' present and former employees.

His Honour Judge John Newey QC said:

> 'No doubt the courts are inclined to show indulgence to parties who are giving evidence on their own behalf, especially if they are in person, but, nonetheless, the general rule must apply to them as to others, namely that they can only give opinion evidence if it concerns, to use the words of Saunders J in *Buckley v Rice-Thomas* (1554) 1 Plowd 118—"a science or faculty". The rules in Order 38 refer to "expert evidence" and not to "evidence given by independent experts". They apply generally: to independent experts, to so-called "in-house" experts and to parties themselves.'

Judge Newey extended time for disclosure of the defendants' expert evidence. He said that if the plaintiffs were not to be informed of the defendants' expert evidence in advance when the substance of it comes to be put to the plaintiffs' witnesses in cross-examination, there might well have to be adjournments to enable them to consider it.

Some difficulty is caused in limiting the expert evidence where the action is by a layman against a person who proposes to call his expert employee to give evidence partly of fact as well as an independent expert. In *Taylor v Greening & Sons Ltd* (1956) unreported the Court of Appeal made an order for directions as follows:

> 'A report by an engineer to be agreed if possible, and if not agreed, the expert evidence be limited to two independent witnesses for each party: provided always that either party may call additional expert witnesses (who may be in the employment of or otherwise connected with such party) that such witness or witnesses shall not qualify on taxation for payment as experts.'

This is a fairly unusual order.

The court has power to limit the number of expert witnesses but this does not extend to excluding expert evidence altogether; *Sullivan v West Yorkshire Passenger Transport Executive* [1985] 2 All ER 134, CA.

The expert's involvement with counsel

Very frequently, the expert will be involved in an initial conference with counsel following production of his preliminary report. There may be other experts involved in the case with whom he will have to liaise. Throughout the case he will be required to give his opinion via solicitors upon the pleadings. It is likely that in litigation counsel will settle the statement of claim or in arbitration points of claim, and he will no doubt comment upon the draft. If a Scott Schedule is ordered to be served he will provide much of the input with regard to technical issues, although it is likely that counsel will draft the final version, which will require checking by solicitors, experts and client. It is therefore likely that throughout the course of the litigation or arbitration there will be a number of meetings at which the expert's attendance will be required. His interreaction with counsel and the final drafting of reports and preparation for trial are dealt with in some detail by Anthony Thornton QC and Anthony Speaight.

Discovery

Discovery constitutes the disclosure by one party to another in the action of the existence of relevant documents which are or have been in his power, custody or control. Discovery is usually ordered upon a mutual basis, ie, the date for service of a list of documents will be the same for each party. A party may be required to verify the list by affidavit. Upon service of the list of documents the other party has a right to inspect those which are not privileged. In construction disputes it is commonly the case that there are a huge number of documents many of which will be of a technical nature, or have technical implications, and therefore solicitors often enlist the assistance of experts in carrying out the task of inspection. It is quite usual for a solicitor then to request copies of the documents which he considers are of particular relevance to him, and again reliance in this respect will often be placed upon the expert, who will better be able to judge the significance of particular documents and their contents. He will also be able to point to any omissions from the list pursuant to which a solicitor will then be able to request from the other party a further and better list. Failing such production an application can be made to the court who will usually order that such a list is produced, which might well be ordered to be verified by affidavit. Alternatively, the court may make an order for specific discovery where a particular category of documents has been omitted. An application for particular discovery is made pursuant to Order 24, rule 7 and must be supported by an affidavit describing a particular document or class of documents and stating reasonable grounds for believing that the document or class is relevant and is likely to be or has been in the respondent's possession, custody or power.

Exchange of experts' reports

Exchange will take place in accordance with the order of the court or arbitrator. It is generally believed that meetings of experts should take place prior to exchange of reports since after exchange some entrenchment of views can occur. A meeting of experts can produce some form of settlement. The solicitor's task is to meet with the expert and client and perhaps counsel and to carry out a general review of the action if the experts have agreed a without prejudice draft statement setting out common grounds between them and the issues which remain unresolved. The expert will have no doubt agreed the statement subject to his client's instructions and the scrutiny of the lawyers. The meeting of experts is often an opportunity to commence negotiations and very often there is one meeting with consultation with clients and lawyers in the intervening periods between the meetings of experts.

Advice on evidence

It is likely that as the date for trial or arbitration draws closer, instructing solicitors will seek the advice of counsel in relation to evidence. This will include not only documentary and factual evidence but also evidence of the experts. A major conference will usually take place and experts will attend to discuss the presentation of the case. This will take place two to three months prior to the trial or perhaps earlier if necessary. Discussion will take place on matters such as the bundles for trial, proof of evidence of witnesses of fact, expert evidence, any photographs, plans, models to be used in evidence at trial, and counsel will be appraised of any meetings which have taken place between the experts and any negotiations towards a settlement.

Trial

As the trial approaches, the solicitor will be preparing bundles, witness statements and reports and generally taking stock of the case. He will be arranging for counsel to be briefed and for experts and other witnesses to attend trial. It is extremely important that documents are legible, numbered and well presented. He will advise experts as to when and where they will be required to attend.

CHAPTER 4

The expert as advocate

Richard Hawkins FRICS, FCIArb

In construction disputes it is not uncommon for a party to be represented by an expert. In many cases the expert will be able to negotiate on behalf of his client with experts, or representatives of the other party, in order to reach a conclusion to the matter which is satisfactory to both parties. If such a conclusion is not possible or practicable some other method must be adopted to bring about a settlement.

If the parties have chosen arbitration as such a method of settlement of the dispute the expert may conduct the reference on behalf of his client. In this sense he assumes the role of technical advocate. He is appointed to conduct his client's case and this distinguishes him from the expert witness whose function is to act purely independently and to assist the tribunal. The technical advocate cannot be independent and primarily he will be appointed by the client to present his case. In *Multi-Media Productions Ltd v Secretary of State for the Environment* (1988) 5 CLD 03 18 it was held that it is an undesirable practice for one person to combine the roles of the expert witness and advocate. An expert is appointed to give an unbiased opinion, whereas an advocate has to do the best he can for his client. An expert who conducts a case and gives evidence must expect such evidence to be treated with some caution by the tribunal.

Whilst it is desirable that the technical advocate should have a good understanding of the laws of contract and tort, and the rules governing the submission of evidence, he is in no sense a lawyer. He may be dealing with lawyers for the other party, or parties, but that fact should not be allowed to influence him in the manner in which he conducts his client's case. He should neither have illusions of grandeur, nor feel any sense of inferiority or apology. He is there to conduct the case for his client because the circumstances lend themselves to that course of approach.

The type of arbitration which is most suitable for technical advocacy is that in which there are few, if any, matters of law. Where the matters in dispute are largely confined to those of fact, the conduct of the reference is ideally suited to an expert who is able to identify the points at issue from his previous knowledge and experience. This differentiates him from the lawyer who, in general terms, may not be an expert in the particular matters in dispute and may have to rely, to a large extent, on the information with which he is provided.

The standard forms of construction contracts include arbitration agreements, indicating the pre-supposition that disputes which may arise will generally be on matters of fact. The parties to those contracts have therefore chosen for themselves, at the time the contract was made, the means by which the dispute will be determined. A third party, who is both an expert in his field and totally impartial, will receive evidence from the parties to the dispute and decide who is the winner and who is the loser on each of its constituent parts. It is intended that his decision will be final. It is perhaps then a sad reflection on the construction industry generally that it has allowed, what in essence should be a fairly simple and informal process, to become both expensive and protracted, and a mirror image of a High Court action. Parties finding themselves with a dispute which they cannot settle between them, often find their only course of action is arbitration, because of the decision in *Northern Regional Health Authority v Derek Crouch Construction Co Ltd* [1984] QB 644, 26 BLR 1, CA. In this case it was held by the Court of Appeal, inter alia, that the High Court did not possess the same wide jurisdiction with which arbitrators are expressly provided in the Form of Building Contracts, particularly in respect of powers to 'open up, review and revise any certificate, opinion, decision, requirement or notice'. In this regard the arbitrator stands in the shoes of the architect. To a large extent that can introduce a certain resistance. Parties, even though they have entered into an arbitration agreement, then have doubts concerning the desired finality of the arbitrator's award. Their first reaction is often to appoint a lawyer who, because of his training and experience will undoubtedly conduct the reference based on the Rules of the Supreme Court. There is nothing intrinsically wrong in this, but it may not be the most efficient and cost-effective way of conducting his client's case. The arbitrator is appointed by the parties, or their representatives, to decide the issues. Since he is so appointed, he can decide, by referring to the parties if desired, how the reference will proceed. In this sense the flexibility and informality of arbitration is compared with that of a High Court action.

Since the technical advocate is not a lawyer, and consequently does not have any formal legal training, he should be ideally suited to such flexibility and informality. His experience and training has probably involved him in previous examples of the subject matter of the dispute and from this he will know the most effective way of presenting his client's case before the arbitrator. It may be that formal pleadings can be dispensed with; involving the submission of short written statements, augmented by a detailed inspection at the site. In a dispute where very large sums of money are involved, the parties may nevertheless decide the best method of advising the arbitrator of the issues is by means of formal pleadings and the full procedure of discovery, expert witnesses and a formal hearing. Provided the matters of law involved are either minimal or non-existent, the technical advocate may effectively conduct his client's case.

THE APPOINTMENT OF THE EXPERT

The appointment of the expert may come about in one of two ways. The expert may be retained by the client to give general advice and assistance on contractual matters over a long-term period, or the appointment may be made as a result of either a direct approach, or a recommendation by a third party, for the subject matter of the specific dispute.

In the case of the former, the expert will already have established a relationship with the client, and will probably have had a direct involvement with the subject matter of the dispute over a long period. He may already have taken steps to try to achieve a resolution, but without success. It may be on his recommendation that his client has referred the dispute to arbitration. As to the latter appointment no previous relationship will exist between client and expert and he will be introduced to the dispute with no prior knowledge of its history.

In either case the expert's approach should be similar. Before either advising the client to refer the matter to arbitration, or taking a step in the reference he should make a thorough study of the client's documents and papers, and interview members of the client's staff, to establish the content of the case. Even if he has been involved for some time his memory may have caused him to overlook a vital letter or other recorded document which may assist or destroy the credibility of the whole case.

If the expert's opinion is sought as to whether the claim is worth pursuing to arbitration, he should first consider the following before advising his client:

(i) Does the claim have substance and stand a reasonable chance of success?
(ii) If the claim were to fail could the client afford to pay the other side's costs?
(iii) Is there evidence to support the claim? Are witnesses available? If they have left the organisation will they willingly give evidence at a hearing?
(iv) Is there evidence of impecuniosity of the other side? Could it afford to pay both the award and the costs of the reference?
(v) Is there an arbitration agreement?
(vi) Does a dispute exist?

These basic questions are considered in further detail below:

(i) Does the claim have substance and stand a reasonable chance of success?

This is not meant to imply that the technical advocate should only assume responsibility for assignments where there is a high probability of success. The expert should, however, try and analyse in his own mind, from his previous knowledge and experience, whether his client is wasting money in pursuing or defending a claim. No client is going to thank an expert for assuming a commission and accumulating a large fee account, only to see the claim fail. If, having completed his analysis, the expert is of the opinion that the claim stands only a meagre chance of success, or if he considers it will fail completely, he must of course advise the client accordingly. If the client insists on pursuing the matter, it becomes the client's decision and the expert has to do his best, sometimes against his own better judgment, to ensure a just settlement.

In the construction industry it is common for parties to play the game of brinkmanship. This is where one party, rightly or wrongly believing he has a cast-iron case, sets out on the path of arbitration or litigation in the hope the other side will capitulate and together they can reach a negotiated settlement. In this eventuality the expert must learn to tread a very careful line. If he assumes an assignment on these, sometimes flimsy, grounds and unless he takes sufficient measure to protect his position, for example, by warning his client in writing, he may find when things do not work out as his client had hoped that he is on the receiving end of his client's wrath and anger. If this happens he may need to closely inspect his professional indemnity policy.

There is nothing worse for the expert than having to prosecute a claim that stands little chance of any success. Not only is he going to risk his reputation in the eyes of his client, but also in the eyes of the other party and their professional advisers, with whom of course the expert may have other dealings. This is particularly salient in circumstances where a party, having already given notice to the other side to concur in the appointment of an arbitrator, and maybe the arbitrator has actually been appointed, takes the decision that conducting his own case is not as simple as he first thought and seeks to appoint an expert to act on his behalf. Similarly, a party may already be receiving advice from an expert and it may be advice he does not care to act upon, so he takes steps to appoint another who, he presumes, will confirm his rather misguided views. In either of the above examples the expert, if he is to be appointed as technical advocate, must be very wary about assuming responsibility on behalf of his client without first carefully analysing the merits and liabilities of the claim. Such advice is not always easy to heed, especially when the expert is approached by a new and, sometimes seemingly, influential client. It is often too much of a temptation to blindly take the commission, on the presumption that the claim is sound, only to find in the course of the proceedings that it would have been far better to have advised the client at the outset of the flimsy chance of success. Furthermore, at this point it is often very difficult for the expert to receive payment of his fees in full or at all. Clients do not take kindly to having to pay for what they invariably see as wrongful advice.

It sometimes takes a lot of courage for the expert to advise his client, who may be very influential, that his ideas of a claim as a result of some dispute or difference between the parties on a contract which seemingly went wrong from the beginning, and which the client has had to live with every day for the previous three or four years, in fact has no substance at all. However, if the expert considers it to be so he should have no qualms about speaking his mind. He can always invite the client to obtain a second opinion. In the long-run it may save both the client's money and the expert's reputation.

A would-be claimant may have cause to think he has the best claim in the world, but its pursuance by the expert is a waste of time and money if it has no substance, ie there is no evidence to substantiate the claim. As has already been discussed above, the claimant may have lived with a problem for a long time, and may be convinced that he is absolutely correct in what he is claiming. This may or may not be so. The plain fact is the claimant has to prove, on the balance of probabilities, that what he is claiming is valid. Thus, if loss and expense is being claimed, such loss and expense must be proven. It is not sufficient for the claimant to try to charge for a full-time site supervisor, for example, if that individual was at the material time actually controlling two projects. This fact is bound to be known to the opponent or to his professional advisers. In any event, it is a fact which will manifest itself at discovery. Likewise, the claimant may try to charge for a loss of contribution to head office overheads. A calculation based on a purely notional assessment is not acceptable.

The expert must carefully consider the evidence. Of course if all he is provided with is a number of files, and it is left to him to prepare the claim evaluation, he will be mindful of the dubious nature of the examples given above. If, however, the claimant has already produced such an evaluation, and submitted it to the other side, perhaps prior to the matter reaching the stage of a dispute, the expert must be quick to advise his client of the errors or omissions in such calculations. Unless the expert is given carte blanche to recalculate the evaluation he should seriously advise his client of the pitfalls of proceeding on the alternative basis.

(ii) If the claim were to fail could the client afford to pay the other side's costs?

When the expert finds himself in the position where, in spite of his advice, the client insists on pursuing a spurious claim, the expert should ask the client to consider this all important question. Clients have a habit of only looking subjectively at the question of costs. That is, they will consider whether, if they fail, they can afford their own costs, but fail to take into account those of the opposition. Such costs can, of course, be considerable. Whilst the claimant's own costs, if he employs an expert, may be modest, if unsuccessful he may be faced with the costs of a solicitor and counsel, plus of course those of the arbitrator.

The same applies when a settlement is reached part of the way through the arbitration reference. If the terms of settlement are such that the claimant effectively loses, his opponent is naturally going to be looking for reimbursement of the whole of his costs.

It is impossible to accurately predict the outcome of any claim, otherwise there would presumably be no need for recourse to arbitration or litigation and there would be fewer lawyers. However, because of his breadth of experience the expert should be able to detect a poorly supported claim and advise his client accordingly. After all, the expert has presumably been appointed for his expertise and his client would do well to listen to his advice.

(iii) Is there evidence to support the claim?

Any claim, particularly when it reaches the stage of arbitration, is only ever as good as the evidence produced in its support. If it proceeds right the way through a full arbitration reference, the arbitrator who is unable to supply himself with evidence will decide and make his award purely on the evidence adduced before him. Returning to the example of the site supervisor (above), if the claimant is claiming a full-time employee, he must be able to produce evidence by way of time sheets, salary slips, extracts from company accounts, or the like, that such an individual was so employed. Likewise, the claimant may allege that he is entitled to a definable number of weeks of extension of time for completion of the works. Given that the matter has reached the stage of dispute, because up to that point the claimant has been unable to persuade the architect that he is entitled to more time, the burden is clearly on him to produce evidence to support his contentions.

The expert, again because of his knowledge and experience, will be able to assist the claimant to amass the evidence necessary to discharge the burden of proof. He will know how to extract such information from his client's files. He will also be able to quickly recognise when such evidence is not available, often due to the complete absence of suitable correspondence and documents necessary to advance his client's case. In this eventuality he must advise his client of the folly of proceeding.

In each of the previous categories, it is fair to say that in many instances, if one fails, they all fail. Whilst this may be regarded as a rather sweeping generalisation, it is sadly nevertheless true. Some of the most vociferous claimants find, when they commission an expert to conduct their case, that in fact it is just not economically feasible for them to pursue a claim. The expert need not feel despondent. If he has prevented his client from not only making a fool of himself, but has effectively saved him from the folly of throwing good money after bad, the expert has earned his fee. Furthermore, he will have earned his client's respect, in spite of the somewhat unpalatable facts he has had to impart, and probably stood himself in good stead for further work in the future.

If the expert is faced with the problem outlined above in that the claimant's files are devoid of evidence necessary to support the claim, there may be recourse to oral evidence given under oath at an attended hearing in the reference. This line of attack is only good if such oral evidence is available from witnesses to fact. The construction industry is perhaps renowned for the fickle nature of those employed within it and there is a general tendency for staff to move from one company to another with monotonous regularity. The claimant may well be faced with the problem that staff who would have made ideal witnesses have in fact moved to another company and may not even be employed in this country. However, provided the would-be witness is still in the United Kingdom, and is willing and able to give evidence, the claimant can request his new employer to release him, for an appropriate remuneration which will become costs in the arbitration. If he is unwilling the claimant has the option to issue a subpoena compelling the witness to attend, but always runs the risk in so doing of the witness turning hostile. If the individual has left the jurisdiction, for example, he may have undertaken a contract of employment abroad, or cannot be found, the subpoena option is not available. In this eventuality hearsay evidence may be permitted at the hearing.

In any event, even if the witness does volunteer to give evidence in support of the claimant's contentions, there is no guarantee that under oath he will perform as required and 'come up to proof', particularly under cross-examination. Those representing the other side will do their best to impugn the integrity of the witness. Once again the expert's function in the matter of witnesses, particularly where the written evidence is either extremely suspect or at worst non-existent, is to carefully consider whether the claimant is likely to succeed in his claim on this basis, and to give the appropriate advice.

(iv) Is there any evidence or sign of impecuniosity of the other side?

Obviously there is little point in a claimant pursuing a claim, whether through litigation or arbitration, if he has cause to believe his opponent has insufficient funds to pay either the substantive sum, which he hopes the court or the arbitrator will award him, or the claimant's costs of bringing the action.

If such a belief is justified, the expert can assist the claimant to try to establish the current trading position of the other side. A number of agencies exist which will provide a check on the creditworthiness of a limited company for a modest fee, and the expert will undoubtedly have experience of these. Alternatively the expert may elect to make his own enquiries at Company House. But generally the information available by these methods is only as good as the last set of published accounts. Other enquiries should therefore be made to discover if there are any rumours amongst suppliers of goods or services to the particular company concerned, of extended credit, bad debts, etc. It is not always cost effective to question the integrity of the very large companies, public authorities and the like. However, there have been some quite nasty shocks in recent years with the insolvency of some seemingly large companies who had been household names within the construction industry. There is little point in a claimant incurring fees only to be able to proceed as far as a point where he has to stand aside and watch the liquidation or receivership of his opponent in the knowledge that unless the liquidator or receiver adopts the contract personally, there is little hope of his claim and costs being met in full. In such circumstances it is unlikely that a liquidator or receiver would adopt the contract personally unless there was a substantial counterclaim which would have the effect of injecting large sums of money into the insolvent company for the benefit of the creditors.

The expert then, when faced with an opponent of dubious financial standing should do whatever is at his disposal to try and establish for himself, and his client, the financial status of that opponent. If his and his client's fears have any grounds at all he would do well to advise, however unpalatable it might seem at the time, withdrawal from any further action, and put the matter down to experience.

(v) Is there an arbitration agreement?

If it is established that a dispute or difference has arisen, and there is no valid arbitration agreement, the parties can choose whether they nevertheless wish to refer the matter to arbitration or to litigate. If arbitration is chosen the expert should first agree with those representing the other side the terms of such an agreement.

For an arbitration to be under the control of the Arbitration Acts 1950 to 1979 a valid agreement to refer disputes or differences to the decision of an arbitrator must be in writing (Arbitration Act 1950, s 32). Most standard forms of construction contracts contain written arbitration agreements and thus the Acts apply. Likewise the agreements in the standard forms of building contracts define the jurisdiction of the arbitrator and state the time at which certain matters may and may not be referred to arbitration. The fact that the parties to a contract have not formally executed a document is not always a bar to the existence of an arbitration agreement. Provided they have agreed that the terms and conditions of a particular form of contract are to apply, acceptance of such terms and conditions can be by the conduct of the parties in accepting their respective obligations as if an agreement had been formally executed; *Brightside Kilpatrick Engineering Services v Mitchell Construction (1973) Ltd* (1975) 1 BLR 64, [1975] 2 Lloyd's Rep

493, CA. Obviously formal execution removes any doubt as to what the parties have actually agreed.

If the parties to an existing dispute decide to refer the matter to arbitration and enter into an agreement which enables them to do so, they should be careful to ensure it is in writing so that the Arbitration Acts 1950 to 1979 apply.

Some forms of construction contract, generally those which are non-standard and produced by some main contractors and management contractors, deliberately exclude an arbitration agreement so that the parties have to litigate upon any irreconcilable disputes or differences which may rise during the performance of the contract. In these cases the party who drafted the contract will almost certainly not be persuaded to enter into an agreement to refer an existing dispute to arbitration. In like vein the Association of Consultant Architects/British Property Federation Form of Building Agreement provides for the parties to choose at the time the contract is made the alternative between arbitration and litigation for disputes or differences which may arise during the performance of the contract.

Provided the claimant has not already requested the other party to concur in the appointment of an arbitrator prior to the expert having been appointed, the expert should first look to see whether there is a written agreement between the parties to refer disputes to arbitration. He should ask for the contract or, if the original is not available, a copy thereof and inspect it carefully. If there is no written arbitration agreement he should consider why. It may be, as in the examples previously considered, that there has been a deliberate decision by the party who drafted the contract document that disputes should be the subject of litigation. The majority of, but not all, construction arbitrations are primarily concerned with matters of fact. Why parties to construction contracts should wish to refer their disputes to litigation is a matter of some conjecture, unless of course it is to try to preserve their right to appeal from the decision of a lower court. Nevertheless, it is really beyond the scope of this chapter to speculate further.

Having established there is no written agreement between the parties, and there is no good reason why there is none, the expert may set about the process of approaching the other side, or their representatives, to agree to refer the dispute to arbitration. A word of caution is perhaps appropriate here. Any two parties who have reached the stage of a dispute and who cannot settle their differences by negotiation are probably unlikely to be able to settle the terms of such an agreement.

If there is a valid arbitration agreement in existence between the parties the expert should consider whether the subject matter of the dispute or difference falls within any of the categories which stipulate that they cannot be referred to arbitration, except with the express approval of the other party, until after practical completion, or alleged practical completion, or abandonment of the works. Such stipulation is found, for example, in Article 5.2 of the Standard Form of Building Contract 1980 Edition, published by the Joint Contracts Tribunal. There is nothing quite so demoralising for an expert, than, full of confidence in front of his client, to send off a request to the other party to concur in the appointment of an arbitrator, only to receive a response to the effect that such a request is somewhat premature under the terms of the arbitration agreement.

The expert may represent a sub-contractor to a main contractor. If the dispute or difference is one which is wholly between those two parties, and subject to the existence of a valid arbitration agreement, it may be referred to the decision of an arbitrator and following his award that should be where the matter will end. However, if the dispute or difference is one which is wholly or substantially the same as that between main contractor and employer the expert should very carefully study the conditions of the sub-contract to see if there is an enjoinder provision. In a standard form of sub-contract the parties will be reasonably safe as to the apportionment of costs. In non-standard forms the expert should be very cautious about advising his client to avail himself of what purports to be an enjoinder provision. The client may find himself on the receiving end of a complete muddle over the apportionment of costs of the reference and the award.

(vi) Does a dispute or difference exist?

Arbitration agreements in standard forms of building contracts state that disputes and differences between the parties shall be referred to the arbitration and final decision of a person who it is agreed between the parties should act as arbitrator. Such dispute or difference must therefore be capable of being defined in order for the appointed arbitrator to have the necessary jurisdiction to determine the matter. There is often doubt as to what constitutes a genuine dispute or difference in this context. A dispute may arise from a claim. However, the existence of a properly documented claim is not a condition precedent to a dispute. A dispute is sufficient if it is a 'difference of opinion about the central issues' (Mustill and Boyd *Commercial Arbitration*). There must, it is submitted, be at least an exchange between the parties which indicates their disagreement.

For a dispute to exist there must be an assertion by one party and an express rebuttal by the other. If one party claims to be owed a certain sum by the other, and the other party agrees that it is in fact owed, there is no dispute. In short there would be nothing for an arbitrator to decide and issue an award over. Silence, however, by a party to a claim of the other is not in itself a dispute. If faced with this position the expert must elicit some positive response from the other side. In many cases if his client has tried and failed, the very fact that he indicates his involvement may be enough to obtain the required rebuttal. Alternatively, his involvement may be seen by the other party as a threat to a weak defence and may be sufficient to effect the commencement of negotiations towards a satisfactory settlement.

In most cases, if a claimant can show there is a genuine dispute or difference between the parties which is sufficient to satisfy the terms of the arbitration agreement, the formulation and submission of a detailed and documented claim, prior to the delivery of a formal request to the other party to concur in the appointment of an arbitrator, will incur him in additional expense which he will not recover. The expert should be mindful of this and advise his client that once the issues of the dispute are defined, the evaluation of a claim can be delayed until the time comes to reduce the issues to writing for the benefit of both the other side and the arbitrator. In this way the claimant should, under normal circumstances, be able to recover the cost of formulating the claim as costs in the arbitration, provided of course he is successful. The expert should be aware that his costs incurred prior to the notice to concur in the appointment of an arbitrator are not recoverable as legitimate costs in the arbitration (*James Longley & Co Ltd v South West Thames Regional Health Authority* (1983) 25 BLR 56). In this case the costs in an arbitration were referred to a taxing master, who disallowed the costs of the expert in giving general advice in the conduct of the arbitration, apparently on the basis that it was work which should have been carried out by the solicitor. Since a solicitor had been appointed by the party, that is obviously a correct view. It should not, it is submitted, be confused with the situation which is covered by the contents of this chapter, that is the expert acting as a technical advocate. In such circumstances the expert is appointed instead of, not in addition to, a solicitor and there is therefore no reason why if his client is successful in the arbitration his costs should not be met in full, subject of course to taxation.

Taxation of costs has, of course, nothing to do with the Inland Revenue. It is merely a process whereby an inspection and study is made of the bills of costs, submitted by one party to the other, to establish their proper content and validity. This requirement is only necessary in instances where the parties themselves cannot agree upon the amount of such costs. Section 18 (1) of the Arbitration Act 1950 provides that the arbitrator may himself tax the costs, and this subject is considered in further detail later in this chapter.

The expert, when commissioned to act as technical advocate, should look for the dispute or difference. Sometimes this will be a simple task, in others it will not. If he cannot define the dispute he must take steps to establish what it is; in so doing there is of course the chance he might reach a satisfactory settlement.

Should the expert find his appointment has been made subsequent to a notice of arbitration having been given by his client, but prior to the proper establishment that there is a genuine dispute, he must immediately take steps to remedy the matter. This will avoid the embarrassment of attending a preliminary meeting before the arbitrator only to be informed by the learned gentleman that in fact he has no jurisdiction in the matter.

In the foregoing only the role of the expert as advocate for the claimant has been examined in depth. Obviously he can act equally well for the party who is rebutting the claim, who will in effect become the respondent in the arbitration. The questions previously posed can easily be reversed to make them applicable to the respondent to the claim, and to a large extent the same detailed considerations will be a necessary part of the expert's involvement. The main difference between the roles of an expert acting for a claimant, and that for a respondent, will be the latter will in most instances not be merely confined to a defence to the claim, but will have the additional matter of a counterclaim. The counterclaim is capable of standing as a claim in its own right, therefore the comments and considerations mentioned in sections (i) to (vi), above, will be directly applicable and do not require repetition.

As to the defence to the claim, many of the considerations in (i) to (vi), above, will be relevant. However, the expert will not really be in a position to properly advise his respondent client before the notice of arbitration is served because he will not, in most cases, have detailed knowledge of the claimant's claim. The exception to this will of course occur when the claimant has submitted a detailed claim prior to arbitration being contemplated. One of the main differences between the roles of the expert acting for the defence, as opposed to acting for the claimant, is that the defence only has to rebut. The burden of proof is on the claimant; he who asserts must prove. The detailed and thought provoking considerations of the claimant are not therefore strictly relevant. On occasions a defence may be a consequence of the claimant unilaterally seeking the appointment of an arbitrator, and the respondent becomes a reluctant party. Thoughts and detailed considerations which have been examined, above, are hardly relevant in such circumstances. The respondent's major consideration if he has no counterclaim is get out of his newly-found position as cheaply as possible.

One further and important question the expert should ask his client is the subject of his own fees. Experts are generally prevented by the rules and bylaws of their respective professional institutions from charging their fees on a contingency basis, and unless the matter is small and uncomplicated it is not always easy for the expert to provide a forecast of his fees. The alternative is therefore on the basis of an hourly rate. The level of such will depend on the expert's organisation; whether he is a lone practitioner or whether he is employed by a large organisation, and the level and cost of his firm's overheads. The client should be warned by the expert if he requires regular payments on account and the client should be aware that he may be expected to pay out large amounts of money before he sees any signs of recovery. Whatever form of agreement client and expert reach over the expert's fees, it is essential for the expert to keep the client regularly informed of the fee level incurred, and of the activities performed to reach such level. Clients often fail to realise the complexity of the expert's involvement and there is nothing worse in a relationship than for the client to realise part way through an arbitration that he cannot afford to pay his advocate's fees.

When the expert and client are *ad idem* concerning his appointment the agreement should be reduced to writing. This can help to save much misunderstanding at a later date. Such a written agreement should detail the precise terms of reference; the basis upon which the fees of the expert are to be calculated; whether disbursements and expenses are to be charged in addition to the quoted fee; whether the client requires a detailed breakdown of the time spent on each occasion an account is rendered; the intervals when accounts will be rendered and the time following which the client is expected to settle those accounts; whether interest will be charged on overdue payments not made in accordance with the terms of the agreement; whether, in a long-term commission, the expert reserves the right to review the basis of the fee to be charged to increase it in line with inflation or otherwise; whether VAT is to be added to the fee; and whether the expert requires any payment on account of his fee to be provided beforehand. All of this may seem to be the basic rules of a good business relationship, but it is surprising the number of rational, clear-thinking professionals who shrink from the task of having to discuss and detail their remuneration, as though it were all rather vulgar. Nevertheless, it is a subject which must be aired at some stage, and what better time to do so than at the commencement of the relationship before any work has been done. In the majority of cases the client will welcome such a direct and professional approach, since obviously he is made fully cognisant of exactly what he is expected to pay in consideration of the expert acting in his best interests.

THE APPOINTMENT OF THE ARBITRATOR

Once the expert has been appointed, having given detailed consideration and analysis to the foregoing, the next stage is to arrange for the appointment of an arbitrator to whom the dispute or difference is to be referred. One of the big advantages of arbitration over other methods of settling disputes is that the parties, having agreed upon this method, can then further agree upon the arbitrator of their choice. In truth it does not of course often happen that way, but at least the facility is available. Two parties who are already locked into a dispute are hardly likely to agree on anything by that stage. Nevertheless, whereas in litigation the parties will be provided with the next judge who is available; in arbitration they can determine right at the start of the reference exactly who will decide their fate. There is nothing magical or mysterious about arbitration. It is two parties who have a disagreement over a common matter arranging to air their differences in front of a third who, having listened to them, will decide who wins and who loses. As in any adversarial system of deciding commercial disputes, the arbitrator is not there to discover the truth.

It is very rare, in construction contracts for the name of the arbitrator to be included in the arbitration agreement. That is not to say it does not happen. Where it does, it can save much delay and effort when the notice to concur is given. In all standard forms of construction contract, and in most ad hoc conditions produced by main contractors or sub-contractors, it is rare. The first step for the expert is service of a written notice on behalf of his client on the other party, stating a dispute exists and requesting they concur in the appointment of an arbitrator to whom such dispute can be referred. An example of such a notice is reproduced and included at Appendix 2, below. The expert should ensure before despatching the notice that he has fully complied with the terms of the arbitration agreement. For example, the agreement may stipulate the notice has to be sent by registered post, or recorded delivery. If he fails to so comply, and sends it by ordinary mail, or by courier, or by fascimile machine, or even delivers it himself, in such circumstances it will be deemed an invalid notice. Further, the written notice must generally be sent by one party to the other. There is nothing incorrect for the expert to send the notice, provided it makes it plain he has his client's authority to do so. The expert must, however, send it to the other party and not to, for example, the architect, quantity surveyor or engineer named in the contract. If matters have reached the stage where the other side has already instructed representatives to act for them, for example, another expert, or solicitors, and have signified their agreement for those representatives to receive a notice to concur, the expert may presume that by so doing he is serving it upon the other party.

Another aspect of the arbitration agreement of which the expert must be meticulously cautious is the requirement as to when a notice to concur can be given. For example the Standard Form of Building Contract 1980 Edition, Amendment 4 issued July 1987, at condition 30.9.3 gives a limit of 28 days following the issue of the final certificate by the architect. The expert will save a lot of embarrassment with his client if he follows such stipulations. In the case of *Emson Contractors Ltd v Protea Estates Ltd* (1987) 39 BLR 126 it was held that by not issuing a notice to concur within the stipulated time of 14 days, the claimant was not entitled to refer the dispute to the decision of an arbitrator. Further, Emson were not entitled to have the time extended for the commencement of an arbitration under s 27 of the Arbitration Act 1950. This section provides that in a case where the arbitration agreement stipulates a time by which a step must be taken in the arbitration, if the High Court is of the opinion that, in the *circumstances of the case, undue hardship* would otherwise be caused, the court may extend the time of such a period as it thinks proper.

It is good practice for the notice to concur to include more than just a single name. It may subsequently transpire that if the parties do agree upon one name, he may not be able to act and time will have been wasted. A short list of three names is ideal. If practicable each of the three should be contacted beforehand to ascertain if they are willing and able to act should one of them subsequently be appointed. The names chosen for such a list should, as far as possible, be relevant to the matter of the dispute. For example, if the dispute arising out of a building contract is one of quality of workmanship and/or materials, it would generally be more advantageous for the parties to choose an architect rather than, say, a quantity surveyor. Alternatively, if the dispute is one of extensions of time to the period for completion, and/or the incurrence of loss and expense, a quantity surveyor should be able to adequately decide both issues. Naturally the names suggested should not include any which, if the matter were tested, could show or indicate any partiality. The construction industry is a small world, and it is almost impossible to nominate an arbitrator who has not at some stage had some dealings with either parties themselves, or their experts or representatives. This matter is discussd in more detail later in this chapter.

As soon as the notice to concur in the appointment of an arbitrator is given, costs in the arbitration begin to run. Time wasting from now on should be kept to a minimum. The expert acting for the respondent to the dispute, should carefully consider the names suggested by the claimant. His natural reaction may be to dissent from agreement merely because they have been proposed by the opposition, suspecting none of them may be impartial. Unless he has some fundamental reason for objection, he should, if only for the sake of the costs aspect, give serious consideration with his client to the names proposed. Such fundamental reasons for objection could include the following:

(a) The nominees may have excellent credentials in their respective modes of operation, but have little or no experience of arbitration.
(b) There may be more than a hint of suspicion that one or all of the nominees would not act with impartiality.
(c) The respondents may be involved with one or all of the nominees on other contracts.
(d) One or more of the nominees may have been the arbitrator on a previous dispute in which the respondent was involved and thus he may feel this is likely to be prejudicial, for whatever reason.

In respect of (a), whilst lack of experience of conducting arbitrations is not in itself a sound reason for objection, the expert, who will have some experience of these matters, should be very cautious about either nominating or accepting a proposed arbitrator who does not at least have a detailed knowledge of the rules governing the giving and receiving of evidence. The last thing either party wants is an arbitrator who admits evidence from one side and not the other, or who provides himself with his own evidence (*Fox v P G Wellfair Ltd; Fisher v P G Wellfair Ltd* (1982) 19 BLR 52; *Top Shop Estates Ltd v C Danino* (1985) 273 Estates Gazette 197). The Chartered Institute of Arbitrators conduct a structured system of detailed training for arbitrators by examination and assessment, and generally any would-be arbitrator who is a member of their panel of practising arbitrators should be acceptable to both parties.

If the parties cannot agree upon the appointment of an arbitrator the expert for the claimant should examine the arbitration agreement to discover if there is a facility for the nomination to be made by a third party in such an eventuality. The standard forms of construction contract provide for such third party nomination, as follows:

Joint Contracts Tribunal (JCT)

Standard Form of Building Contract 1980 Edition, 1987 Amendment: A President or a Vice-President for the time being of either Royal Institute of British Architects (RIBA), Royal Institution of Chartered Surveyors (RICS), or The Chartered Institute of Arbitrators (CIArb). Parties decide at the time of entering the contract. If none is agreed, then President or a Vice-President of the RIBA.

Intermediate Form, 1984 (IFC84): President or a Vice-President for the time being of either RIBA or RICS. Parties decide at the time of entering the contract. The form is silent as to the procedure if no such decision is taken.

Agreement for Minor Building Works (1980): President or a Vice-President for the time being of either RIBA or RICS. Parties decide at the time of entering the contract. The form is silent as to the procedure if no such decision is taken.

Standard Form of Building Contract with Contractor's Design 1981 Edition, 1987 Amendment: President or a Vice-President for the time being of RIBA, RICS or CIArb. Parties decide at the time of entering the contract. If none is agreed then appointer is the President or a Vice-President of CIArb.

Associated Forms of Sub-Contract for use with JCT forms of main contract: President or a Vice-President for the time being of the RIBA, RICS or CIArb as appropriate.

The foregoing forms provide for nomination by the third party upon application from one, or both parties to the dispute, if they do not agree upon an appointed arbitrator within 14 days of the notice to concur having been served by one on the other.

ICE conditions of contract

The fifth edition (June 1973) (Revised January 1979) provides for a nomination to be made by the President for the time being of the Institution of Civil Engineers if the parties themselves fail to agree upon an appointed arbitrator within one calendar month after a notice to concur in the appointment of an arbitrator has been served by one party to the other.

General Conditions of Government Contracts for Building and Civil Engineering Works (GC/Works/1) Edition 2— September 1977

Provides for a nomination to be made at the request of the authority by the President of such one of the following as the authority may decide: The Law Society; RIBA; RICS; the Royal Incorporation of Architects in Scotland; the Institutions of Civil Engineers, Mechanical Engineers, Heating and Ventilating Engineers, Electrical Engineers, or Structural Engineers.

Having established the identity of the third party nominating body, the experts must first make contact with it on behalf of his client. In general a pro forma will require completion, and sometimes a fee paid. Such fee will almost certainly be considered a cost in the arbitration. The pro forma will request such details as the following:

(i) the names of the respective parties, and identification as to which is the claimant and which is the respondent;
(ii) the names and identities of the parties' representatives. Here the expert should be careful so as not to be identified as his client's solicitor. He is also advised to avoid using the term 'agent'. The laws of agency could cause him some difficulty here. It is best if he just identifies himself as the claimant's 'representative';
(iii) whether the application is a unilateral one, or a joint one endorsed by both parties;
(iv) a brief outline of the dispute;
(v) some bodies, such as the RICS, like the applicant to identify within the body of the pro forma any arbitrators which it is felt would be inappropriate at the outset.

When the details on the pro forma have been completed to the best of the expert's knowledge he should obtain his client's signature and a cheque for the fee if appropriate. If his client is a corporate body, the expert must ascertain that whoever signs the application is authorised in every respect to do so, and that the individual is not *ultra vires* the authority bestowed on him, or her. Having obtained the completed application the expert then sends it, together with photocopies of both the arbitration agreement and the notice to concur, to the appropriate third party nominating body. The parties await the nomination made by the president of that body. This usually takes two or three weeks and both parties, or their representatives, are advised simultaneously. Prior to that event, the president's staff will approach the nominee and ask him to accept the appointment. When this has been done in writing, the president will advise both parties, or their representatives, simultaneously of the appointed arbitrator, and request that they make direct contact in order to proceed with the reference. There is no appeal from the decision of the third party nominating body. The parties have agreed, in the arbitration agreement, that in the event of their being unable to decide between themselves upon the appointment of an arbitrator, they will ask a third party to do so for them. If the procedure results in either one, or both parties, finding themselves with an arbitrator who is unsuitable, the only way he can be removed is by the High Court (Arbitration Act 1950, s 1). The arbitrator's appointment is irrevocable except by leave of the High Court, unless a contrary intention is expressed in the arbitration agreement. Thus, an aggrieved party should have an extremely sound reason before it considers it worthwhile making application to the court for removal of an arbitrator who had been appointed by such a method.

If there is no agreed method of third party nomination in the arbitration agreement the court will so appoint (Arbitration Act 1950, s 10(1)). When the other party rejects the expert's three suggested names, the expert should serve a written notice on the respondent to appoint, or concur in appointing, a named arbitrator. If the appointment is not made within seven clear days from the date of such notice, the expert, on behalf of his client, should consult a solicitor and instruct him to make application to the High Court to make an appointment. In such eventuality it is wise, though not essential, to supply the court with some suggested names, although different from those contained in the original notice to concur, having established first if they are willing and able to act. When the High Court makes such an appointment, it is worthy of note that the arbitrator so appointed has 'the like powers to act in the reference and make an Award as if he had been appointed in accordance with the terms of the [arbitration] agreement'.

When a third party nominating body refuses to make an appointment, or does not make it in the time specified, or if no time is specified, within a reasonable time, either party to the agreement may serve a written notice on the other to appoint. As in the preceding paragraph, if the appointment is not made within seven clear days after service of the notice, the party who served the notice may make application to the High Court to make an appointment (Arbitration Act 1979, s 6(4), incorporating Arbitration Act 1950, s 10(2)).

Section 10(1) of the Arbitration Act 1950 also provides for the High Court to make an appointment in the event of the appointed arbitrator refusing to act, being incapable of acting, or dying, as long as the arbitration agreement does not express a contrary intention.

THE ARBITRATION REFERENCE

During the time taken to agree or obtain the appointment of the arbitrator the expert for the claimant will not be idle. He should use this time to prepare the foundation of his case, both from a factual and legal aspect. He will already have defined the dispute and subdivided it, if necessary, into its constituent parts. He should be considering how he will present his client's assertions to both the respondent and the arbitrator. He can commence this preparation by conducting interviews with those who have been involved with the construction project, to establish the detailed background of the subject matter of the dispute. It will also give him the benefit of deciding, at an early stage, who of these will make the most credible witnesses.

Another invaluable form of preparation the expert can and should involve himself with is that of preparing a programme of the complete reference. Such a programme is capable of production on the basis of a bar-chart, the form of which the expert will be most familiar with as that utilised by contractors for indicating their intentions in respect to the phasing of construction sequences. An example of such is reproduced at Appendix 1. Whilst there is no absolute guarantee the reference will proceed in accordance with the programme prepared by the expert, which, at the time of preparation can take no real account of delays, it will serve as a useful tool to remind him of the status of the reference at any given time. That is providing he keeps it updated as each variation to his estimated or agreed time period occurs.

Once the arbitrator has been appointed he will, in all probability, want to meet the parties and/or their representatives to discuss the form of the reference. This is usually known as the preliminary meeting.

The preliminary meeting

The arbitrator will generally formally advise the parties of his appointment and invite them, and/or their representatives to attend a preliminary meeting. This meeting is important, both for the parties and the arbitrator. The expert who is skilled at advocacy will see the importance of such a meeting, and persuade his client to attend with him. As well as giving all concerned an opportunity to meet the arbitrator who is to decide their fate, it also gives the parties the opportunity to meet together. Some arbitrators deliberately leave the parties in a waiting room or reception area together, presumably in the hope they might talk about things other than the weather in an effort to try and settle their differences. It is not unknown for the parties to leave a preliminary meeting with the intention to meet again in the near future to seriously consider settlement. Such discussion before the commencement of the main meeting will give the advocates an opportunity to jointly agree upon a timetable for exchange of pleadings, discovery, number of experts, et al.

The arbitrator will generally leave the arrangement for the date, time and venue for the preliminary meeting to the parties' representatives. This avoids the need for him to get involved in the detail. The expert will therefore have to agree the necessary arrangements with the other side and notify the arbitrator when complete.

During the meeting the arbitrator will normally keep strictly to a prepared agenda, the typical format of which will be familiar to the expert. If no agreement has been reached on a timetable this will be dealt with in discussion with the arbitrator. Some arbitrators are reluctant to deal with finality on matters such as the number of expert witnesses, the time for a view of the site (if appropriate) or the date and time of the attended hearing. Admittedly, the product of the meeting normally provides both parties leave to apply for an amendment, but it will be in the best interests of the claimant if his expert as advocate can try to engender some spirit of urgency and pace into the reference by at least tabling a date for the hearing. Psychologically it gives the parties something to aim for. If the date is left in abeyance all too often the reference results in a rather relaxed affair which lacks any kind of impetus and wastes time and therefore costs. The expert, if he is acting for the respondent will of course be well aware of this, and will do his utmost to try and remove any psychological advantage his opponent might hope to achieve.

As to the agreement of a timetable, the expert should beware of being encouraged to adopt an unrealistic time period. He should try and aim for one which is neither too long nor too short. If he already has a reasonable idea of the issues involved he should not find an estimate too difficult to forecast. He will obviously be in greater difficulty if he has not managed to grasp a basic understanding of the issues before attending the preliminary meeting. It is difficult here to say what is a realistic timetable and what is not. It will depend to a large extent on the preparation time required in view of the complexity of the issues. Some arbitrations lend themselves to a reduction of the matters in dispute to categories, and for those categories to be the subjects of separate hearings with the arbitrator being asked to make interim awards on each one. Others may call for a large part to be decided on documents-only, with oral submission forming only a small part of the whole reference. Others of course will be the straightforward type of exchanged pleadings, discovery, inspection, and formal hearing of all of the issues, followed by the arbitrator's one final award. Thus the expert should learn to recognise the different types and to plan his timetable to suit. He must remember that, generally, whatever period he might require for himself, he should be prepared to give the other side the same. The timetable for a straightforward hearing might be as follows, although it is stressed this cannot be rigidly followed in all circumstances:

(1) Points of Claim: to be served on the respondent within six weeks of the date of the preliminary meeting.
(2) Defence and counterclaim (if any): to be served on the claimant within six weeks of receipt of the points of claim.
(3) Reply to defence and defence to counterclaim (if any): to be served on the respondent within 21 days of receipt of the defence and counterclaim.
(4) Reply to defence to counterclaim: to be served on the claimant within 14 days of receipt of the reply to defence and defence to counterclaim.
(5) Further and better particulars to be provided by one party to the other within 21 days of receipt of a request.
(6) Discovery: 14 days after close of pleadings.
(7) Inspection of documents: seven days thereafter.
(8) Expert witnesses (independent experts who will give opinion evidence) to meet during [month, year].
(9) Experts' reports to be exchanged by [date].
(10) Scott Schedule (if appropriate) to be produced by [date].
(11) Inspection of the site by the arbitrator (if not to be combined with the hearing) on [date].
(12) Agreed bundle of documents to be submitted to the arbitrator not less than 14 days prior to the hearing.
(13) Date for the hearing (approximately 26 weeks from date of preliminary meeting—if the parties keep to the agreed timetable).

The expert should remember to take with him to the preliminary meeting his client's copy of the contract, to avoid any mistake. It will be the first time the arbitrator has an opportunity to view the document and it will give him the chance to ensure he has jurisdiction to act. If there is no formally executed document in existence, the expert should ensure he has a copy of the relevant standard form of contract conditions with him, together with, if applicable, the correspondence between the parties which signified their initial agreement. The arbitrator should be able to tell from these documents whether he has jurisdiction to act in the reference. In disputes arising from standard form building contracts, for example, the arbitrator has the power to put himself into the shoes of the architect and to open-up, review and revise any previous decision of that architect. The expert as advocate for the respondent should be mindful of the matter of the arbitrator's jurisdiction and if in any doubt at all should question and raise the matter with the arbitrator. If doubt arises, such question of jurisdiction can be determined by application to the High Court, not by the arbitrator himself.

The expert should attend the preliminary meeting well prepared. His approach at the meeting itself should be positive, and at its conclusion the arbitrator should be left in no doubt as to what the expert and his client expect of him. Likewise, the expert should be left in no doubt as to what is expected of him and his client. For example, the arbitrator may have been appointed by the President of The Chartered Institute of Arbitrators, as a third party nomination, and he may be in some doubt as to whether the parties have adopted the Rules of that Chartered Institute. Normally in construction disputes the answer would be negative, but neither the parties nor the arbitrator should be left in any doubt if they are all to avoid the pitfalls which befell the hapless arbitrator in the case of *Pratt v Swanmore Builders Ltd and Baker* (1980) 15 BLR 37, [1980] 2 Lloyd's Rep 504. In that particular case the court held that the arbitrator had so misconducted himself and the proceedings that he must be removed since he had by his mistakes allowed the arbitration to be reduced to such a state that there was no prospect of justice being done if it continued. One of the matters of which the arbitrator was guilty, in the court's opinion, was that whilst he had been appointed by the President of The Institute of Arbitrators (as it then was) he presumed that by the sending to both of the parties a copy of the Regulations for the Conduct of Arbitrations, published by the Institute of Arbitrators, they would automatically be bound by the regulations. He made no attempt to get the parties to actually accept those regulations. Further, the arbitrator took no steps to ascertain what was the scope of the arbitration agreement or whether it included agreement that the regulations should apply.

Following the preliminary meeting, the arbitrator will generally reduce the product of the meeting in writing in the form of an order for directions. This document will order the parties to abide by the agreed timetable for the exchange of pleadings, discovery, inspection of documents, exchange of experts' reports and the date, or provisional date, for the hearing. A copy will be sent simultaneously to the representatives for each party. On receipt the expert should carefully study the order to ensure it corresponds exactly with the agreements, as he understood them, which had been made at the meeting. If there is any variation he should immediately notify both the other side and the arbitrator, in an effort to rectify the error.

Although the arbitrator may order such, the expert should always remember when communicating with the arbitrator to ensure a copy is automatically and simultaneously sent to the other side. Further, the expert should avoid making telephone calls direct to the arbitrator or attempt to meet with him unless a representative of the other party is present with him. Most arbitrators will not accept telephone calls unilaterally from one party. If there is a need for the expert to make urgent contact by telephone he should speak with the arbitrator's secretary and let the other side know what he has done. It should go without saying that if the expert and the arbitrator meet socially, as does happen, they should not attempt to discuss the reference or the matters in issue, however tempting it may be.

Points of claim

Following the agreement made at the preliminary meeting as regards the timetable, as confirmed in the arbitrator's first order for directions, the first step in the reference is for the claimant to deliver his points of claim to the respondent within the stipulated time period. A copy will also be sent simultaneously to the arbitrator. Some arbitrators like to depart from the recognised standard wording of court procedure and the Rules of the Supreme Court as laid down in the White Book. Instead of points of claim they state a preference for the use of such terminology as statement of case. Whether there is any advantage in using this alternative is a matter of conjecture. By using the standard terminology everyone knows where they stand. When non-standard words and phrases are used a reason for discord and misunderstanding is introduced. It is accepted that the claimant's claim and the respondent's defence and counterclaim have to be reduced to writing to acquaint the arbitrator and each party of the other's case. It is further accepted that arbitration should not mimic or mirror litigation. However, since lawyers are almost certainly involved by one party or the other, there is some justification for using the terminology everyone understands. In defence of such reasoning there has been at least one instance where the expert, as advocate, has assumed the responsibility for the conduct of his client's case in a reference to arbitration wherein, at the commencement it was considered the dispute was almost entirely over matters of fact. He later found, during the reference, that the other side introduced many matters of law. In such circumstances there is every justification for the expert, or his client, to request assistance from a lawyer. If the documentation between the parties is in a form the lawyer cannot easily understand, or identify, costs will be wasted whilst he familiarises himself with the way the claim and defence have been settled. For the foregoing reasons, and for the sake of clarity therefore, the widely used terminology will be referred to throughout this chapter.

The expert has a time period of, perhaps three, four or six weeks to prepare and settle his client's points of claim, as stated in the arbitrator's order for directions. If he has already produced a claim for his client prior to the notice to concur having been served, his work should be relatively straightforward. He will need to tidy-up the contents of the document into a form of pleadings which can be identified as such by the respondent and the arbitrator. He will also have to carefully consider the contents of the claim evaluation to ensure that the figures inserted therein are capable of being properly substantiated. Obviously if no claim had been submitted prior to the commencement of the reference, he will have to begin from scratch.

In this case, and providing the expert has undertaken the task of understanding the basic issues and has conducted interviews with witnesses to fact during the early stages before the preliminary meeting, he should have no difficulty in meeting the deadline for serving his points of claim in accordance with the agreed timetable. On the other hand, when the expert is acting for the respondent in an arbitration reference, he is somewhat limited in the amount of preparation he can achieve prior to receipt of his opponent's claim. Obviously he will have quite a considerable grasp of the matters in dispute, but in interviewing witnesses to fact he will have to cover the ground in a global fashion without necessarily being able to confine it strictly to the issues. However, unless he does do this he may find himself in some difficulty in being able to serve his points of claim, together with a cogent defence within the agreed timetable. If, in this eventuality there is to be a counterclaim in addition to the defence, the expert's task will to some extent be made easier, in that he will have to interview witnesses in order to compile the counterclaim, and he will hope to cover the points to be raised in his defence at the same time.

On a procedural point, what should the expert do if faced with a request from his opponent for an extension to the agreed timetable for serving his pleadings? The final decision rests with the arbitrator, if the parties' representatives find they cannot sort it out amongst themselves. If such a request is made, it is common courtesy to agree to it, provided it is not for an outrageously long period out of all proportion with that which has previously been agreed. The sanction to such requests is costs, and neither party is going to do their cause a great deal of good, either in front of the other or the arbitrator, if they persistently ask for extensions of time. If the expert is minded not to accede to his opponent's request, the chances are that he will be served with a claim, or defence, which is deficient and for which the other side will inevitably seek leave to amend, in which case a reasonable request for time might just as well be granted in the first place.

In preparing his points of claim the expert should be aware of the functions of pleadings, which are best summarised as follows:

(1) To identify the areas of dispute. The basic theory is that the pleadings should summarise the facts and issues in a case as briefly and as clearly as possible.
(2) To allow the arbitrator to understand exactly what is being alleged, what is being asked for and the nature of the defence. Effectively it sets the limits of his jurisdiction.
(3) To allow the other side to understand precisely the nature of the case against them and in particular the exact allegations which are made against them and which they should answer.
(4) Good pleadings assist the drafter to clarify his own case and should help to keep down costs.

Much could be written about the form of pleadings, most of which would be beyond the scope of this book. There are excellent textbooks on the subject, and if the expert is in any doubt as to what will be expected of him, he should consult one of these. It is sufficient, in addition to the foregoing list of basic functions, to draw attention to the following practical aspects which will be of use in the settlement of pleadings:

(a) Only material facts should be pleaded. A material fact is one which must be established to win the claim. All the material facts must be pleaded.
(b) The defence to any allegation should not be pre-empted.
(c) Facts should be pleaded, not law.
(d) Facts should be pleaded, not evidence. It is often difficult to distinguish facts from evidence, but as a general rule the pleadings are meant to set out the facts, not to prove them.
(e) Facts should be pleaded, not argument.
(f) Particulars: the other side should be given some idea of the general allegations against them; sufficient that they can establish exactly of what it is they are accused. Sometimes it will be an advantage and enhance the chances of settlement if the expert does much work at an early stage and fully particularises the claim, for example, in matters of direct loss and/or expense.

(g) The expert is advised to use his own words and to keep the language as simple and non-technical as possible. The use of plain English is recommended, and the inclusion of legal jargon, particularly if by using it the expert clearly indicates his ignorance for its proper meaning or intent, should generally be avoided. In this context it is not good practice for the expert to try and adapt someone else's pleadings. Generally such practice does not work, however attractive the notion may appear.

The settlement of pleadings has much to do with style. The expert, if he is not familiar with their production, will probably need to spend some time drafting and re-drafting until he has a document which he considers will serve his needs. In practice he will very soon discover whether it has served its purpose effectively and efficiently. If it has not, and the other side cannot determine what allegations are being levied at them, or its contents are so much gobbledegook, the expert may quickly find himself on the receiving end of a lengthy request for further and better particulars of the points of claim or, if he is acting for the respondent, of the defence and counter-claim (if any). Also, he will not create a good impression with the arbitrator who, if on the receiving end of pleadings he cannot fully understand, will be in some difficulty in deciding the issues. If his pleadings have achieved the required intention any such request, if served at all, should be short and concise.

As has already been suggested (above) the expert should have already carried-out his own analysis of what his client is seeking to claim. If it has not already been done by this stage in the reference, the expert will need to undertake it as part of the compilation of his points of claim or counter-claim as appropriate. This may put him in some difficulty in meeting the timetable. In any event when the analysis is complete, the expert should decide on the most suitable structure for its inclusion into his points of claim or counterclaim. It may be appropriate, for example, for schedules to be used. These can often help to clarify the issues and may be of more benefit than a thousand words. It should also be remembered at all times that the major part of the advocate's role, as well as identifying to the other side the allegations being levied against them, is to bring his client's assertions to the attention of one individual, the arbitrator, who up to that point will know nothing about the material facts or the real points of the dispute. The easier these matters are portrayed to the arbitrator therefore, the easier will be his grasp of the matters being raised. It should also help to reduce his costs.

The points of claim therefore should contain no submissions of law or opinions; only the basic facts upon which the claim is being referred to arbitration, and only known facts from instructions and documents. Assumptions about what may have happened, or what probably happened, form no part of well presented points of claim. It is also important for the expert to include in the prayer, that part at the end of the points of claim, or counterclaim, which summarises the claim in clear terms, just what is sought. This may include for example: extension of time to the period for completion; a declaration that liquidated and ascertained damages are being wrongfully withheld by the respondent; moneys due under the contract; direct loss and/or expense; alternatively damages for breaches of obligations under the contract; financing charges (if applicable to the particular form of contract); statutory interest; and costs. Any facts which may give rise to any special or unusual loss or damage must be separately pleaded. It should be remembered that if a matter is not pleaded the arbitrator, if he subsequently awards on it, will be in excess of jurisdiction, and therefore guilty of misconducting himself on the reference. This is perhaps a point worth considering by experts when acting as advocate for the respondent.

Where financing charges are claimed, perhaps following the authority in *F G Minter v Welsh Health Technical Services Organisation (WHTSO)* (1980) 13 BLR 1, CA, these must be pleaded separately from statutory interest. Financing charges are part of general loss and/or expense for which the express conditions of the contract may provide recovery. Statutory interest is that which the arbitrator has an absolute discretion as to whether to award and in what sum, in accordance with s 19A of the Arbitration Act 1950. This is considered in more detail later.

Upon completion, the points of claim should be read through, revising or deleting as necessary. All arithmetic should be checked thoroughly, preferably by someone other than the expert himself. It is always embarrassing to have to amend a claim after service for the sake of a minor arithmetical error which could have been avoided. When the expert is satisfied all is in order arrangements are made for copying and delivery to both the respondent and the arbitrator simultaneously.

If the expert subsequently finds after service that it is desirable to amend his points of claim the procedure for so doing will depend largely on whether the procedure of the reference strictly follows the Rules of the Supreme Court (commonly known as the White Book). If not, it is up to the parties to agree between themselves as to how to approach amendments, with the final decision vesting in the arbitrator. If the White Book is followed, under Ord 20 the points of claim can be amended once up to the close of pleadings. Thereafter leave must first be obtained. When amending, the practice is to delete in red and underline all additions in red. This readily identifies the parts that have been changed from the original document. Subsequent amendments, if desirable, are done in green, then blue and so on.

The expert is recommended to check his pleadings at least once between the close of pleadings and the hearing. However, the sanction for late amendments is costs against the party seeking to do so. When and if the expert needs to obtain leave to amend, he should first submit a copy of the amended document to the other side for their comments and objections. If none the amended document should be sent to the arbitrator requesting leave and advising him the other side have raised no objections. When granted the amended pleading is served on the opposition. If objections are raised by the other side the expert will have to apply for leave and request a hearing date to argue his case before the arbitrator. In practice arbitrators rarely refuse leave, and few applications are seriously contested. Once leave has been granted the expert should identify such at the bottom of the pleading when it is re-served, with the legend 'Amended by leave of the arbitrator granted on . . .'.

Arbitrations in construction disputes invariably involve claims to overcome an alleged undervaluation of variations. Alternatively, the point of claim may generally involve much figure work and arithmetic. In such circumstances during his analysis of the claim, or counterclaim as appropriate, the expert may conclude a simpler means of expressing himself and particularising his claim by the use of a Scott Schedule (so-called after an official referee of the same name). The usage and benefit of such a schedule is discussed in chapter 6. Its purpose is to bring together in one document either all the issues between the parties or the issues regarding a particular aspect of the dispute. Its layout, in schedule form, enables the claimant to itemise in clear, concise terms the monetary form he is claiming under each relevant heading in the first column. The next column enables the respondent to comment on the principle and the quantum and insert his own assessment of the quantum. The final column is left blank for the arbitrator's comments when either hearing evidence on the schedule or when considering his award. The most convenient approach for the use of the schedule is agreement with the other side on the principle either prior to, or at, the preliminary meeting, and requesting the arbitrator to order its use in his order for directions. Alternatively, if the expert only realises its potential as he is drafting his points of claim he can easily apply to the arbitrator for an order, having first advised the other party of his intention and having obtained their approval. If such approval is withheld, the expert will have to make a case to the arbitrator in the form of a formal submission based on the savings in cost to be gained from the use of such a schedule. It will then be up to the arbitrator to make his decision.

Defence

When acting for the respondent the expert's first task on receipt of the claimant's points of claim is to understand just what the claimant is seeking. A well drafted claim will assist considerably in this respect; a badly drafted one will entail having to waste time and expend cost in trying to understand its contents and will undoubtedly lead to a lengthy request for further and better particulars of the points of claim. The purpose of the defence is largely to reduce and define the areas of the dispute, and to outline and establish the lines of argument in defence of the claim.

The expert, having first conducted his analysis of the contents of the claim, should arrange to meet with his client and study the issues in detail. He and his client must establish which parts, if any, of the claim are admitted. This will leave those sections upon which further information may be required and those which are denied completely. In some instances it may be the respondent will admit parts in principle but will not accept the quantum. In others he will deny both.

The expert, when defending a claim, should be mindful of the accepted terminology in such circumstances. To 'deny' conveys a final meaning: the respondent disputes a part or section of the claim in its entirety. The respondent must have very good grounds for pleading with such finality. The sanction for false denials is of course costs thrown away. When denying, the expert will be well advised to consider whether he should include the respondent's own version of the events after the denial. If part of the claim is agreed, the reply is that it is 'admitted'. Once admitted, unless the respondent subsequently amends the defence, again at the risk of costs being awarded against him for causing unnecessary time wasting due to indecision, there is nothing for the arbitrator to decide. If there is a part of the claim upon which the respondent can neither admit, and equally, cannot deny, usually because of a lack of knowledge, the expert must put the claimant to strict proof. In this case the accepted phrase used is either

'The respondent does not admit . . .', or '(this part of the claim) is not admitted'.

Rules of the Supreme Court Order 18, rule 8 sets out the positive allegations which should be pleaded in a defence; viz:

(i) any act or matter which makes a claim untenable. For example, a fundamental matter of law such as limitation; or a lack of proper notice;
(ii) any matter which if not pleaded might take the other side by surprise at the hearing, and which might therefore necessitate an adjournment;
(iii) facts or matters which, although not arising out of a previous pleading, may put a different complexion on the claimant's allegations.

It should be appreciated by the expert when analysing the points of claim unless something is expressly denied or not admitted it will be deemed to be admitted. For this reason what is termed a general traverse is used in the defence (see below).

A defence to a claim may take the following form, for example:

(1) Paragraphs 1, 2, 5, and 8 of the points of claim are admitted.
(2) Paragraph 3 of the points of claim is admitted save that it is denied (for example) the architect was at all material times Mr L Smith. From 9 September 1986 to 15 May 1987 the architect was Mr H Jones.
(3) Paragraph 4 is not admitted.
(4) The respondent denies each and every allegation in paragraph 6 save that it is admitted the claimant did give notice of delay to the regular progress of the works.
(5) The respondent denies each and every allegation in paragraph 7 save that it is not admitted the claimant did give written notice to the architect of their incurrence of loss and/or expense.

and so on . . . ending with the general traverse, as follows:

(17) Save as herein expressly admitted or not admitted the respondent denies each and every allegation contained in the points of claim as though the same were set out herein and separately traversed.

Commonly used phrases, which the expert may find useful when employed to represent either claimant or respondent, are as follows:

Further or in the alternative . . . This is a useful phrase where there are alternatives in a case, be it alternative causes of action, alternative breaches, alternative types of negligence, et seq. The phrase indicates the allegation following it is either in addition to, or an alternative to the allegation already made, giving the pleader the option of succeeding with one, or either, or both.

As alleged or at all . . . A phrase which is especially useful in a defence where one is denying how or why an occurrence happened. It can be used as a wide denial of any specific causation particularised by the claimant, or any other causation which might make the respondent liable. For example: 'The respondent denies he is indebted to the claimant in the sum of £50,000 as alleged or at all.' This tells the claimant that the respondent thinks he owes him nothing, whether the sum as alleged or any sum.

If, which is denied . . . Another useful phrase in a defence, which will effectively allow two alternative lines of argument. The first indicates the allegation is denied. The second shows that if the first is subsequently found to be right, there is a further argument on the facts or the law to indicate the respondent is not liable. For example: 'If, which is denied, the architect did issue a certificate pursuant to condition 35.15.1 of the contract [first line of argument] he did not at the same time send a copy to the nominated sub-contractor [second line of argument]'.

In the premises ... A phrase which draws a conclusion from allegations made in previous paragraphs.

By reason of the matters aforesaid... An alternative to 'in the premises' with a similar meaning.

At all material times ... Alleges that a particular relationship or statement of facts continued throughout the period covered by the pleading. For example: 'At all material times the claimants were building and civil engineering contractors operating from 115 High Street, Basingchester.'

As before with the claim, once the defence is completed the whole document should be carefully checked, particularly if it contains any arithmetic, before being despatched to both the claimant and arbitrator simultaneously. In most, but not all cases, there will be a counterclaim to accompany the defence. This is considered in the next section, below.

It may appear from the foregoing that the time for preparation of the defence should be shorter than that for the claim. The expert should consider, before agreeing to what is ostensibly a short period that, as has already been noted, to a large extent he will not be able to commence the defence in earnest until he receives the claimant's points of claim. Additionally, the expert will almost certainly find himself with the same time period as that for the points of claim, in which to serve both the respondent's defence and counterclaim. The expert should therefore beware of being encouraged to agree to an unrealistically short period for service of the defence.

Counterclaim

A counterclaim is a claim which would stand in its own right. 'A counterclaim is to be treated, for all purposes for which justice requires it to be so treated, as an independent action' (per Bowen LJ in *Amon v Bobbett* (1889) 22 QBD 543, CA). However, as such, a counterclaim is entirely dependent upon the claim of the claimant, since a counterclaim cannot be pleaded after the claimant has obtained an arbitrator's award (*CSI International Co Ltd v Archway Personnel (Middle East) Ltd* [1980] 3 All ER 215, [1980] 1 WLR 1069). There are occasions where a respondent requires to serve notice to concur in the appointment of an arbitrator but is beaten to it by the claimant. Such action does not deny the respondent the right to make his own claim, except it is usual procedure for him to await receipt of the claimant's points of claim and to serve it together with the defence. There are times of course when the respondent will only make a counterclaim because he has received a claim from the claimant.

A counterclaim is subject to the same rules for its drafting as those for a claim. The expert acting for the respondent is therefore put in the same position, in the drafting of a counterclaim, as if he were acting for the claimant. There is, however, one major point worthy of consideration, which is the difference between a counterclaim and set-off. As has been stated, above, a counterclaim is a claim which stands in its own right. As such its content does not need to arise from the same facts as the points of claim. It can relate to anything about which the parties are in dispute. Conversely a set-off must relate to and arise from the same facts as that of the points of claim and should therefore be pleaded as the ultimate paragraph of the defence. The distinction is that a set-off is not a claim in its own right. It is not a separate action, and again in comparison with a counterclaim it cannot be adjudicated upon and awarded if the claimant subsequently withdraws. Further, if a set-off exceeds a claim it can only be set-off against the claim, not awarded on separately. An illustration of the difficulty the expert could find himself in is found in the case of *British Anzani (Felixstowe) v International Marine Management (UK) Ltd* [1980] QB 137, [1979] 2 All ER 1063.

> The plaintiff agreed to build a warehouse for the defendant to lease, and eventually there were claims for rent arrears by the plaintiff and for the defects in the building by the defendant. It was held that the defendant's claim on defects might be a set-off, but that although the set-off did not need to come from the plaintiff's cause of action, it should be factually connected with it. Here it was not, so the defendant should have pleaded a counterclaim rather than a set-off.

See also *Business Computers Ltd v Anglo-African Leasing Ltd* [1977] 2 All ER 741, [1977] 1 WLR 578. If the expert is in any doubt it is often best that he pleads a counterclaim.

On a matter of procedure, when pleading a counterclaim if the expert is alleging facts already pleaded in the defence, or admissions made to the points of claim, these can be repeated in summary form rather than setting out the whole matters again, for example:

> The respondent repeats paragraphs 1 to 17 inclusive of the defence. In the premises the respondent has suffered loss and damage, particulars of which are summarised in Schedule 1 annexed hereto.

The expert must remember to include in the prayer to the counterclaim costs and statutory interest, in the same manner as it would be in the points of claim.

Reply and the defence to the counterclaim

There is a distinction between a reply and a defence to counterclaim, of which the expert should be aware. A reply to the defence is rarely necessary since generally its object is to deny what the respondent has already said in the defence. In the absence of a reply there is an implied joinder of issues. Rules of the Supreme Court Order 18, rule 14:

(i) if there is no reply to a defence there is an implied joinder of issue on it;
(ii) a joinder of issue means that each and every allegation is deemed to be denied;
(iii) there can be no joinder of issue, implied or express, on a statement of claim or counterclaim.

The expert could therefore simply draft a defence to the counterclaim and ignore the reply. However, if the respondent has raised some new issues or made new allegations which need to be considered and dealt with, a reply should be pleaded. A reply can also be useful where it is desirable to admit allegations pleaded in the defence or where it is appropriate to admit and avoid. If a reply is pleaded it should not raise any new issues which, in hindsight, should have been pleaded in the points of claim. In this eventuality it is better that the claim be amended (see above). Finally, a reply should conclude with a general denial of everything else in the defence, for example:

> The claimant joins issue with the respondent upon his defence save insofar as the same consists of admissions and save for any admissions contained herein.

When drafting the defence to the counterclaim the expert stands in the shoes of the expert acting for the respondent. That is, he pleads in exactly the same manner as if he were acting for the respondent, working on the premise the counterclaim is a claim in its own right. If the reply and the defence to the counterclaim are both pleaded, they must appear in the same document.

Further and better particulars

There will be many instances when the expert, acting for either the claimant or respondent, will not be able to answer the other's pleadings until he can obtain more information. Generally his client will not be able to provide it; he may be as much in the dark as his technical advocate. It is not going to really achieve a great deal for the expert to make an educated guess; this may only lead to a requirement for amendment later. The expert must therefore approach his opponent and formally request this information. This is done procedurally by issuing a request for further and better particulars (of the points of claim, or the defence). Naturally if the claim is well drafted, and fully particularised, any such formal request will be seen by the respondent's representative as a fishing exercise, and the reply may not actually achieve the claimant's expert's desired objective. Likewise, it is not always beneficial to request further and better particulars just because it is considered the pleadings were badly drafted. In so doing the expert may put the other side on their guard, with the end result they prepare a better case.

Where the matter of requests for further and better particulars has been anticipated in the timetable agreed at the preliminary meeting, the arbitrator should have included a provision for such in his order for directions. In this eventuality the party upon whom the request is served has to reply to it within the time stipulated for that purpose. Any delay will be subject to a request for an extension, alternatively a penalty as to costs. For this latter consideration, an expert faced with a request would do well to answer it in a reasonable time.

If the expert considers it will be of real value, within the considerations of time, speed and cost, to serve a request for further and better particulars, he should only ask for that which he really needs to know. He is only allowed to request such particulars as should have been in the original pleading; nothing more. Further, he will not be entitled to receive evidence, although the dividing line between evidence and fact is an extremely slim one.

Upon receipt of a request for further and better particulars, the expert should first consider if he wants to resist giving information, and if so whether there are good reasons for such resistance. Further consideration should be given, in the light of the questions received, whether the expert's pleading is weak in any area and if it can be improved upon, even to the extent of seeking leave to amend. The expert can also look to see if his opponent is trying to interrogate him on any matter without leave, although in practice this can be difficult to appreciate, particularly to an untrained eye. If the expert is minded to resist, especially if he considers he is being asked for evidence, or is being interrogated, he can simply answer 'The claimant/respondent is not entitled.' There is no requirement to explain why. Often the other side will not come back again, in which case the expert can see it was a 'fishing expedition'. Conversely, if they do come back, and the expert is at all unsure how he should deal with the matter, for both his sake and for his client's, he would be well advised to consult a lawyer. If the other side make application, the expert should consider carefully the costs aspect of arguing that application, which could easily fall to his client.

Close of pleadings

When the pleadings are closed, that is when both parties have served on the other their formal claims and defences, the expert and his client should take stock of their position. A large amount of costs will have been incurred by this time, but in relation to the whole reference with a full hearing, those costs will only be a fraction of the total. For the expert it is an ideal time to think seriously about the wisdom of continuing with the reference. Much work has still to be contemplated: discovery, inspection of documents, agreement of figures as figures, preparation for the hearing and the hearing itself.

For the expert acting for the claimant, having seen and studied the defence and counterclaim (if any) the claim of his client may not seem so attractive as it had when he first served the notice to concur in the appointment of an arbitrator. The point about brinkmanship has already been made (see above); the expert should avoid leading his client further into a large bill of costs if there is a strong hint of the claim failing. Even if a small part were to succeed, there is no guarantee that the claimant will recover his costs. The arbitrator may decide, in his absolute discretion, that costs will not follow the event and may penalise the claimant on costs if he considers much of the claim had no real chance of success in any event and was grossly exaggerated. There is much legal authority upon which the arbitrator can base such a decision: *Re Fearon and Flinn* (1869) LR 5 CP 34; *Matheson & Co Ltd v A Tabah & Sons* [1963] 2 Lloyd's Rep 270; *Perry v Stopher* [1959] 1 All ER 713, [1959] 1 WLR 415; and others. The expert, having considered the foregoing, may find this an appropriate point to approach the question of settlement. He may find his opponent just as anxious to do likewise, in which case they should meet as soon as possible to try and reach a compromise. Any meetings, or exchanges of correspondence should of course be made clearly without prejudice, to keep alive the strict legal and contractual rights of each of the parties.

The same applies to the expert acting for the respondent. He may persuade his client that to continue with the reference would be futile and risk not only his own costs but those of his opponent. In addition, for some parties to arbitration and litigation, the time involvement invariably results in some detrimental effect on the day-to-day running of the business. Although invariably hidden, this is also a cost to which the party is put. Again, if minded to approach the other side to consider reaching a settlement, it must be done without prejudice.

As an alternative to compromise the expert may wish to make an offer of settlement without discussion. Such can be in the form of an 'open offer', in which case the arbitrator can be shown its form and content, or a 'sealed offer', the form and content of which will only be declared to the arbitrator after he has made his award. The open offer has a disadvantage in that, if not accepted, it can jeopardise the further case of the party making the offer, in that the arbitrator will have seen that a weakness exists, to which he may have difficulty in closing his mind. The sealed offer usually takes the form of an offer of settlement, in which costs up to that point are taken into consideration, the form and content of which the arbitrator is debarred access to. If the other party accepts the offer, the parties duly advise the arbitrator and he publishes a consent award without any further action being taken in the reference. The consent award will deal with the costs of the award (the arbitrator's costs) and its publication signals the arbitrator as *functus officio* as regards any further action in the arbitration. If the party to whom the sealed offer is made is not minded to accept, and wishes to continue with the reference, then, providing he is ultimately awarded as the substantive part of the arbitrator's award at least the amount of the offer, or a greater sum, he should get the majority of his costs back (subject to the arbitrator following the general rule that costs follow the event). On the other hand, if the party to whom the offer is directed does not accept it, continues with the reference, but is awarded a substantive sum which is less than the amount offered, he will only be awarded his costs up to the date of the offer. The machinery for advising the arbitrator of the existence of a sealed offer, and the timing thereof, is discussed in a later section.

If expert witnesses have not already been appointed, the close of pleadings is perhaps a good time to do so. The expert as advocate will have a good idea of the kind of expert he should appoint to act as a witness of opinion evidence to assist the arbitrator in reaching his decision. On the other hand, it can be argued that the expert as advocate is in an ideal position to undertake that task himself. This depends to a large extent on the format the arbitration reference adopts. Unless the arbitrator has himself decided, or the parties have themselves agreed, to dispense with the formalities of the High Court procedure, and the strict laws of evidence, then the expert is advised to follow the normally accepted procedure and appoint an expert witness to give opinion evidence. There is little merit in a technical advocate, who is, for example, a quantity surveyor, appointing another quantity surveyor to give expert opinion evidence on the evaluation of loss and/or expense which the technical advocate has himself prepared as part of the particulars in the points of claim, or counterclaim, as the case may be. Such experts, when appointed, must appreciate the purpose of their appointment, which is not to act as any kind of advocate, but to give expert opinion evidence to assist the arbitrator.

Discovery

Discovery is perhaps one of the most difficult of legal definitions and processes for the non-lawyer to understand. Doubt has been raised as to whether there is any real or beneficial requirement for discovery in arbitration references. Section 12(1) of the Arbitration Act 1950 contains a provision to the effect that, unless a contrary intention is expressed in the arbitration agreement, all parties to the reference 'shall . . . produce before the arbitrator . . . all documents within their possession or power . . . which may be required or called for . . .'. This is analogous with the Rules of the Supreme Court Order 24, which entitles the parties to civil action, begun by writ, to discovery all documents 'which are or have been in their possession, custody or power relating to the matters in question'. However, the analogy ends there. In a High Court action discovery takes place automatically after the exchange of pleadings, unless there is an express order to the contrary. In an arbitration reference discovery is at the discretion of the arbitrator; an order so directing the parties will be included in his order for directions.

The fundamental purpose of discovery is to enable the parties to assist their own cases in the reference by the process of disclosure by one to the other and subsequent inspection of documents which they may or may not have already seen. It is often a complete anathema to a claimant contractor to be told he must make all his correspondence with, say, his sub-contractors available to the other side for inspection. Such action may of course be totally prejudicial to the claimant's case, nevertheless if discovery is ordered, it must be done. Likewise, there is no point the claimant contractor claiming a cost of £1,000, if in his cost records for all the world, and particularly his opponent, to see, it only shows £800. The only documents the parties do not have to disclose one to the other are (a) those which are in their possession, custody or power, but which they no longer have, and (b) those for which they claim privilege. In the case of the former the claimant must say when they left his possession, custody or power and where they have gone since then. The latter category will include correspondence of a confidential nature between the parties themselves and their professional and, strictly speaking, legal advisers. However, where non-legal advisers are employed, privilege is allowable for communications written in contemplation of arbitration. In any event, where a technical advocate is employed by one of the parties to represent him it is unlikely the opposing party's representatives would seriously object to privilege being claimed for communications between the party and his advocate. Another category under which privilege from disclosure may be claimed is for documents marked 'without prejudice', the full meaning of which is 'without prejudice to strict legal rights' and which the arbitrator should not see as it will be prejudicial to the party's case. However, for privilege to be successfully claimed for such documents, they must relate to an offer by one party to the other to settle the matters in dispute in whole or in part. Once one communication has borne the legend, all future communications from that party on the subject of settlement will be deemed to have also borne it whether expressly stated or not. Documents or communication bearing the legend which are not offers of settlement will not be classified as privileged from discovery and disclosure. The most obvious form of 'without prejudice' letter is that which contains an offer of settlement after the reference to arbitration has commenced, in the form of a Sealed Offer (see above). Clearly the party making the offer does not want the arbitrator to know what he has done, so he claims privilege from disclosure, not necessarily to the other party, but to the arbitrator.

There are two types of discovery: general discovery and specific discovery. General discovery means the disclosure by each party to the reference to the other of all relevant documents which are, or have been, in their possession, custody or power and which are material to the dispute. It will generally include all correspondence between the parties; minutes of meetings; accounts details, including wages sheets, cost records, orders, invoices, et al; drawings; photographs; site records; diaries; valuations; certificates; instructions and variation orders; and all correspondence, sub-contracts, directions, valuations and payments between a contractor and his sub-contractors. The process of specific discovery is normally applied when one party has good reason to suspect the other of not having disclosed all documents in the general discovery. It may be that the party wishes to inspect one or more specific papers he knows he sent to the other side but of which he kept no copies. The party wishing to inspect informs the other of the specific documents and expects to receive an invitation to inspect. If no invitation is received the first party may apply to the arbitrator with a request that he orders the second to make the specific document, or documents, available. Any violation of that order will provide grounds for the first party to make application to the High Court under s 12(6) of the Arbitration Act 1950. In which case the expert must involve the services of a lawyer.

It will depend on the matters in dispute, their complexity, and the wishes of the parties as to whether the arbitrator considers it appropriate to order general discovery. The technical advocate should not feel compelled to request general discovery in a dispute of a simple nature. Any ensuing order from the arbitrator may only serve as a costly exercise in which the volume of paper to be inspected may far outweigh any furtherance of his client's case. As an alternative, he may, with or without the consent of the other side, prefer to settle for an order which will allow both parties to restrict discovery to those specific documents which they would both wish to inspect.

If an order for general discovery is made, usually with inspection of documents either seven or 14 days thereafter, the expert should prepare lists for service on the other side. It would be wholly appropriate to follow the list of documents which are applicable to a High Court action, if only for the succinct and clear way in which its contents are conveniently conveyed to the other party to the reference. An example of such listing is as follows:

> The following is a list of the documents relating to the matters in dispute in this arbitration reference which are or have been in the possession, custody or power of the claimant(respondent) and which is served in compliance with the arbitrator's order for directions dated ....:
>
> (1) The claimant(respondent) has in his possession, custody or power the documents relating to matters in question in this arbitration reference which are enumerated in Schedule 1 annexed hereto.
>
> (2) The claimant(respondent) objects to produce the documents

which are enumerated in Part 2 of the said Schedule 1 on the grounds they are privileged. They consist of professional communications of a confidential nature made to the claimant(respondent) by his technical advocate for the purposes of giving him advice in this arbitration reference, prepared and given in anticipation of and during the progress of this arbitration reference.

(3) The claimant(respondent) has had, but has not now, in his possession, custody or power the documents relating to the matters in dispute in this arbitration reference enumerated in Schedule 2 annexed hereto.

(4) Of the documents in the said Schedule 2, those numbered 1 and 2 in that Schedule were last in the claimant's (respondent's) possession, custody or power in April 1986 and the others in October 1986.

(5) Neither the claimant(respondent) nor his technical advocate nor any other person on his behalf has now, or ever had, in his possession, custody or power any document of any description whatever relating to any matter in dispute in this arbitration reference other than the documents enumerated in Schedules 1 and 2 annexed hereto.

The list is compiled from documents which are conveniently arranged in files appertaining to their contents. All the documents within each file are numbered consecutively. So, for example, all correspondence between contractor and architect will be separately enumerated within one set of files. Other classes of documents, such as meeting minutes, instructions, certificates, et al will be dealt with in a similar manner.

At the same time as the expert serves the list on the other party he should advise them when and where inspection of the documents can be made. Whilst in a High Court action it is customary to serve formal notice of inspection, it is submitted such formality is not necessary in arbitration.

The expert, if on the receiving end of the list, may have good reason to believe the other party has no proper grounds for claiming privilege for one or more documents. If he genuinely believes this, and thinks it will assist his party's case to inspect those documents he can challenge the other side's claim to privilege. If such challenge is defended, and he wishes to continue with his assertion, he can appeal to the arbitrator. Before doing so, however, he will do well to remember it will be the arbitrator who will make the decision. To do so the arbitrator will need to see the documents, and if he decides the claim to privilege is upheld, he will have to cast the contents from his mind. The arbitrator, however clever he may be, is still only human, and there is little doubt that this is asking the impossible.

The expert should, whenever practicable to do so, conduct the inspection of the documents himself, and not follow what is customary practice in legal circles of sending a junior to inspect. This practice usually ends up with thousands of copies of documents which may, or more often, need not, be required. The expert, because of his technical knowledge and experience will be in a far better position to assess just what he needs to look at, what is missing from his own client's files, and therefore of what documents he needs copies to be made. He only really needs copies of those papers which he knows he may need to refer to during the hearing. With others it may be sufficient for him to merely make a note of their contents. In any event, once he knows the existence of a particular document he can ask for a copy at any time. Inspection is an aspect of the reference which should be taken seriously. A lot of useful information can be gleaned from carefully reading the files of the opposition, and much can be gained by the expert spending time over the whole exercise. For example, where the expert is acting for the respondent employer his client would not have seen any correspondence between the claimant contractor and his sub-contractors and suppliers. The contractor might be claiming an extension of time, or loss and expense, or both from the employer. However, inspection of his files may declare that a problem with one of his sub-contractors was the root cause of the delay and the claim against the employer is spurious in any event. Conversely, the expert who is acting for the claimant contractor may equally discover documents in the files of the architect or quantity surveyor which could just as easily destroy the respondent employer's counterclaim.

If for any reason the expert suspects the other side have not disclosed all of their documents at discovery he can require them to swear an affidavit as to the completeness of their list.

Agreement of figures as figures

Unless the parties have a real objection, the arbitrator will generally order that figures be agreed as figures. This is often a process which is both misunderstood, and abused. If conducted correctly it can prove to be a time, and therefore a cost, conserving exercise. Once again, because of his knowledge and experience the expert as advocate is in a good position to conduct this agreement personally. The process is designed to allow the parties, or their advisers, to make agreement on figures, documents, drawings, photographs, maps, et al irrespective of liability in order to reduce the time at the hearing. In an arbitration reference which involves a claim for an extension of time and reimbursement of loss and expense, there will inevitably be a large number of documents appertaining to the dispute. There will also be the evaluation of the claim, containing many arithmetic calculations and items of cost headings. Clearly, if the arbitrator has to hear evidence at the hearing to try and prove each of those documents, calculations and costs it will not only prove time consuming but the arbitrator will have to make his own decision as to their validity, which will inevitably increase his own costs of the award. Since most, if not all, of the aforementioned items will be a matter of record, it will obviously be to each party's advantage to reach agreement prior to the hearing, leaving only the liability to be decided by the arbitrator. The expert should make arrangements to meet the other side in order to try and reach agreement. If the other party is represented by lawyers, they will generally appoint their own expert to meet with the technical advocate. In many instances when two experts meet together on these exercises it signals the start, if not the conclusion, of a settlement between the parties. If nothing else it may introduce a relationship between the parties which has not existed since the start of the dispute.

If and when agreement on figures as figures has been reached the expert should reduce such agreement to writing. This document should clearly indicate those items upon which agreement has been reached, and those upon which it has not. It could include for the guidance of the arbitrator the reasons why it has been impossible to reach agreement on certain items. A signature of the individual acting for the other party should be obtained to the document. This document will indicate to the arbitrator what agreement has been reached between the parties and what is therefore left for him to decide.

Following such agreement it should be possible for the parties to define more clearly the issues they want the arbitrator to consider. During the process of agreeing figures as figures, negotiation and settlement of certain facts and matters is always possible and common ground may be reached between the parties. The expert is well placed to define these issues and he should not be afraid to encourage agreement and settlement if at all practicable. Providing the expert has obtained the confidence of his client, be it claimant or respondent, he will in many cases be given the authority to make such settlements, even to the point of settling the whole dispute and thereby bringing a conclusion to the arbitration reference. A problem ensues when the expert's client will not properly consider the advice given to him, and refuses to allow his advocate to settle aspects of the dispute which clearly should be settled. This often is a result of the client becoming emotionally involved and unable to take the same objective view that the expert can take from his detached position. Nevertheless, if and when agreement has been reached, the expert and those representing the other party should, wherever possible, produce a statement of issues in the dispute upon which they require the arbitrator to adjudicate. The advantages of this are obvious; the arbitrator will be forewarned of the matters upon which to consider evidence and the parties' advocates will be able to confine their adducement of evidence to that which is only concerned with those issues. The result in time and cost savings can only be beneficial to both parties.

As a sequel to the agreement of figures as figures the expert should attempt to consider with the other side an agreed 'working bundle'. After the process of discovery and inspection of documents (see above) both sides will have many files all containing the abundance of documents which are necessarily amassed during a typical construction project. In addition, their contents will be swelled by the copies obtained each by one party from the other as a result of inspection of the other's documents. Whilst many will be germane to the dispute and therefore to the arbitration reference, the majority will not. It is in neither party's interest to have their advocates wade through thick files of largely irrelevant papers during the hearing; it will only prolong matters during what is the most costly part of the arbitration reference. An agreed working bundle, particularly when used in conjunction with a statement of issues to be decided (see above), will limit the number of documents and papers to be considered to a manageable proportion. As with the agreement of figures as figures, the parties' terms of agreement to an agreed bundle is restricted to their cognisance of the existence of the documents within it and of their contents. It is not an indication of either party's advocate's agreement as to the intention of any document or the interpretation thereof. Any documents upon which such agreement cannot be reached must be proved before the arbitrator.

The working bundle should be made available for the hearing in four copies; one for the arbitrator, one for each of the advocates and one for the witness box.

Interlocutory applications

During the period between the preliminary meeting and the hearing, generally known as the interlocutory period, the procedure is rarely as plain and straightforward as has been outlined above. The expert may have good reason for suspecting that, for example, the property which is the subject matter of the dispute is going to be, or is likely to be, destroyed, altered, or sold before the arbitrator has had an opportunity to either view it or make his award. Or the other party is intending to transfer funds out of the United Kingdom. Or, where the expert is acting for the respondent, the other party is impecunious and is unlikely to be able to pay the claimant's costs if they lose. In each of these instances, and provided the grounds can be proven, applications can be made to the High Court under s 12(6) of the Arbitration Act 1950 for the appropriate orders, being respectively an '*Anton Pillar* Order', a '*Mareva* Injunction', and an order for security for costs. In each case the expert will need to involve the services of a lawyer; he must not even attempt to try and make application himself. He should first discuss his concern with his client and obtain definite instructions to refer the matter initially to a solicitor. Once the solicitor is satisfied that there are sufficient grounds to make application to the court matters can proceed. The actual form of the application and the procedure is beyond the scope of this book.

The subject of security for costs is not always a matter for the High Court, and can be considered in more detail. As stated above, if the expert has good reasons to suspect the other party, if they were to lose the arbitration, could not pay his own party's costs of the reference and the award, application can be made for such security. Generally only the respondent can seek security for costs. However, if the respondent has made a counterclaim, then the claimant, being a defendant of that claim, may make application in certain limited circumstances. The expert seeking the order should have good grounds before involving his client in what could potentially be additional costs. Whilst impecuniosity is a good ground for seeking an order, it is not always sufficient. The court has absolute discretion in its assessment as to whether to order security for costs, having consideration for the merits of the dispute, including:

(1) the *bona fides* of the claimant's case;
(2) the claimant's prospects of success;
(3) whether there is an admission in the pleadings or elsewhere by the respondent that money is due;
(4) whether the application is being made oppressively;
(5) whether the claimant's want of means was brought about by the respondent's alleged conduct;
(6) the stage of the reference when the application is made.

Having considered the above, the court may feel disposed to make an order for security for costs, either in the total sum of the application, or for some part of it; perhaps up to the next stage of the reference, for example, discovery or the hearing. When such security is ordered, it is usually a term of the order that further proceedings in the reference are stayed pending the provision of such security to the satisfaction of the party in whose favour the order is made.

Whilst the court, by the power granted to it under s 12(6) of the 1950 Act, provides a sufficient means of obtaining an order for security for costs, the time aspect involved may be detrimental to the party seeking such security. Before taking this course of action, the expert should carefully examine the terms of the arbitration agreement to consider whether it provides the arbitrator with the power to make such an order. If it does, the expert may dispense with the procedure of appointing a solicitor to make application to the court, and instead deal with the matter himself by direct application to the arbitrator. However, this situation would be unusual. For example, none of the standard forms of building contract provide the arbitrator with such power. In some instances, however, given that application is to be made, it may be worthwhile, and in the interests of time and cost conservation, for the expert to seek the approval of the other party or their representatives to make a joint approach to the arbitrator and to vest in him the power to order security for costs. He is, after all, the individual the parties have chosen to decide their dispute, and he is probably in the best position to decide whether, in the circumstances of which he will be familiar, such an order should be made. Conversely, there will be occasions when it would be more advantageous for an independent body, such as the court, to consider an application for security for costs, if only for the very reason that it will not know all the details of the dispute. Before the expert takes either course he should first weigh these matters carefully in his mind.

Sometimes the expert, when acting for an enthusiastic claimant, finds himself in the position of having a reluctant respondent. In many instances, the respondent will not only be reluctant, but will consider he has been drawn into a reference to arbitration by a claim which he considers is spurious. As a result he not only wants no active part in the reference, but also becomes disruptive. The expert for the claimant will have recognised that his client has been held out of his money for long enough, the parties having probably been in dispute for some considerable time before the notice to concur in the appointment of the arbitrator was served. The respondent pays lip-service to the whole affair, delays in replying to correspondence, tries to deal with the matter himself without appointing lawyers or an expert to represent him, and generally adopts a detached and intransigent attitude towards the whole affair. As for the claimant, he has not wanted to take the dispute to arbitration, but the respondent's attitude is symptomatic of why the dispute has arisen in the first place and of the respondent's general regard for him. He just wants to proceed with the reference and obtain an award in his favour.

When the parties made the contract between them, they agreed that in the event of a dispute or difference arising between them such dispute of difference would be referred to the final decision of a single arbitrator. Having made that agreement the parties have chosen their own remedy. Further, having had an arbitrator appointed to hear their dispute, whether by agreement or by a third party nomination, his authority is irrevocable except by leave of the High Court (Arbitration Act 1950, s 1). Of course, if he felt so disposed the reluctant respondent could make application to the court for removal of the arbitrator, providing he had sufficient grounds to make such application worthwhile. However, it would not remove the agreement to arbitrate. The result would be a considerable delay whilst the application was heard, and even if upheld, the appointment of a new arbitrator. Given the scenario in the preceding paragraph, the expert for the claimant is faced with two alternatives. The first, and least attractive, is to not be intimidated by his opponent's combined lack of interest and real progress and to adopt a philosophical view that the costs arising from the delay will, hopefully, be awarded to his client. That cannot always be guaranteed and presupposes his client can actually afford to wait. The second alternative is to make application to the arbitrator for an order, or a series of orders, to encourage the respondent to comply with some kind of programme which will provide the reference with the required momentum to guide it towards a conclusion. Whilst this in itself will not remove the delays which seem inherent in even the best-run references, it will at least indicate to the respondent that neither the claimant nor the arbitrator are prepared to tolerate his incessant delaying tactics. After all, the arbitrator has a vested interest in concluding the matter; he will want to recover his fee. In any event he will probably be a busy man who does not want dates allocated for action in the reference to be continually set aside.

The sanction for non-compliance with an order of the arbitrator is an application to the High Court under s 5(1) of the Arbitration Act 1979 to extend the powers of the arbitrator notwithstanding the express provision of the arbitration agreement between parties. If such application is upheld by the court, it gives the arbitrator the power, subject to any conditions specified in the order, to continue with the reference in default of appearance of the reluctant party in a like manner as a judge of the High Court might continue *ex parte* (s 5(2) of the 1979 Act). The procedure to be followed in making such application to the court should be made by the claimant party, and not the arbitrator. The expert should advise his client of the course of action to be followed and instruct a solicitor to notify the reluctant respondent of the intended proceedings. If subsequently the powers of the arbitrator are extended and he proceeds *ex parte* he will only hear evidence from the claimant upon which to base his award. Nevertheless, his award will still be valid and have all the same powers as an award given after a conventional reference. It is likely that when the reluctant party sees that the expert and his client are not prepared to be intimidated by his continual delay and refusal to co-operate he will actually comply with the orders of the arbitrator without the need for any application to be made to the High Court. There cannot be many parties who would risk having an award made against them without having been given an opportunity to present their own defence.

During the interlocutory period the expert may find himself having to deal with any number of applications to the arbitrator for procedural orders or for decisions on preliminary issues. Some of these may emanate from himself, or from the other party to the dispute, or from the arbitrator. In large arbitrations some arbitrators and/or advocates like to narrow down the issues into a number of preliminary issues or 'sub-trials', where specific aspects of the dispute are heard. In a typical arbitration reference arising from a dispute on a construction contract where there is a claim for an extension of time to the period for completion of the construction works, a claim for loss and/or expense arising from disruption to the regular progress of the works, a claim for increased value of variations, together with all the associated defences, and a counterclaim for liquidated damages and contribution towards the cost of faulty workmanship, the arbitrator may wish to deal with each of the issues separately. Thus the technical advocate will find himself in front of the arbitrator and the representatives of the other party on a number of separate occasions. Alternatively, the arbitrator may decide it is appropriate to have more than one preliminary meeting in order to review progress and plan future progress towards one main hearing. In any event, the expert as advocate should be prepared for the probability that few references proceed with textbook regularity. It is perhaps inevitable that parties to a dispute which have chosen arbitration as a means of settlement are unlikely to be able to agree on anything, least of all the way and manner in which the reference will be conducted. In many cases the arbitrator will keep the parties on the straight and narrow, but whilst he can coax and encourage them, he is not generally in a position to dictate.

One further matter which can happen at any stage of the reference, not just during the interlocutory period, but which it is convenient to examine here, is the matter of the arbitrator misconducting himself or the proceedings. In this respect, the term 'misconducting himself' is nothing to do with any moral misdemeanour. Examples of misconduct include such occurrences as failure to hear evidence from both sides; giving himself evidence; failure to conduct the reference in a manner expressly or impliedly prescribed; behaviour in a way which is contrary to public policy; bias towards one party to the detriment of the other. If the expert is of the opinion that the arbitrator appointed is guilty of misconduct he should, having considered the matter with his client, and where appropriate with the representatives of the other party, arrange for a solicitor to institute proceedings in the High Court for removal under s 23 of the Arbitration Act 1950.

Expert witnesses

If the technical advocate considers the dispute to be of such nature that it would advantage his case to appoint an expert witness, such an expert should be appointed as early as possible in the reference. If the matter of expert witnesses has not been dealt with at the preliminary meeting and therefore the arbitrator's order for directions is silent on the point, the technical advocate should apply for an order dealing with the subject, after notification to the other party of his intention to do so. Once appointed, the technical advocate should obtain as much assistance from the expert witness in building his case as he can muster, particularly if it covers aspects which are beyond the experience and knowledge of the advocate. The advocate should instruct the expert witness to prepare a report containing his opinion evidence as soon as possible. The arbitrator will, in an order for directions, order the expert's report to be exchanged with that from the expert witness appointed by the other side, usually seven or 14 days at the latest prior to the commencement of the hearing.

Having received the report from the expert witness, or witnesses appointed by the other party, the technical advocate should, with his own expert(s) consider the contents very carefully; all the time looking for signs of either an early settlement opportunity, or anything which might mean he has to amend his pleadings, even at this late stage. He can rest in the knowledge that the other side will be doing exactly the same.

The hearing

The date for the hearing will have been set at a preliminary meeting. In any event, it will come all too soon and cause a last minute rush to ensure everything is ready. The expert must of course strive to make certain he is going to be ready. There will be things that go wrong at the eleventh hour; no one can predict what they will be, but the expert must, as far as is possible, be prepared for such an eventuality and try and programme his timetable to allow for it. Time will be at a premium, and the adrenalin will flow, but he must not allow himself to be so unprepared and nervous that he fails to execute that which he is there to do: present his client's case to the best of his ability. The key-word before, during, and at the hearing is preparation. An ill-prepared advocate, whatever his discipline, is an annoyance to his client, the other advocate(s) and of course to the arbitrator and it will not assist his cause. If the expert has to travel for any longer than an hour in each direction to the hearing, he would do well to consider staying overnight in an hotel as near to the venue as will make life comfortable for him. As most will realise, travel can be very tiring and public transport is exposed to all manner of delays and hold-ups. The last thing the expert will want is to arrive at the hearing either so tired he is unable to devote all of his concentration to the matters in hand, or to be late due to an unforeseen delay on the train service or due to a hold-up in traffic.

Most arbitrators like to follow the practice of the courts and set the times for the hearing between 10.00 am and 4.00 pm, or 4.30 pm, with an adjournment for an hour between 1.00 pm and 2.00 pm and short adjournments for coffee and tea during the morning and afternoon sessions. Superficially this may seem a short day, but in fact it is quite long enough for anyone to maintain their concentration. It also provides valuable time at the start and end of the day for the parties and their representatives to discuss tactics and to deal with any fresh evidence. It also provides time, although perhaps not so obviously, for the parties to talk to each other and assess the chances of reaching a settlement.

If it is left to the parties to agree upon the venue for the hearing between themselves, the expert should try and obtain approval to one which is going to be convenient for not only all concerned, but also within reasonable distance of the subject matter of the dispute as it may be necessary for the arbitrator, accompanied by the parties' representatives, to view this during the course of the hearing.

If there are voluminous files of documents which the expert will need at the hearing, he should arrange for these to be delivered to the chosen venue at least by the day prior to the hearing. He does not want to be bothered with carrying huge boxes of documents on the first morning: there are bound to be more pressing demands on his time. He should also remember to take with him any textbooks, legal authorities and the like which he might need. Also such obvious things as pens, ink, non-sticky part-adhesive pads (for paginating files and books) and a supply of notebooks. These latter requirements are of course most essential, as is the whole process of note-taking.

It will be helpful at the hearing if the technical advocate can have an assistant with him, if only to help with noting. If it is not possible, then the expert will have to do his own. The purpose of noting is twofold: to provide a record of the proceedings and as an aid to the advocate in cross-examination, re-examination and his closing speech. The expert should always aim to be neat, legible and accurate; illegible and untidy scrawl is not going to prove helpful. Noting should ideally be done in a bound A4 size notebook. The infamous counsel's notebooks are ideal, but not essential. Something similar obtained from the High Street stationers is just as effective, provided the pages are ruled on both sides and the leaves are reasonably well secured to the spine or entered into a loose leaf binder. All the right-hand pages should be numbered, leaving the first blank to act as an index. Each notebook should be separately identified with a code-letter. Notes should be taken on the right-hand pages of the book, which is best divided 2/3:1/3; 2/3 for the note and 1/3 for any comments on cross-examination or re-examination. Other, more detailed comments can be written against the notes using the left-hand page, perhaps using a different colour ink. The best way of noting during the giving of evidence by a witness is to telescope the answer. So, instead of writing a verbatim question and then the answer, and running the high risk of missing the next question, reduce the two to a statement. Careful note should be made on any objection and/or applications and the arbitrator's directions thereon.

Unless the arbitrator orders otherwise, the order of speeches generally follows the procedure in a court action, namely:

(1) Claimant opens.
(2) Claimant's witnesses; respondent cross-examines; claimant re-examines.
(3) Respondent's witnesses; claimant cross-examines; respondent re-examines.
(4) Respondent closes.
(5) Claimant closes.

However, if the defence and counterclaim is likely to, or does, exceed the claim, the respondent may open.

The opening speech

The expert as technical advocate should remember that he is addressing a fellow expert who will be well versed in the matters on which he is expressing himself. He will not, therefore, have to explain in great detail to the arbitrator terms which are generic to a construction project, or outline in detail the clauses in standard conditions of contract, unless he wishes to place a particular emphasis on wording or intent. He should also learn to be brief and relevant; there is nothing more likely to put an arbitrator off than an opening which is boring in content and repeats the same ground over and over again. Furthermore, the whole point of the opening speech is going to be lost. As a last general point, the expert should watch the arbitrator especially if he is taking hand-written notes; time must be given for the arbitrator to complete his note before moving on to the next topic. The opening speech is a means by which the expert, who may be dealing with an arbitrator who is used to, or prefers to be addressed by, lawyers, can usefully give the arbitrator the first impressions that in fact he is capable of conducting his client's case and does know with what he is dealing.

As to the content of the opening speech, the following will serve as a brief guide. The expert should first remember he is there to assist the arbitrator to decide in favour of his client. The arbitrator will have only the brief outline of the matters in dispute from the pleadings, with very little by way of explanation to their form or content. The hearing will explain and amplify the pleadings, by means of evidence. The expert should begin by outlining the basic facts of the case: the name and place of the contract works, the form of the contract and its conditions and any amendments to the standard text (although this should all be done in the pleadings it will do no harm to repeat it briefly), the name of the architect and, if relevant, the quantity surveyor, the commencement, duration and completion date and the approximate value of the contract. He should outline the areas and matters in dispute between the parties, and the reason why they are appearing before the arbitrator. Again, this will be evident from the pleadings, but will assist the arbitrator to hear it rather than read it. The expert can then introduce the evidence he intends to adduce.

As an alternative to an opening speech delivered orally, a way of saving time, and therefore considerable cost, at the hearing is for the parties' advocates to deliver the text of such speech directly to the arbitrator, with a copy to the other side. The same procedure can of course be conducted with the closing address and final submissions. Whether such actions will have the same impact and effect as an orally delivered speech will very much depend on the individual circumstances and generalisation would be inappropriate as to whether written speeches are good or otherwise.

Some arbitrators order the parties to serve on them, and to each other, a list of the witnesses they intend to produce at the hearing seven, or 14 days before the due date. Whether this actually achieves anything constructive is a matter of conjecture. It may serve as a guide to the parties, or it may assist the arbitrator to assess whether the time set aside for the hearing is sufficient. In the absence of such an order, the expert should carefully consider whether he wishes the other side to have prior knowledge of whom his witnesses will be. With such prior knowledge, preparation of cross-examination will be made that much easier as they will undoubtedly be able to pre-empt to a large extent the examination-in-chief of those witnesses.

During the opening the expert should beware of anticipating what his witnesses will say. It may be appropriate merely to advise the arbitrator that he proposes calling Mr Jackson, the site agent, to assist him in relation to a particular matter. Alternatively, he may just advise the arbitrator of the name and designation of the individual and leave it to the arbitrator's and the other side's imagination as to why he is going to be called. However, by advising the arbitrator of the witnesses at the opening stage and their order of appearance will give him an indication of how the hearing will be conducted.

The expert advocate must not try to give evidence himself. He must not tell the arbitrator what he thought happened, as if it were a matter of fact. Instead he should advise the arbitrator that he hopes by calling a particular witness to demonstrate that a certain fact took place. Any documents which the expert intends to refer to throughout the hearing, for example, progress charts, particular drawings, etc, should be introduced at the opening. Providing these have been agreed as documents by the other side they may be given an exhibit number, in agreement with the arbitrator. If they have not been so agreed as documents, the expert will have to wait until he calls witnesses to prove them. When all that needs to be said at the opening address has been said, the expert should close it by saying that unless he can help the arbitrator further, then with his permission he would like to call his first witness. The arbitrator will either ask some questions on the content of the opening, or simply allow the first witness to be called.

Examination-in-chief

Section 12(2) of the Arbitration Act 1950 provides that witnesses on the reference shall, if the arbitrator thinks fit, be examined on oath or affirmation. Some arbitrators do, some do not. Nevertheless, to save any embarrassment at the hearing the technical advocate should warn his witnesses beforehand about the possibility they will be required to take the oath, or an affirmation. Once the witness has taken his seat in the witness 'box', which is usually a table and a chair set apart from the main table, the expert should make him feel as much at ease as is possible under the circumstances. Undoubtedly it will be a strange environment and the expert wants to get the best out of the witness, not see him reduced to a nervous wreck. The expert will first verify the name and place of residence or business of the witness, the position within the organisation for whom he works, and the length of time so employed. There will normally not be any objection to the expert leading the witness through these questions. After that, the expert must not lead witnesses during examination-in-chief. He must learn to progressively question the witness until the point is reached that he wants the arbitrator to hear. In some arbitrations the advocates may agree to ask leading questions until the other objects. However, the expert should not take this informal procedure for granted. Generally, unless a contrary intention is either expressed in the arbitration agreement or between the parties and the arbitrator, arbitrators are governed by the Law of Evidence. The expert should be prepared therefore to ask his questions of the witness without leading.

The expert should be aware of those of his witnesses who are apt to either say too much when answering his questions and those whose answers will be what they want him to hear, rather than what he wants to hear. In either instance, neither of these classes of witness should ideally be allowed into the arbitration room whilst other witnesses are giving their evidence. This will only confuse matters even further. Likewise, if the expert sees witnesses for the other side present in the room during the giving of evidence by other witnesses for that side, and he has reason to think answers to questions may be tailored to corroborate each other's evidence such that it may be prejudicial to his own client's case, he may object to the arbitrator. If the arbitrator upholds the objections he will order that witnesses enter the room one at a time to give their evidence. The expert may see a witness to fact for the other side referring to notes. If he is not aware of the existence of such notes or they have not been agreed he can point out the fact to the arbitrator and ask him to ascertain the validity of such notes in terms of contemporaneity.

As a matter of preparation, it is advisable before the hearing for the expert to make a list of the topics he wishes to cover with each witness. Evidence and the order of the witnesses should be dealt with in an orderly and logical sequence. During questioning the foundations should be laid for any comments which may be made during the closing address. Most importantly the expert advocate acting for the claimant, must ensure his questioning of his witnesses covers all the material facts he needs to prove his client's case. He who asserts must prove. Finally, the expert should not himself become unsettled by the advocate for the other side, particularly by a lawyer who is used to appearing in the courts. If he is challenged on a point of principle, or more particularly on a point of law, which appears to be prejudicial to his client's case, he should consider seeking an adjournment during which he can consult a lawyer.

When each witness has been examined-in-chief, the expert should thank him and ask him to remain where he is whilst the other side's advocate asks his questions.

Cross-examination

Cross-examination is a complete change in technique from examination-in-chief. For one thing it is permissible to ask leading questions of the witness. It is sometimes feasible to anticipate the examination-in-chief of the other side's advocate, and therefore the expert as advocate can to some limited extent prepare his cross-examination questions. Generally though such questions will emanate directly from the opposition's examination of their witnesses, and the expert will have to carefully note the answers to such questions and concurrently decide which of the answers he wishes to challenge. Such is the importance of strict note-taking. The expert is advised to adopt an approach of gentle persuasion, rather than be too aggressive. Aggression is likely to alienate him with the arbitrator, particularly if in using it he manages to reduce each witness to a nervous wreck. Such tactics are unlikely to assist the arbitrator to decide the matters in issue. He should therefore be calm, polite, but above all, persistent. If the witness tends to wander off the point of the question, it is often wise to let him, and then rein him in and get to the point that needs to be made. A good advocate will also get to know the arbitrator. If he sees the arbitrator shifting about and obviously getting bored by a particular line of questioning, he might stop and change tack. That will please the arbitrator, and the advocate can always go back to the original line of questioning later if in the meantime subsequent answers have not satisfied the point.

Cross-examination should impugn the credibility of the witness's evidence, not attack the witness as an individual. Such bully-boy tactics are best reserved for American television court-room dramas and have no real place in arbitration. In the event the arbitrator may have sympathy for the witness, and any points made by the advocate will therefore be lost.

Unless the advocate has a note-taker, he will of course have to make his own notes of the cross-examination as he proceeds. It is advisable for him to try to note simple words or short phrases, in a kind of code, which will assist him to decipher what the witness has said when he comes to read them back later. Some form of notes are needed, and the expert should not attempt to rely purely on his memory. Cross-examination of a witness can take the equivalent of a day, or more, and it is doubtful if anyone could remember all the answers for that length of time. During cross-examination the advocate for the party not examining the witness will be taking notes in readiness for re-examination (see below).

Finally, any issue can be raised in cross-examination, even if it has not been raised during the witness's examination-in-chief, providing it can fairly be said to arise from or is relevant to the issues in the pleadings.

Re-examination

Re-examination should ideally be short and limited. It can be a sensitive stage in the hearing, and is prone to more objections than any other. It should be avoided unless it is absolutely vital to re-examine. If re-examination is necessary, the expert should remember, like examination-in-chief, he is not allowed to lead the witness. Secondly, all questions must relate to points raised or dealt with during the cross-examination of the witness, and not any other witness. The advocate is not allowed to raise any new issues at all. If he has forgotten to ask a question on a particular topic during examination-in-chief, that point will have to be thrown away, unless he can obtain leave to recall the witness later in the hearing.

The process of re-examination can be useful in two main ways. First, to allow the witness to elaborate on an answer given during cross-examination, if he was stifled from giving what might be described as an adequate answer. Secondly, to allow the witness to correct himself on an answer if he has been misled by the other side's advocate, or where he may not have fully understood the question.

At the end of this process, when each advocate has concluded his questioning of the witness, the expert should ask the witness to remain in the box until the arbitrator has asked any questions he may have of the witness. When that is concluded, the witness may stand down and generally be excused the remainder of the hearing.

The closing address

This is the time when the expert as advocate can make a résumé of the proceedings and draw to the attention of the arbitrator all the points he wishes to make in order to prove his case. As with the opening speech, the tendency is to make it too long. There is little point in boring the arbitrator with a long address which catalogues in fine detail the whole hearing and thus repeating what he should have recorded in note form anyway. The expert should go through the issues in dispute and the evidence related thereto, commenting on the strong points in his own case, and the weak points in that of his opponent. It is permissible for him to both comment and draw his own conclusions on each. It is not permissible for him to comment on matters which have not been produced in evidence. No new issues or allegations can be raised at this stage. Furthermore, comments may only be made on points on which evidence has been given; in the case of witnesses for the other side, only when they have been given the opportunity to answer during their cross-examination. For this reason the expert should ensure that he puts all the material elements of his own client's case to the relevant witnesses for the other side.

The expert should not give his own opinion of the evidence given: he is there to act as advocate not as an independent expert witness. Such opinions are not evidence, are not relevant, not admissible, and the other side will have no opportunity to cross-examine on them. However, the arbitrator may be invited to draw his own conclusions. If the respondent to a claim or counterclaim brings no evidence on an issue therein, the expert acting for the claimant may point this out, and at the same time comment on the respondent's advocate's examination of the witnesses for the claimant or on the same issue.

The closing address is the ideal time for the expert to make his submissions of law. It is a good idea on the previous day to deliver to the arbitrator, and the other side, a list of the cases to which he intends to refer. Some arbitrators make an order to this effect as a matter of course, but the time for delivery is usually seven days prior to the hearing. This can be restrictive. In any event, such advice will enable copies of relevant law reports to be taken to the hearing. Some arbitrators will prefer not to refer to them at the time but later when they actually make their award. It is a good idea for the arbitrator, whether he has access to the law report or not, to be taken through the respective case, with any relevant passages read aloud to show how and why the case is relevant to the matters in issue.

The closing address, as the name suggests, is a time for drawing towards a conclusion. A time for reminding the arbitrator, briefly, of the various points of evidence which were adduced during the preceding days of what, may have been, a long and sometimes tedious hearing. And a time for asking the arbitrator to make his award in favour of the expert's client in accordance with the claim as pleaded, finishing with a phrase to the effect that his case is concluded, unless the expert can assist the arbitrator further.

Procedural matters

Matters of general importance on procedure throughout the hearing which may be of interest and use to the expert as advocate are as follows:

(1) He should always aim to be brief, concise and to the point. It is boring and pointless to reiterate and repeat over and over again.
(2) The arbitrator should always be referred to as 'Sir', or if a woman, 'Madam'.
(3) The advocate for the other side may be referred to as 'Mr (Mrs, Miss, M/s) X', or if he/she is of counsel 'My Learned Friend'.
(4) The expert as advocate should always aim to keep a straight face. Smiles, laughter, mirth, facial expressions and mannerisms are all part of the play-acting, but they can equally convey the wrong message to both the arbitrator and the other side.
(5) The expert should always be polite and deferring to the arbitrator, who should be thanked for any assistance given, however small or trivial.
(6) Objections should be raised as little as possible, and then only when the expert is absolutely sure of his ground.
(7) Direct questions of the arbitrator should be avoided. For example, if the time is approaching the end of the morning session, and either the expert has finished with a witness, or it is a convenient point to temporarily break the examination of a witness, it is better to say to the arbitrator, 'Sir, that would be a convenient point to break my line of questioning and I wonder whether you might like to take the lunch adjournment now', rather than 'Can we take lunch now, Sir?'
(8) Droning monotones are best avoided, especially during speeches. Pauses and variations in tone and pitch prevent boredom, as long as they are in keeping with the solemnity of the situation.
(9) Apologies should be made for loss of words; in any event this gains time.
(10) The expert should adopt the principle of the 'honest guide', and strive to be fair in order to gain the sympathy of the arbitrator. Merely appearing opposite a lawyer will not necessarily gain such sympathy per se. Thus:
    (i) good points made by the other side should be conceded as such;
    (ii) during a submission on a point of law, any decided case which goes against the claim should be referred to by the expert, and not ignored in the vain hope that it has escaped the other side's attention and they will not refer to it;

(iii) 'muzzling' of a witness in an attempt to hide some matter is to be avoided. The other side, or the arbitrator will almost certainly notice;
(iv) evidence must never be misquoted.

(11) Problems in the expert's own case should be identified and dealt with openly before the other side can capitalise on them.
(12) The throwing down of gauntlets should be avoided, for example, 'Sir, on the facts I submit you cannot award against my client' is not a good tactic.
(13) To a large extent, conduct at the hearing is a matter of style.

Arbitrations on documents-only

So far in this chapter the procedure has been outlined around a typical arbitration (if such a thing exists) culminating in an attended hearing. However, there is scope within disputes arising from construction contracts for arbitrations to be conducted on documents-only. In many ways this procedure may suit the expert who finds difficulty in addressing an audience, but is nevertheless perfectly capable of expressing himself in writing. However, the expert who is contemplating such an approach should always consider whether it will be in the best interests of his client. Documents-only arbitrations have their advantages, as well as their disadvantages. They can be conducted purely on the production of documents in support of each party's case. Or these can be augmented by short submissions by the advocates for each side, rather in the form of a combined opening speech and closing address. In any event there will be no examination of witnesses. This type of arbitration procedure is ideally suited to the dispute involving relatively small sums of money, or where the disagreement turns on matters which can be easily acquired from the relevant documents. Given that a hearing involves the major cost of any arbitration reference, such a procedure will negate the need for high expenditure in order to obtain a decision which will be just as binding as if witnesses had been examined. The advantages are obvious. The parties' advocates can produce their pleadings and written submissions, albeit to an ordered timetable, but without the need for arrangements for everyone concerned to be available on the same day at the same venue. It would be naturally well-suited to disputes where, say, there were no, or only unreliable, witnesses to fact and where the correspondence between the parties was capable of expressing and supporting the parties' case. The procedures outlined earlier in this chapter would still be relevant and be followed right up to, but stop short of, the point of the hearing. There could still be, for example, discovery. In fact it could be argued discovery is an even more important process in this type of arbitration reference than that with an attended hearing; great reliance being placed on any piece of paper having relevance to the matters in dispute. There are, however, disadvantages of the documents-only method. For one thing, it has often been said, word-processors do not tell lies. That is to say, there is no chance for either side to examine and cross-examine witnesses who, invariably tend to manipulate the facts and often alter their approach to any particular matter under close cross-examination. Furthermore, the attended hearing approach to arbitration does give the parties, through their advocates, the opportunity to be seen and heard and whatever the outcome of the arbitrator's award, at least they will have had a sight and sound of the issues. In documents-only references they have none of that satisfaction, and a doubt may fester with the losing party as to whether the written words did actually convey the intended meaning.

Arbitrations on documents only are still within the ambit of the Arbitration Acts 1950 to 1979. The arbitrator still has the same powers as he would under a reference with a hearing, and he still has to publish an award which is final and binding on the parties.

The award

Following the conclusion of the hearing there is nothing further the expert can, or should, do until the arbitrator has published his award. Depending on the number of issues, this will generally take approximately one month. During this time the expert will undoubtedly be badgered by his client to know the outcome and to suggest the arbitrator is constantly encouraged to waste no further time. Naturally the expert should resist such temptation. Only if the time taken to publish the award is inordinately protracted should the expert even contemplate making contact with the arbitrator. When the arbitrator has completed his award, he will write simultaneously to both parties' representatives to notify them the award is published. Either party, upon payment of the costs of the award, may take up the award. The costs of the award are the fees of the arbitrator, and are quite separate from the costs incurred by the parties in the conduct of the reference which, not unnaturally, are known as the costs of the reference. If, in order to take up the award, the party to whom the arbitrator has awarded the costs of the award actually pays them, there will be a clause included in the award to the effect that the other party will reimburse the first. At the same time as the arbitrator sends his award to the party who pays his costs, he will simultaneously send a certified copy to the other party. Section 20 of the Arbitration Act 1950 provides that a sum directed to be paid by an award shall, unless the award directs otherwise, carry interest as and from the date of the award and at the same rate as a judgment debt.

Upon receipt of either the award, or a certified copy thereof, the expert will notify his client of the good, or not so good news. There remains to be concluded the matter of the costs of the reference. If the claimant has been successful on the claim, he will normally be awarded reimbursement of his costs; costs following the event. If the claimant has been successful on his claim, and the respondent successful on his counterclaim, both parties will be awarded reimbursement of their respective costs.

It should be noted it is not only the outright net winner who receives his costs (*Tramountana Armadora SA v Atlantic Shipping Co SA* [1978] 1 Lloyd's Rep 391 at 399). Where there is a claim and counterclaim on which each party has succeeded wholly or in part, the most usual form of order is that the claimant shall have the costs of the claim and the respondent shall have the costs of the counterclaim. But if the counterclaim is in substance only a defence to the claim, it is generally preferable to order that one or other or neither party should be awarded some or all or some proportion of the total costs of the reference.

Section 18(1) of the Arbitration Act 1950 provides that the costs of the reference and the award shall be at the discretion of the arbitrator who may direct to and by whom and in what manner such costs shall be paid. The arbitrator must deal with the question of costs in order for his award to be considered final and therefore binding. There will be occasions when it is appropriate for the arbitrator to make an interim award, dealing with the questions of liability and quantum, but deferring his decision as to costs until a later, final award. This happens most often when a sealed offer has been made earlier in the reference, and the party making the offer wishes to address the arbitrator on the subject of costs after the publication of the interim award so described above.

Section 18(1) of the 1950 Act further provides that the arbitrator may himself tax and settle the amount of costs to be paid in the event of the parties failing to agree between themselves upon the quantum of such costs. The alternative is the parties have the costs agreed by a taxing master in the High Court. This can be a laborious process, sometimes taking years. Furthermore, the parties really need to employ costs draftsmen, adding further cost and time, for it to be done properly. The parties should be able to agree costs between themselves, usually with a bit of negotiation. Many arbitrators now will agree to tax costs, and notify this in their award in the event the parties fail to agree. It is sensible that the arbitrator should tax and settle costs; he will know the detail of the reference, and will have a better idea than any other third person appointed by the parties of the amount of work and time which has been expended by them in bringing the reference to a conclusion.

The expert's first task will be to summarise all the items of costs. From the date notice to concur was served on the other party he will have anticipated such a task. All time spent by him in connection with the reference should have been logged, with a note of how such time was spent. Whilst diary notes are useful, they are generally insufficient to meet this requirement. He should anticipate the need for scrutiny by either the other side, or by the arbitrator if he has agreed to tax the costs, or failing which a taxing master. A good system which should satisfy the requirement is the use of a short pro forma time allocation, setting out the following:

(a) title of the arbitration;
(b) date of the time allocated;
(c) note of telephone calls, both in and out;
(d) note of meetings held and with whom?
(e) note of tasks undertaken;

each with as full a description as possible. If necessary these forms can be made available to the third party who conducts taxation, in the full knowledge they contain all the relevant information as to how the expert spent his time.

Initially the expert should summarise the time from these time pro formas into a bill of costs, together with any additional expenditure and disbursements to give a total of his client's costs in the reference. This should be submitted to the other party for either payment or comment. It would be unusual, but not unknown, for the other party to pay without questioning at least some part of the bill of costs, and a period of negotiation will probably ensue. If agreement is not reached either side will suggest taxation, either by the arbitrator or failing which, the High Court. In this event, the expert should carefully double check all his time records to make certain there is no duplication of time, or time recorded which was not absolutely necessary to the reference. His bill of costs and records will be forwarded to either the arbitrator, or to a costs draftsman prior to High Court taxation, as appropriate and all the expert can do is await the outcome.

Upon receipt of the award, the expert, or his client, may have reason to challenge either all or part of it. This can be a dangerous path to tread, and the expert must be absolutely certain of his ground before giving any advice to his client in its regard. It may be just a simple error by the arbitrator such as an incorrect reference to either or both parties, for example, calling the claimant the respondent, or vice versa. When this happens either the arbitrator may notice it himself, or upon notice by either party he is allowed to correct such errors under the slip rule in s 17 of the Arbitration Act 1950. Any more serious matter giving rise to the desire for the award to be either remitted to the arbitrator for reconsideration, or to be set aside, should not be considered without the expert and his client first consulting a lawyer. Such matters are really beyond the scope of this book, but the expert should consider in any event there can be no appeal to the High Court on any finding of fact on the face of an arbitrator's award, unless he is so wrong he could never be right and has been negligent in coming to his decision. In general terms the court will take the view that the parties have chosen for themselves the course of arbitration to decide and settle their dispute and have agreed beforehand that the arbitrator's award will be final. Unless therefore there are very strong grounds for upsetting that final award the expert should not embark on a course which will inevitably involve his client in further time and cost with perhaps no certain outcome in his favour.

Other forms of technical advocacy

In addition to acting as a technical advocate in arbitrations, the expert may also act in a similar manner in other tribunals of a lay nature. These may include acting for a party in a valuation tribunal, where the decision is to be taken for two parties by a third and where a valuation is required, but where there is no dispute. In this case the parties choose a person to provide a valuation for them, not to make a decision in a dispute. As such the tribunal is not governed by or subject to the Arbitration Acts 1950 to 1979.

Another source of lay advocacy in the construction industry occurs where an adjudicator is appointed. Under the latest provisions of the JCT Standard Form of Contract With Contractor's Design, 1981 Edition, Amendment 3, 1988 there is an optional adjudication provision contained therein. The ACA/BPF Form of Building Agreement also contains provision for the appointment of an adjudicator. But probably the most commonly used form of adjudication provision is contained in the BEC/FASS and JCT Standard Forms of Sub-Contract conditions. In these forms the adjudicator should be agreed at the time of execution of the agreement. He is appointed to act when the sub-contractor does not agree with the main contractor's right to set-off alleged loss and/or expense from moneys due and owing under the sub-contract, and/or the quantum of such loss and/or expense. In each of these examples of adjudication they are not arbitration references and as such are not governed by the Arbitration Acts 1950 to 1979. However, the money and costs involved may be considerable. When faced with the requirement for adjudication, parties often employ an expert conversant with construction contracts to present their case. Most forms of adjudication, certainly those connected with the procedure for set-off under the respective forms of sub-contract, are completed on written representations, and there is no opportunity for the expert to make an oral submission. Nevertheless, it does involve making written statements with supporting calculations and the expert must be sufficiently conversant with the contract, or sub-contract, conditions to be able to provide an efficient and cheap service. In this respect, there is no award as such. The adjudicator merely advises whom shall pay whom and his costs, in the case of the standard forms of sub-contract, are borne by the sub-contractor subject to a later decision of an arbitrator. The ACA/BPF form is silent as to the costs of the adjudicator; the optional adjudication provisions in the JCT CD81 contract for use with contractor's design requires the parties to share the costs of the adjudicator in equal proportions.

CONCLUSION

This chapter outlines the role of the expert as a technical advocate in a generally straightforward arbitration reference. Few arbitrations are conducted in such textbook fashion and, perhaps by the very fact that the parties have reached a dispute arising from a construction contract, they are unlikely to assist each other in all cases to reach a speedy conclusion to their differences, particularly if it may be prejudicial to their respective case to do so. There are many examples of delaying tactics and there are a number of ways in which either party may protect themselves from such tactics during the course of the reference. Some of these have been anticipated and described in the body of this chapter. There will be others and the expert is advised to observe the early signs and if he thinks he cannot cope with the matter himself, advise his client accordingly and seek immediate assistance from a lawyer. As long as the lawyer is made aware the expert has the conduct of the reference and legal assistance is required only to overcome a procedural point within that reference, together with if appropriate, a watching brief, it is unlikely that the lawyer will seek to take the matter out of the hands of the expert against his, or his client's will. As was outlined at the start of the chapter, the expert may find himself surrounded by lawyers acting for the other side. In such event he should feel neither intimidation nor should he seek humility. He is there to act in the best interests of his client and providing the dispute turns on matters of fact, rather than law, his knowledge and experience will provide him with the necessary qualifications needed.

However, this alone will probably not be sufficient. The expert will need to gain experience in arbitration procedure. This may come from a variety of sources. His firm may involve itself in the business of arbitration, in which eventually he will come across terms and procedures almost as a matter of course. He may be encouraged to assist and be involved with his colleagues, perhaps learning the technique of the hearing from note-taking for a leader. If this is not available, he can obtain much valuable knowledge from the examination structure of the Chartered Institute of Arbitrators. This will obviously give him the dual advantage of the opportunity to qualify as an arbitrator under their scheme, and to learn the procedure. Visits to the local courts will also give valuable insight into good advocacy.

Above all, he will need to gain experience in structuring a case, sometimes from the barest of information. Parties to arbitration invariably, but not always, have appallingly bad records and files. He must learn therefore to build up a case from scraps of information, often relying on oral evidence in its support. He must also be able to conduct a contractual analysis from the information presented to him from which to construct his basic claim and argument. Above all he must be presentable, confident and honest. All these are qualities which will assist him in his conduct, and about which further comment in a book of this nature is unnecessary.

Throughout the text the male gender has been used. There is nothing significant in this, and it has been done both for ease and consistency. There is nothing inherently masculine about the nature of the work of the expert as technical advocate. Although it is usually carried out by men, because they form the predominant gender in the construction industry, it may just as easily be conducted by women.

APPENDIX 1: ARBITRATION PROGRAMME

		Year																																		
		Month																																		
		W/e																																		
EVENT	Staff																																			
Appoint arbitrator																																				
Preliminary meeting																																				
Points of claim																																				
F & B P of P C																																				
Defence & CC																																				
F & B P of D CC																																				
Reply																																				
Listing docs. for discovery																																				
Exchange and Inspection																																				
Prep. of legal case																																				
Expert witness reports																																				
Statements from witnesses																																				
Prep. case for hearing																																				
Hearing																																				

Note: There should be 52 columns for the year

APPENDIX 2: NOTICE OF ARBITRATION

Our Ref:
Your Ref:

9th April 1988

Name & Address of other party
[Employer]

Dear Sirs,

Title of Contract

We (I) act for [name of contractor] with whom you are in contract on the above named project.

As you are aware, the Conditions of Contract provide for a number of obligations to be observed by the architect named therein. Our (my) clients claim an entitlement to the following:

1) an extension of time to the date for completion; and
2) repayment by yourselves of liquidated and ascertained damages, consequent upon (1) above; and
3) ascertainment and reimbursement of direct loss and/or expense incurred as a result of delay and disruption to the regular progress of the works.

At the date hereof the architect has refused to make any further consideration of any of the matters outlined above.

A dispute exists therefore, and pursuant to the arbitration agreement in the contract, and with our (my) clients' full authority we (I) write to request that you concur in the appointment of an arbitrator to whom the dispute can be referred for his final decision.

We (I) suggest:

First name, address and qualifications
or,
Second name, address and qualifications,
or,
Third name, address and qualifications,

as suitable arbitrators. We (I) shall of course be pleased to consider any names you may care to suggest as alternatives. We (I) remind you that if the parties do not agree upon an arbitrator within 14 days of the date hereof, we (I) may make application to the President or a Vice-President of [name of the third party nominating body named in the contract] to make such an appointment.

Yours faithfully,

[signed by expert]

(a copy may be sent to the architect [or engineer as appropriate] named in the contract)

CHAPTER 5

View from counsel

Anthony Thornton QC, Assistant Recorder, MA, BCL (Oxon)
Anthony Speaight MA (Oxon), Barrister

In no field of work currently being litigated in the High Court does the expert witness play a more important role than in cases heard before official referees. In Official Referees' business experts are called in almost every case. In many cases each side will call three or four experts. Furthermore, the evidence of these experts will normally go to the very heart of what is in issue between the parties, both as to liability and as to quantum. One exception is perhaps the rare case in which the issue is confined to the interpretation of a contractual document. But most construction disputes revolve around the existence or otherwise of defects in a building or of the liability of different parties for such defects or complicated calculations of measurement of payment owing or costs for delay: it is hard to imagine a court resolving such issues without assistance from a relevant expert.

The position is different in other fields of work. For example, whilst there are many similarities between litigation in the official referees' corridor and the Commercial Court, one of the differences is that experts are by no means a standard feature of Commercial Court trials. In the Chancery Division experts are probably even less of a regular feature. In criminal trials experts are quite common: one will have scenes of police officers producing particles found at the scene, and Home Office chemists commenting on them; fingerprint experts in burglary cases, pathologists in murder cases, and police surgeons in drink drivings. But it is rare indeed for the entire prosecution case in a criminal trial to depend on forensic scientists: more typically, the expert evidence will form a small, and uncontroverted part of the Crown's case. One has to turn to personal injury to find another field in which expert evidence is essential. But even here the role of the expert is far less central than in construction cases. Although one must always have a medical report to support quantum in a personal injury case, these reports are agreed in most such actions: and it is unusual for a doctor to see counsel in conference before such a trial. Moreover, the medical evidence does not play any part in the question whether liability for the accident is established, and governs only the general damages part of the quantum. Experts on factory safety are, indeed, a regular feature in accident at work cases, but if the injury was sustained, as is so often the case, in a road accident, the judge will not need an expert to help him decide which driver was to blame.

So when one asks how barristers view experts, the answer received from the construction bar will have a different emphasis from that which might be given by barristers in general. In construction cases an expert is quite simply an indispensable member of the team. A barrister can no more mount or defend such a case without an expert, or maybe several, than he could without a solicitor to instruct him or a lay client to act for.

For this reason barristers take a great interest in who the experts in a construction case are. Most barristers keep or have access to records on expert witnesses. Some barristers keep their own personal file. In other cases barristers pool information into a chambers directory. It will contain comments like 'does good reports for plaintiffs' or 'pathetically weak in the box'. In some cases the comments will be of an even more confidential nature, such as 'watch out: not straight' or 'this man's evidence has been rejected so many times one wonders why anyone still calls him'. No document in a set of barristers' chambers is more carefully guarded: barristers outside the chambers are most unlikely to be allowed to see it: its very existence may be denied. But whenever a solicitor asks a barrister if he has any views on who might be an appropriate expert in some field, the reply is likely to be enthusiastic and positive. Most barristers regret that their pool of knowledge on experts is not more often tapped by solicitors, especially those solicitors with little experience in a particular field. For if one goes into battle with a poor expert the case is already gravely weakened.

What, then, is it that a barrister is looking for in an expert? And what will earn a favourable notice in the confidential file? It is to answering those questions that the bulk of this chapter is directed. We shall endeavour to provide a few basic ground rules. We do not promise that we can turn a High Street architect into an experienced expert. But we do believe that most professional men, who are skilled in their own particular discipline, but inexperienced in litigation or arbitration, should by absorbing our principles become competent and useful experts in construction disputes. We hope, too, that a number of our suggestions will be of interest to solicitors, especially those inexperienced in this field of work.

Judges, however, are *not* intended to read this chapter. If any official referee or other member of Her Majesty's judiciary should chance to let the book fall open at this page, and if, despite the last sentence, the learned judge's eye runs on down the text, then we must ask for the application of that exercise of judicial facility, so incomprehensible to the outsider, but so natural to the bench—putting something completely out of your mind. Read on if you must, but do so strictly 'de bene'. The next time we appear before you, we shall deny all knowledge of anything that here is said.

This chapter is largely written in the language of litigation. Almost everything we say is just as true for arbitration. But it would be tedious to keep on saying 'judge or arbitrator', 'statement of claim or points of claim', 'plaintiff or claimant' and so on. So we shall be speaking in litigation vocabulary.

So far as the barrister is concerned there are two main phases for the expert. The first may be called the pleadings and report phase. The second is actually giving evidence at trial. The first phase is mostly concerned with drafting documents—either the experts' own report, or pleadings drafted by counsel with the expert's help. The second phase, by contrast, involves the expert entering upon the public stage by going into the witness box. Some experts are excellent at one phase and weak in the other. For the talents and skills required for paperwork may not co-exist with an impressive demeanour under cross-examination.

THE PLEADINGS AND REPORT PHASE

Rule 1: bring together barrister and expert as early as possible

How soon should the involvement of an expert begin in a construction case? The answer is that it cannot begin too early. In the case of a prospective plaintiff the ideal course is for the barrister and expert to be brought together before the statement of claim is drafted. Often a satisfactory course is to hold a conference on site. Since the plaintiff owns the building in which it is believed that defects exist, access is often readily arranged. This procedure has a second advantage in giving the barrister at an early stage the opportunity himself to see the subject matter of the dispute: such a view of what lawyers call the 'locus in quo' almost always proves helpful to the barrister. If the barrister and expert are at the 'locus' together the expert can point out the details which are relevant to the issues: he will probably find it easier that way to explain the technical matters.

The task at a plaintiff's conference before proceedings is in the first place to decide whether the case should be commenced at all. If there are weaknesses in the case it is far better that that should come to light now, before heavy legal expenses are incurred. On the other hand, if the decision is to proceed with a claim, it will strengthen the plaintiff's hand if his pleadings from the outset reflect the case which he actually presents at trial. If the statement of claim is flimsy in detailed allegations, it will create a poor impression on the defendants. They will feel that they are against amateurs and that they have a good chance of defeating the claim: the plaintiff will have handed them the psychological advantage. Whereas if the statement of claim is fully pleaded and is served to the accompaniment of schedules setting out all material details in a manner which demonstrates both thought and hard work, it is the plaintiffs who will have the psychological advantage in the early rounds. The defendants will then know that they are up against opponents who are well prepared and probably determined.

An even worse scenario than the flimsy statement of claim which has to be fleshed out as the case goes along is the statement of claim which has to be seriously altered. *Kelly v Norwich Union* [1989] 2 AER 889 was a case in which a householder sued an insurance company on a home policy alleging that his house was subsiding. On the second day of the trial, having overnight received new advice from the expert, counsel for the plaintiff applied to amend his pleadings to allege that the house was suffering from heave: that is the phenomenon when a swelling clay sub-soil moves a house upwards whereas subsidence occurs when a shrinking clay sub-soil permits a building to descend. The defendants lost little time in saying that the plaintiff's case had been turned on its head. The new advice from the expert in that case was the direct result of completely fresh information coming to him by chance on the previous day, and even the best preparation cannot prevent the unexpected turning up. But this is a vivid illustration of the type of change of tack which it is better for a plaintiff not to have to make.

There is, of course, almost always some technical report placed before counsel when settling an initial pleading. Where things so often go wrong is that this initial report is from someone other than the expert who at a later stage is instructed to turn up at the trial. Sometimes the initial report comes from an employee on the staff of the plaintiffs: such a person may be, say, a qualified surveyor but without any previous experience of consultancy, still less litigation, work. It may well seem a commercially sensible decision to use the employee's report at the outset to save the costs of a top expert unless or until it proves really necessary to incur them. Another common reason for a second expert coming in is the following course of events: the first expert is the person engaged to supervise remedial works before a claim is envisaged; then when the proceedings are underway this expert's remedy is attacked by the defendants as unnecessary or wholly mistaken; so the plaintiff goes to a top consultant for a completely independent view. It may be that the second, independent consultant wholly backs up the first expert's opinion. In that case all is well. But not infrequently the new expert has a somewhat different approach: he may point out fundamental failures by the defendants which have not yet been alleged. By this stage it may be altogether too late to introduce the new allegation; but, even if it is not too late, costs will have been wasted and the momentum of the plaintiff's case will be damaged. Time and again we have found ourselves lamenting that we did not have at the outset of a case a first-class report which arrives when the case is well advanced. In individual cases the course which events take is often completely understandable. But without doubt the general principle is: at as early a stage as possible bring together the barrister and the expert who will shoulder the giving of evidence at the trial.

Rule 2: the expert must be constantly at hand

In construction cases pleadings and expert evidence interrelate. In any professional negligence claim, the heart of the plaintiff's pleading will be the particulars of negligence. If it is a rather complex or technical case, they may be transferred from the statement of claim to a separate schedule: but the principle is the same. It is one of the few rules of pleading set out in the *Supreme Court Practice*:

> 'Particulars must always be given in the pleading, showing in what respects the defendant was negligent.'
>
> (18/12/24)

This part of the pleading is one which the barrister cannot draft without guidance from the expert. It would not be professionally proper for a barrister to do so, for the Code of Conduct for the Bar states:

> 'A barrister instructed to settle a pleading is under responsibilities to the court as well as to his client. He may not make an allegation unsupported by his instructions.'

Nor without such guidance could a barrister in any event set out the details of professional negligence.

It is often very desirable for the expert to read counsel's draft statement of claim or schedule entries before they are served and to supply comments on them. Such comments should not be limited to the correction of straight errors. Any suggestion should be made which will contribute to the pleading clearly and comprehensively setting out the case. It makes for an impressive pleading if the more serious or central allegations appear before minor or peripheral ones: so it is useful if an expert will propose a more logical order if counsel has put something peripheral at the head of the particulars of negligence.

It is every bit as important that an expert should be closely involved in the drafting of a defence. It is true that a defendant does not bear the plaintiff's obligation to prove a case. If he wishes, a defendant can enter a bare denial. But in the modern climate of full pre-trial disclosure there are fewer and fewer defendants who consider this to be the tactically desirable course. A judge reading a bare denial defence is likely to conclude that the defendant has no good case to advance. And, indeed, the plaintiff upon whom such a defence is served will conclude that his adversary has little ammunition in his locker: this will give the plaintiff a crucial psychological advantage just as much as the flimsy statement of claim gives that advantage to the defendant. So the wise defendant will wish to plead in detail to the plaintiff's allegations as soon as possible. Even if he does not do so in the first instance, it may not be long before the judge orders him to plead to a schedule. Insufficient attention has in the past been paid to Order 18, rule 8(1) of the Rules of the Supreme Court ('RSC'), the effect of which is that a defendant who proposes to raise an affirmative case must plead it. So the wise solicitor acting for a defendant will give counsel as much assistance as possible from an expert in the drafting of the defence. Time can be a constraint. The Rules stipulate a time period of 14 days (RSC Order 18, rule 2), and although extensions of four to six weeks are readily obtainable, the time available may not be sufficient to instruct an expert from scratch and obtain his mature conclusions. Increasingly, insurers who are notified of building claims commission full expert reports when the claim is notified so that there is the material to hand to plead a proper defence if the claimant launches proceedings.

If the defence sets out the defendant's case on technical matters in detail, it will generally be wise for the plaintiff to obtain his expert's comments on the defence as soon as possible and supply them to the barrister, or arrange a conference to discuss them, so that the barrister can consider whether a reply will be of tactical assistance. Views vary on the tactical wisdom of pleading replies in situations where it is not obligatory to do so. All that can be said in general terms is that in the present climate of judicial thinking, which so strongly favours parties setting out their case in writing, there are an increasing number of occasions when the barrister may incline to plead some reply. Even if he does not, the time spent studying the defence with the expert is not time wasted. The stage will now be approaching when the expert must produce the version of his report which is to be disclosed to the other side. A careful analysis of the pleaded issues will assist the expert to decide on what to focus when he prepares this report. It may be worth emphasising that experts cannot be expected to give the guidance for which they are asked if they are not given the necessary background materials to read: a selection of these documents will vary from case to case, but in almost any situation will include all the pleadings. Experts need to do a good deal of 'homework', but it is the responsibility of the legal team to ensure that they receive the documents which will brief them on the nature of the case.

After the initial pleadings the next stage is normally further and better particulars. Some people consider current practices in this respect unsatisfactory. At present judges tend to give an order in support of almost any request for further particularisation of pleadings. It is almost invariably tactically advantageous to raise as many requests as one can think of against the other side. That is so for two reasons. The first is purely negative: it is a confounded nuisance answering these requests, so one is inclined to put the other side to as much trouble as possible. The second is more positive: it is beneficial to tie the hands of one's opponent. The consequence is that much time and cost is taken up in producing pleadings running to many pages which are totally indigestible. A better regime might be to refuse such requests in most circumstances but at the same time to apply strictly the rules debarring parties from advancing cases which had not been pleaded. Then it would be in the interests of parties themselves to ensure that their case was fully pleaded; and if they added detail later it would come into the main pleading in the form of an amended draft, with the beneficial result that everything would be in one document.

However, so long as the present practice of further and better particulars remains, practitioners will exploit it and experts should play their part in doing so. They can do this at both stages. The first stage is the drafting of the request. In practice it is rare for experts to give ideas at this stage. But we believe it can be valuable for experts to do so and sometimes have asked experts in conference if they have any suggestions. Occasionally, an expert will spot a curious phrasing of an allegation and be able to make a suggestion as to a valuable way of clarifying the pleaded case one has to meet. The second stage is answering the request: here the role of the expert is indispensable. All too often it is not until now that a party sets out the proper detail of his allegations of workmanship defects, professional negligence or the like. If the further and better particulars contain a large amount of technical material it can be especially valuable if the expert checks the draft before it is served.

Some cases do not proceed in the conventional way to a full trial because the plaintiff believes that the defendant has no good defence. In building and engineering cases this normally arises when the plaintiff is a contractor suing on a certificate for payment. In such a situation the plaintiff will apply for summary judgment under Order 14 or for an interim payment under Order 29. If the defendant wishes to defend the claim he must put in a full affidavit setting out his defence. If the defence consists of a set-off of a counterclaim for defects, then the defendant will do well to secure the support of an expert. The defendant may exhibit an expert report, or, better, file an affidavit from the expert. Here, then, is yet another situation in which the input from an expert will provide the very heart of the material with which the barrister is concerned at an interlocutory stage.

By this stage it will be becoming apparent to any consultant reading this chapter that a heavy workload is involved in the task of acting as an expert witness. If a professional man is unable to devote to a case the time which will be required, it is better that he should not accept the instructions to act as an expert in the first place. Many litigants have suffered because their expert was unable to devote the time month after month to deal with the repeated requests from the lawyers for comments on one document after another. It is far, far better that a professional man should at the outset decline to act in the capacity of a litigation expert than half way through the case by reason of his pressure of other work let down a client for whom, perhaps, professional reputation as well as much of his worldly wealth is at stake.

Rule 3: experts should aim above all for clarity and should start from readily comprehensible principles

During the course of a case an expert will probably be asked to write several reports or several versions of the same report. An early version, supplemented perhaps by explanations in conference, will form the basis of the pleaded case. A later version will be disclosed to the other side and read by the judge. Those experts who produce first-class reports are a priceless asset to the party employing them.

It should be emphasised at the outset that reports for litigation purposes must deal with matters which technical experts may not be accustomed to dealing with: in their normal work they may write reports advising what remedial works are required, whereas in litigation the court will very often be concerned to discover not merely what works need to be done, but who was responsible and why are these works now being required. The absence of any discussion of 'liability' aspects is one of the most common shortcomings of reports written by experts who are inexperienced in the requirements of litigation reports. The ingredients of a good litigation report will be discussed at some length in this chapter.

The judge may well read the experts' reports before he comes into court on the first morning of the case. If that occurs, the party whose reports impress the judge most will have secured an invaluable early advantage. The hard truth is that judges are swayed by first impressions just like anybody else. Indeed, although judges do not complete making up their minds until the end of all the argument, they will begin to form assessments at a very early stage. An American judge visiting London was heard in Middle Temple Hall one lunch time to explain: 'Of course, I make up my mind in advance: otherwise how could I know which parts of the evidence to take a note of?' Needless to say English judges are very different. But one official referee recently told a London audience: 'Judges like to keep ahead of the barristers in a trial'. Even if the judge has not read the reports before the start of the case he will certainly read them at an early stage.

This is all part of the mysterious process of 'getting the judge's ear'. Barristers find from experience that in some cases everything they say seems to slip down like well matured port. Other days one can say nothing right and one's opponent appears to have an invisible hot-line to the bench. Few objectives are as prominent in a barrister's mind in preparing a case than to get on the judge's wavelength. To achieve this objective, attention will be paid to a whole range of tactics: from noting individual quirks, such as which series of law reports a particular judge may like to have cited to him, to major decisions like abandoning a weak head of claim. None, however, is more important than ensuring that the paperwork placed under a judge's nose to read presents the case in an attractive way. Whereas traditionally a barrister would have sought to secure a favourable first impression by the manner in which he summarised his expert's evidence in his opening speech, today, with so much of any civil action, and most particularly official referee actions, set out on paper, the good or bad first impressions will be made by the expert's own words in the report he has written.

Because the other side are aware of all this, a first-class report will have a major impact on the atmosphere of a case as soon as it is served on them. What we said about good pleadings and gaining the psychological advantage again applies here.

What then makes a first-class report? Naturally one will hope that the expert's conclusions will be strongly favourable to the client. But whether they are or not depends on the technical issues in the case. Nothing written in this chapter can affect that. What this chapter does seek to give guidance on is the manner of presentation. Perhaps few experts realise what a range there is between the most cogent reports one sees in the course of litigation and the most incomprehensible.

What, then, are the qualities of presentation to which an expert should aspire in drafting his reports? The foremost quality is: clarity.

Most building and engineering cases concern subject-matter which is potentially complicated for one or both of two reasons. The first potential reason is that the subject-matter is very extensive. Typically this is so when there are a large number of defects in a building case. A claim relating to a single dwelling house may easily produce a schedule with over one hundred different defects—and that is amongst the simplest kind of building case. In practice one may be dealing with an entire housing estate constructed for a housing association or local authority with dozens of different defects in each of many units of accommodation.

In such a situation the expert reports are bound to be long and complicated. Nevertheless our experience is that there are some experts who are capable of producing reports so logically ordered that despite their scale such cases never get out of hand. Other experts, though of great competence in their field, produce volumes of data, which can be so dense and tangled that it can take a barrister literally several days of analysing them before he begins to see what the main areas of defect really are.

The second potential reason why the subject-matter may be complicated is that, even if it concerns only a single item, it is highly technical. Whenever this is so, it is desirable that the expert's report should be addressed with a lay reader in mind. An obvious example of a type of case where this is appropriate is air conditioning. With a range of different kinds of air conditioning in use, the workings of none of which are readily understood by laymen, a good report in an air conditioning case should begin by explaining the principles on which the system in question operates. Another example of technically complicated subject-matter is the case which concerns structural calculations. It is true that there are one or two barristers practising at the construction bar who are also qualified in a profession relevant to the construction industry. Such rare birds may already have a complete grasp of the technical background to a case. But the typical barrister, even if he had been regularly handling construction cases for a number of years, will welcome an expert report which addresses itself to the lay reader for at least two reasons.

The first is that he is aware, if he is wise, that his own little technical knowledge, picked up in earlier cases, may be a dangerous thing. He may, for example, have a reasonable grasp from a case he did last year of the application of holding down straps for securing light roofs; but if he undertakes a fresh case in which a roof blew away on the assumption that the design will be based on the same approach he may go seriously wrong should the new case concern, say, purlins at eaves level secured into reinforced concrete piers.

The second reason is that even if the barrister does not need such explanation, the judge may do so. What, it may be asked, is the purpose of having specialist official referees if they do not understand basic principles of construction? The short answer is that, although the official referees who have been sitting for a number of years have an impressive knowledge of the technical side of construction work, one has no guarantee who will end up trying the case. With the present pressure of business before official referees there are often three or four deputies sitting. In some cases these will be circuit judges or Queen's counsel whose professional experience has been in fields other than construction. Furthermore even an experienced official referee cannot be expected to be familiar with all the technical fields which play a part in the increasingly complicated processes of modern building and engineering. So the safer course is always to assume that the reader of an expert report will be a layman.

One of the authors recalls a striking illustration of the difference between clear exposition from an expert and the absence of it. It was, again, an air conditioning case. The system's performance was unimpressive, but there were inevitably a range of theories as to who might be to blame and why. Junior counsel had over quite a period of time churned out only half-understood pleadings, schedules and further and better particulars concerning chillers and valves, baffle plates and nozzles. These drafts had been based on hundreds of pages of expert report describing defects supplemented by some discussion in conference. Then leading counsel was brought in. The silk had had many years' experience in which he had handled many building cases. His first move was to order a seminar to instruct him on the principles of the system; he announced that before anyone tried to brief him about the things which might or might not be wrong he needed to be taught how the system was supposed to operate if everything was right. The seminar lasted about four hours. Visual aids in the form of vast charts had been prepared and were produced to illustrate the instruction. The education started with the simplest first principles. But by the time it was over the defects and counter-allegations, which for months had been in such a fog, seemed entirely straightforward. The wisdom of this silk lay in his humility. He did not posture as having 'a rough grasp' of highly technical matters in which he was not qualified. Going back to first principles was the key which led to the true strengths and weaknesses in that case being for the first time clearly perceived. The lesson can be regularly applied in technically complicated cases: the expert should explain how a system is intended to operate before setting out what is wrong with it.

Since this chapter is intended to be of use to experts as a 'nuts and bolts' guide, we hope it will assist to make some practical suggestions of techniques by which experts can improve the clarity of their reports, at the same time as discussing the format which these reports should take.

Rule 4: develop a report in the format required for a trial

Reports disclosed in litigation today are more than merely technical reports of a consultant. They are intended to form part of the evidence in a case. The Rules were set out in chapter 2. Order 38, rule 38 speaks of a report containing 'the substance of any expert evidence'. Whatever the Rules Committee may have had in mind in 1974 when this rule was introduced, an official referee today is likely to regard 'the substance' of an expert's evidence as meaning the whole of the expert's evidence. Additional comments by way of evidence in chief may be permitted if something unexpected arises after the report was written. But a party would be presumptuous and unwise if he thought that he could treat his expert report as a mere summary to be developed in the witness box.

The proposition that an expert's report is also to be his evidence in chief is not without its difficulties. Traditionally evidence in chief has been led by counsel. It was their job to know what to ask and in what order to do so. Working this out was part of getting up a brief for trial. Until very recently it was regarded as improper for a barrister to play any direct role in drafting an expert's proof. That view was based on certain comments made by Lord Denning and Lord Wilberforce in *Whitehouse v Jordan* [1980] 1 All ER 650, CA and [1981] 1 All ER 267, [1981] 1 WLR 246, HL. That was a medical negligence case and the remarks were made in a very different context. This situation was potentially thoroughly unfair: one party in a case might have an expert who was very familiar with litigation, whilst the other might have an expert who had never been involved in litigation before and simply had no idea of what was needed to be included to constitute evidence in chief. In such a situation the party with the inexperienced expert was denied the assistance of counsel in adducing evidence in chief from a crucial witness. Happily, this problem has now been resolved. In March 1988 the Bar Council amended the Code of Conduct by adopting a new rule in these terms:

> 'In a civil case a barrister may settle . . . the report of an expert witness which is to be disclosed to another party.'

It is worth noting that, at the same time, the Code of Conduct was amended to permit a barrister to settle the written statement of a witness of fact which was to be served on another party pursuant to a direction of the court.

However, it is not anticipated that it will become normal practice for barristers to draft expert reports. It would certainly add to the cost of litigation if that were to become the practice. The barrister will be available to give as much help as may be necessary. But one hopes that in general the expert will be able to draft at least the majority of the report himself. The suggestions which follow are intended to help the inexperienced in doing so.

Firstly, it is better if the report is written in the first person singular by John Know-all than a document published in the plural by Know-all and Partners. When evidence is given in court it is given by human beings who enter the witness box one at a time. Mr Know-all may well have been assisted in his work by several other people. If it is a foundation case, for example, there will have been labourers to dig trial pits, underlings to note and measure every crack in the building, and chemists in laboratories to analyse soil samples. Preferably Mr Know-all, the consulting engineer, will indicate exactly what has been done by himself and what by others, though in fact reports rarely make that clear. In theory the other side could insist on the others coming to court, but in practice that scarcely ever happens.

Secondly, the report should give the qualifications and experience of the witness. Here all modesty must be cast aside. The other side's expert will crack himself up to be the top man. So do not allow yourself to be outdone. Some regular expert witnesses have up to a couple of pages on a word processor describing their experience and listing obscure articles. Establishing relevant qualifications and experience is more than a bit of window dressing: it is an essential part of the expert's evidence, since, as explained in chapter 2, a witness cannot start expressing opinions until the ground has been laid by proving that he is an expert in the particular field.

Thirdly, there is a good deal to be said for a witness setting out at an early stage of his report the information on which it is based. This can be done by listing the categories of documents read, stating the date on which the expert was instructed, and saying whether, and, if so, when, a site visit has been made. An area of some difficulty can sometimes be what to state about instructions from the lay client. It has been known for experts to write a report saying they have read the client's proof of evidence and for the other side to say that privilege in the proof is thereby waived. That is almost certainly a bad point in law. And, even if a good point, it will not cause any worry in an official referee case in which the proofs of evidence are to be disclosed later in any event. But it is obviously unsatisfactory if an expert says that he is basing his conclusion on the lay client's instructions and does not summarise those instructions. So, if the relevant contentions of fact are not apparent from the pleadings (which should always be one of the categories of documents read by the expert) the best course is probably to summarise the facts instructed.

Fourthly, as a self-discipline as well as for the assistance of the reader there is something to be said for setting out the issues with which the expert proposes to deal. The relevant issues will be those emerging from the pleadings.

Now comes the body of the report. Its format will vary depending on the case. We repeat our suggestion that if the subject-matter is of any technical complexity, the expert should first set out the principles upon which it is supposed to work. With a view to enhancing clarity we offer the following suggestions:

Photographs

(1) Provide a photograph of the building or engineering work in question. Even if the case is concerned with such hidden-from-view items as plumbing or electric wiring, it will help the barrister and judge or arbitrator coming fresh to the case to see a photograph of the outside of the building. It helps to set the scene. One gets an impression of the age and quality of the structure. It gives a feel of the standard of electrical installation or radiators which one might expect.

(2) Provide photographs of the areas manifesting defects. This sounds obvious, but in many cases it does not happen. If there is any possibility of remedial works being carried out before a hearing, photographs of the defects may assume considerable evidential importance.

(3) Give every photograph a number, that is to say a unique number. If the plaintiff calls his first photograph 'P1', his second photograph 'P2', and so on each photograph can thereafter immediately be identified by number. This also sounds obvious but is virtually never done. In

practice one finds that there are sheets with three or four photographs mounted on them, the sheet having a number but the individual photographs not. Or one finds that the early numbers '1, 2, 3, 4' have been used several times over so that 'photograph 3' can mean several quite different pictures.

(4) Mark each photograph with the date on which it was taken and the name of the person who took it. When the photograph is taken, no one may imagine that the appearance will change. But over the years which may elapse before a hearing there may be some change: then it could become crucial to establish the date when the photograph was taken. Assume, too, that every photograph will have to be strictly proved. That requires the photographer to go into the witness box. Of course, in 99 cases out of 100 the photographs will be agreed. But you can never tell in advance which will be the 100th case, and if no record has been kept of who took a photograph proving it may become impossible.

(5) Supply a plan on which is marked the position of the photographer for each photograph and the direction in which he was looking. This is very much easier if each has its unique number. One can put that inside a circle with an arrow indicating direction.

(6) Supply sufficient copies so that every copy of the report contains original photographs and not photocopies.

British Standards, Codes of Practice etc

One of the most satisfactory ways of establishing an allegation of design or workmanship negligence is to demonstrate a departure from a standard document. The documents which are normally relevant for this purpose are: Building Regulations or as the case may be by-laws, British Standards, Codes of Practice, Building Research Establishment publications and manufacturers' instructions. Always consider whether a complaint can be supported by reference to such a document. If it can be, produce in an appendix the relevant page of the publication. Bring the whole document to court with you for the trial, but there is no need to photocopy more than the relevant extract for the report. What is unhelpful, though very common, is a vague statement in a report like 'This contravenes IEE regulations'.

Plan and drawings

Many building defects can be understood by a layman only with the assistance of plans or drawings. An example is water penetration to the inside of a building. The criticism will doubtless relate to a detail of a roof window or the like. It is very difficult to explain the channel by which water is finding its way without a large-scale drawing. A useful method of presentation is to use numbered arrows to point to features on such a drawing and on the facing page to set out comments by each number.

In a clay heave foundations case photo-transparencies can be very useful to demonstrate by superimposition the location of former vegetation, ascertained perhaps from aerial photographs or ordnance survey maps, in relation to the buildings.

Schedules and cross-referencing

Judges love schedules. Draft as many as possible. If part of the evidence relates to costings, figures should be given in respect of each individual pleaded defect. This may involve an artificial exercise of breaking down costs, and, if you think that, by all means say so. But do nevertheless give a separate figure by each item. The reason is that the judge may find one way on one item and another way on a different item; and one cannot know in advance which items of defect will end up in which column.

Cross-referencing can be very helpful in the factually complex case, such as allegations of defects in many different houses on the same estate.

Rule 5: beware the 'without prejudice' meeting[1]

A recent innovation in English civil procedure is a court direction that experts meet 'without prejudice' to narrow issues and agree facts. Subsequent to the meeting the experts will very possibly be required to produce a list of matters which are agreed and matters in dispute. This innovation, like so many others, was pioneered by the official referees.

The use of the expression 'without prejudice' is potentially misleading. There is little in common with the 'without prejudice' letter, which contains an offer of settlement without prejudice to a denial of liability being maintained. The explanation for the use of the expression is that what is said will not be as such admitted in evidence at trial, just as the 'without prejudice' letter will not be read by the judge. In other words, it means 'off the record'. But the outcome of the meeting is very much on the record.

Our advice is: approach these meetings with the utmost circumspection. It sounds like a cosy chat. With everything said 'off the record', what can be the danger? In fact, the pitfalls are deadly.

Firstly, realise that, although what you say at such a meeting will not be 'taken down and given in evidence against you', it will in all probability be taken down. That is to say, it may very well be reported by your opposite number to the lawyers on the other side. So if an expert casually mentions at such a meeting that he does not consider, say, his wall ties complaints to be particularly strong, it should come as no surprise to him if in cross-examination the barrister for the other side looks him straight in the eye and says, 'I do not suppose, Mr Know-all, that you would pretend that your wall tie complaints are exactly the strongest part of your case?' The barrister will know that he has you on the run, . . . and you will be.

Secondly, do not 'agree' anything. Explain your opinion. If your opposite number says he holds the same opinion, well and good. You can write down your opinion on the point, and if your opposite number still accepts the words when they are in black and white, you can send this to the lawyers as something 'agreed'. But this is not the moment for 'give and take'. If your view is that remedial works will cost, say £10,000, you stick at that figure. If your opposite number says he thinks that they will cost £20,000, do not 'agree' that they will cost £15,000. Leave that type of agreement, that is to say partial compromises, to the lawyers: you have no authority to enter into them. Of course, if your opposite number points out to you something you had overlooked which leads you to alter your opinion, that is quite a different matter. In that case you certainly do not want to delay the revelation until you are being cross-examined at the trial: you will not be thanked if you change your story in the witness box. But on the other hand, do not be too hasty to concede that your initial view should be altered. We would suggest that if you do feel in such a meeting that you

1 See pp 75–76, supra

may need to modify an opinion, you simply say to your opposite number that you will think about the point and will let him know subsequently. That way you avoid the risk of being talked into a concession which you may later regret.

On no account assent to any proposition which is other than a matter of professional opinion within your own field. Enormous difficulties have been created recently for litigants by their experts purporting to agree matters of fact, upon which there might be conflicting evidence. What status do such agreements have? On one view they bind no one other than the expert. On another view, however, such agreements constitute an agreement binding on the lay client, since they are entered into by someone who is his authorised agent within the scope of that agent's authority. In *Richard Robert Holdings Ltd v Douglas Smith Stimpson Partnership* (31 July 1989, unreported)[2] H.H. Judge Newey QC held that an expert had no automatic power to bind his client at the conclusion of a without prejudice meeting.

Similarly, beware of accepting any proposition which is within the expertise of a discipline other than your own. Furthermore, even if a matter is within your own competence do not deal with it, unless it is a matter on which you are being asked to give evidence. For example, if a quantity surveyor is being called to give costings evidence, then a building surveyor, who is being asked to give evidence to prove the existence of the defects ought not to enter into any discussion about costs, even though he doubtless would have abundant professional experience of prices.

Rule 6: maintain your objectivity

It may be believed that the way to succeed as a professional witness is to bend the advice to suit the client's interests. And it is true that there are a very small number of experts who regularly appear in the courts who do give the impression of living by that maxim. It is a true story of the valuation surveyor, who, upon being asked by a solicitor whether he would accept instructions to give a valuation on a particular property, replied 'Delighted to. Do you want a high valuation or a low valuation?'

But do not be led astray. Our advice as barristers to our lay clients is: select an expert who maintains his objectivity. If one's expert appears partisan, it tarnishes one's entire case. The best person to choose as an expert is a man whose evidence will be so balanced and careful that the judge will feel readily able to accept it. One takes a risk in a sense by instructing such an expert in the first place, since he may tell the client that he has no case. But, if that is the truth, it is better to learn that at the outset. If, on the other hand, such an expert advises that a client's case has merits, then one can pursue it with reasonable confidence that one's evidence will be accepted at trial.

An expert without integrity is a liability to the team. There is no more to be said.

Rule 7: study the evidence of the other experts

As the trial approaches, it is vital that experts in two respects study what other experts are saying. Firstly, all the experts on the same side must

2 See pp75–76, supra.

ensure that they are singing in tune. Up to this stage, they may have been working separately in their different fields. However, it is very likely that their expertise will overlap. There may be inconsistencies between their reports. If there are, this is not necessarily a disaster, but it is important to recognise the inconsistency. Then the team as a whole, led by the barrister, will form a decision as to which opinion to invite the court to accept: if this be the view less favourable to the client, then there will be no problem; if it is the view more favourable, then an explanation doubtless will be prepared why this is to be preferred to the other. If there are a number of experts on the same side giving evidence on closely related areas, for example, as to the negligence of different members of the design team, it may be a good idea to convene a meeting of all the experts to enable them to meet each other. In practice most inconsistencies can fairly readily be ironed out. Inconsistencies between experts are unlikely to be a problem, provided they are identified in time. But if one allows them to surface for the first time at trial, one will be giving the other side undeserved fun at one's own expense.

The second aspect of studying what other experts say is in relation to the other side's experts. After all the labour of getting one's own expert reports together, the day will come when a thick bundle of papers will be received from the other side. There is a temptation to relax at this point, or to concentrate on one's own next task in the timetable such as proofs of witnesses of fact. In fact, prompt detailed analysis of the contents of the other side's experts' reports is one of the most important tasks in the entire process of pre-trial preparation. In consequence of their contents one may, for example, require more factual evidence. Or further investigations at the site may be necessary.

It is becoming quite common for experts to produce supplementary reports commenting on their opposite number's reports. Provision for this has even been observed creeping into official referees' directions. It seems a useful practice for experts to write such further reports for disclosure when they feel they have something to say, but one hopes that this will not become hallowed as an invariable part of every action; or else we shall have even more paperwork than we have already.

In addition to briefing the barrister as to weaknesses in the reports of the other side's experts, it is useful for there to be a briefing about the other side's expert himself. If the discipline is a highly specialised one, the experts probably know each other. They may even have heard each other give evidence before. At any rate the other side's expert may be known by reputation. If he is not known to the lawyers then information about him will assist. In the most extreme case, it may be that the other side's expert has been castigated for the way in which he has approached his evidence in previous cases. Some years ago there was a well-known fire expert who was criticised in a series of cases. This came to light after a man had been convicted of an insurance fraud in a trial at which this expert had given evidence for the Crown. The Court of Appeal set aside the conviction, saying that if the jury had been aware of the criticism in previous cases they might well have evaluated his evidence in a different light. Therefore, distasteful as it is, it forms part of the duty of an expert to inform those instructing him of anything he knows which seriously reflects upon the professional standing of his opposite number. Such situations will, of course, be rare. But in most cases there will be some information about the man's style or weaknesses or, indeed, strengths which can be supplied, and which may assist a barrister as background when considering how to cross-examine him.

THE TRIAL PHASE

Nowadays the main role of the expert at trial is to be cross-examined. The evidence-in-chief will already be furnished by the version of the report which has been exchanged together with any supplementary report. One respect in which something more may usefully be done by the expert at this stage is the preparation of visual aids such as three-dimensional models or large diagrams on flip-charts. Cross-examination is the part of their job which many experts, especially inexperienced experts, dread. We hope that a few comments may assist expert witnesses to ensure that they do themselves justice in what can feel an uncomfortable situation.

This part of the chapter is concerned with how to answer questions in cross-examination, not with how to pose them. But in order to consider how questions can best be answered, it may be revealing to consider cross-examination from a barrister's point of view. The techniques of advocacy are not often discussed by barristers. Most of the books on the subject on the shelves of the bookshop have been written by academics, or Americans, or solicitors. Those books about advocacy which barristers do write tend to be stories of great advocates of the past, rather than how-to-do-it guides to techniques. It seems to parallel the fact that books on the technique of acting are almost always by critics, or directors, or teachers, rather than by actors themselves. Perhaps part of the reason is that advocacy is so much a matter of experience, and, therefore, guided by instinct more than conscious technique. And perhaps the reason why some expert witnesses seem to have so little idea what is going on when they are cross-examined is because of the relative infrequency of a public discussion by barristers of what they are about.

It is a sad truth that very often eminent and careful specialists create a poor impression in the witness box, whereas other expert witnesses whose opinions are perhaps inherently of less weight come over very well. The authors of this chapter were once against each other in an official referee action where one of us had to call two members of a professional firm accused of negligence. The firm was duly and happily cleared of the imputation. But the surprise was that of the two professional men the more senior and highly qualified proved a less good witness than the other. Good experts do not necessarily do themselves justice in the unfamiliar setting of a courtroom. The main purpose of our suggestions in this part of the chapter is to help experts, who do not have great experience in the witness-box, to avoid pitfalls and to explain their opinions in terms which will enable their true worth to be assessed.

Rule 8: do not agree to propositions too readily

Recognise first of all that the other side's barrister will not be cross-examining you at all, unless there is something in your evidence which he cannot reconcile with his case. One avoids cross-examining if one possibly can. There is always the risk that by cross-examining a witness one ends up strengthening his evidence. If a witness for the other side proves impressive or brings out in answer to questions further material supporting his conclusions, one is worse off at the end than the beginning. That is why, for example, the chemist who analyses our soil samples is unlikely to be called to court to be challenged, however inconvenient his results may be: the other side will realise that there is little prospect of shaking his evidence, so their best course is to fit their own theories around it.

In accordance with a similar tactical sense, when barristers do have to cross-examine, they will, if possible, try to avoid head on collisions with the witness. A favourite opening tactic when cross-examining an expert is to try to get him to agree with as much as possible of one's own case. A variant on that is to seek to get him to agree that, where there are differences, one's own expert's views are as valid as his own. These approaches can be devastatingly successful with the type of witness who is too amenable.

Here is an example. It is imaginary, though many real life episodes have been very similar. Mr Know-all is the expert for the plaintiff in a professional negligence action: he says that the defendant's design was inherently risky and a prudent designer should not have attempted it. The defendant's expert, Dr Egg-head, says that at the date in question, although some members of the profession would have taken Mr Know-all's view, there was another reputable body of professional opinion which would have regarded the design as perfectly acceptable. The law is that if such a body of opinion had existed, then, even if the design can today be shown to have been unsatisfactory, the defendant was not negligent. Counsel for the defendant may hope that his cross-examination will go like this:

COUNSEL: Now, Mr Know-all, I dare say that you would agree that my client's expert, Dr Egg-head, is a well qualified and most experienced specialist in this field?
OVER-AMENABLE EXPERT: Oh certainly.
COUNSEL: In fact, if I may say so with respect, Dr Egg-head's standing in the field could be compared with your own distinguished reputation?
OVER-AMENABLE EXPERT: You are very kind.
COUNSEL: Of course, it sometimes happens that two experts, both of high standing, form different opinions.
OVER-AMENABLE EXPERT: Yes, indeed.
COUNSEL: Both then are perfectly valid views.
OVER-AMENABLE EXPERT: Oh, yes.
COUNSEL: Thus in this case Dr Egg-head's views must be as valid and entitled to respect as yours.
OVER-AMENABLE EXPERT: Well, yes.

At that point counsel scarcely needs to ask any more questions. If he has the nerve, he will sit down at once, before the witness has a chance to try to wriggle out of the mess. If his opponent tries to repair the damage by re-examining as to whether anything alters the witness's view that any designer at the time must have realised that the design was risky, counsel will be entitled to object: 'I asked no question as to the merits of this witness's views: I asked him only as to the weight to be accorded to Dr Egg-head's.' In two brief minutes Mr Know-all has probably thrown away his client's entire case.

Pausing here, one or two features are worth careful attention. First, beware the excessively flattering cross-examiner. He is trying to lure you into a false sense of security. Indeed, he will know that many people when flattered in public feel so embarrassed that they can readily be persuaded to say something thoroughly silly. Second, beware the attractively wrapped proposition which you are invited to assent to. This is one of the most fundamental gambits of the cross-examiner—to wrap up his own case in such pretty paper that the other side's expert will agree with it.

How then should the expert have answered these questions? Could he, it may be asked, have answered them any differently without lying? Perhaps this would have done more justice to his opinion:

COUNSEL: Now, Mr Know-all, I dare say that you would agree that my client's expert, Dr Egg-head, is a well qualified and most experienced specialist in this field?
SOLID EXPERT: Oh certainly.
COUNSEL: In fact, if I may say so with respect, Dr Egg-head's standing in the field could be compared with your own distinguished reputation?
SOLID EXPERT: Dr Egg-head is certainly a well-regarded specialist.
COUNSEL: Of course, it sometimes happens that two experts, both of high standing, form different opinions.
SOLID EXPERT: Yes.
COUNSEL: Both then are perfectly valid views.
SOLID EXPERT: No, not necessarily. One may be quite wrong and may be proved wrong. The fact that it was sincerely held does not make a mistaken view correct.
COUNSEL: But in this case Dr Egg-head's views must be as valid and entitled to respect as yours.
SOLID EXPERT: I would regard any opinion of Dr Egg-head as entitled to respect in the sense that it would deserve to be examined carefully to see whether it was correct. But upon examination it might, as in this case, prove to be unfounded

That line of answers would put counsel right back at square one. It would also give a more truthful impression of Mr Know-all's opinion.

Beware, also, the 'isn't it possible' line of questioning. For example:

COUNSEL: But it's possible isn't it that some members of the profession at that date considered it a satisfactory design?
OVER-AMENABLE WITNESS: Oh yes, of course it's possible.

A more accurate answer may be:

SOLID WITNESS: I am not aware of any such body of opinion.

Another instance in which the 'isn't it possible' lines of questioning may be used is when an unlikely alternative explanation for a building failure is being advanced. The cross-examiner hopes that he can score a point whatever the witness answers. If the witness agrees that the explanation is possible then counsel has advanced his own case; whereas if the witness says it is quite impossible then the credibility of the witness will be shaken when it is later proved that it is not totally impossible. One regular expert witness used to answer these types of questions by saying, 'Sir, if you mean a million to one chance, I'd agree with you'. An even better answer, shorn of the exaggerated statistic, might be, 'Your hypothesis is just possible, but in my opinion extremely unlikely in view of . . .'

One of the most famous duels between counsel and an expert occurred in the trial of the murderer, Seddon. Sir Edward Marshall Hall QC, appearing for the defence, had to cross-examine Sir William Wilcox about traces of arsenic in the body of the deceased. Marshall Hall produced an alternative and previously completely unconsidered theory, which, if tenable, would have created at least sufficient doubt to justify an acquittal. At first the expert admitted the possibility of Marshall Hall's theory. It was always said that if he had sat down at once Marshall Hall would have won the case. But he stayed on his feet and sought to press home his advantage. As he did so, Wilcox began to think of a method of disproving the thesis; he asked for the opportunity to do a further test. He did the test, disproved the thesis and Seddon was convicted. The lesson for all expert witnesses is: think carefully if asked to consider a theory for the first time and do not hesitate to suggest any further investigation which might help you form an opinion on it. In other words once again, do not agree with a proposition unless and until you are satisfied that it is balanced and correctly stated.

Above all, beware the 'false assumption' question. That is a question which involves a wholly unproved assertion of fact. This is not a legitimate gambit. It is a trick. Decent members of the bar will not ask such questions, and judges will certainly disallow them. But unfortunately advocates do often ask such questions, and especially before non-lawyer arbitrators such questions may not be stopped. For example:

ADVOCATE: But when there is a body of opinion that such a design was satisfactory you cannot say that a prudent member of the profession could not have made such a design?
OVER-AMENABLE WITNESS: No, I suppose not.

The proper way to advance such a line of questioning is:

COUNSEL: If it were proved that there was a body of opinion that such a design was satisfactory, then you could not say . . .

If the false assumption question, however, does have to be answered, an accurate answer may be:

SOLID WITNESS: Sir, I am not aware of any such body of opinion having existed. If it were established to have existed, then, of course, a prudent member of the profession could have been part of it.

Having said all that about the dangers of too readily assenting to propositions, do not go to the opposite extreme of refusing to accept a proposition which is quite obviously correct. Some experts do behave like this in the witness-box. Their evidence ends up being utterly tedious, and they create the impression that they have so little confidence in their professional work that they are afraid to enter into any intelligent discussion of the case. The judge will be unlikely to repose great confidence in their evidence.

Rule 9: answer as accurately as possible

If the cross-examiner cannot persuade the witness to accept his own case, then he has to move to frontal attack. One possible approach is to attack the expert's experience. It is not often that this can be done successfully with an expert witness. But there have been occasions when it has been used with devastating effect.

There is a famous instance of Lord Carson destroying the credibility of a witness who was called on the basis that he had a lifetime's experience of the conventions in a certain form of entertainment:

CARSON: How long have you been in the music-hall business, Mr Cox?
WITNESS: Theatres and music-halls, 21 years.
CARSON: Mr Cox, how long have you been in the *music-hall* business?
WITNESS: (Pause) Seven months.

This witness made one of the most elementary mistakes. He prevaricated. He tried to get away from answering the question accurately. He would have done much better to have answered in the first place, 'I have been in the music-hall business only seven months, but I have been in theatres generally for 21 years . . .', and then gone on to explain, if it were the case, that he considered his experience of theatres to be perfectly germane to the issues.

Another example of an attack on an expert witness's competence was provided by Mr John Tackaberry at the trial of the famous case of *Anns v Merton London Borough Council* [1978] AC 728, [1977] 2 All ER 492, HL. The plaintiffs called a witness who had had many years' experience in a local authority building control department to state as an expert what standard of care ought to be achieved. The first question in cross-examination was, 'I think that three negligence claims have already been notified against your department'. Any witness who has had the misfortune to be involved in a claim ought not to allow himself to be taken by surprise if he is questioned about it.

A common approach of a cross-examiner seeking to shake a witness's credibility is to find an inconsistency. This may be an internal inconsistency in the witness's own evidence or an inconsistency with another witness called on the same side. If the evidence-in-chief contains an inconsistency, which is not explained, then the cross-examiner is handed ammunition on a plate and the expert has only himself to blame. But if there is no such patent inconsistency, the cross-examiner may explore to see if he can uncover one. Witnesses cannot go wrong so long as they listen to the questions and answer them accurately. If the witness does not know the answer he should say so. Where witnesses so often make fools of themselves is by guessing an answer in a situation where they are unsure. At other times they quite innocently go wrong through not having understood a question. If ever in the slightest doubt what a question means, always clarify before proceeding to give an answer.

Not infrequently, experts have to give evidence on potentially disputed matters of fact. A common example arises when a building surveyor or engineer inspected a property at an early stage of a dispute and describes what the state of the works then was. The other side may, for example, be seeking to establish that the defects arose subsequently. In such circumstances any witness may find something to learn from the manner of giving evidence developed over the years by police forces, whose members are, of course, daily giving evidence where the facts of what occurred are in dispute. Police officers make what are termed 'contemporaneous notes'. Sometimes such notes are made literally as an interview is taking place: on other occasions they are made as soon after an incident as an officer has a chance to make up his notebook. That would generally mean within two or three hours. The rule is that a witness may refresh his memory in the witness box from notes made while matters were still fresh in his memory. In practice police officers simply read out what is in their notebooks. This produces a method of giving evidence somewhat lacking in a sense of freshness. But the evidence is very hard to attack. Whenever it is suggested to a police officer in cross-examination that he is mistaken, he simply reads out again what is in his notebook and asserts that he made the note when matters were very fresh in his memory. If two officers were present at an incident they general write up their notes together. They pool their recollection in doing so. When this happens they normally each write up their own note in their own handwriting, but each note is identical to the other. This eliminates the risk of inconsistencies in their evidence. Sometimes only one makes the note, the other signing it when complete to indicate that he adopts it and agrees with it.

This approach can readily be used when taking any kind of schedule of conditions. It would also be thoroughly appropriate in a foundations case where an engineer as part of his investigation asks the owners of a building when they first saw cracks appear in a building. It is far from unknown for plaintiffs in such cases to say in court that they first saw cracks at a later date than the date they mentioned to the engineer. The outcome of a defendant's limitation defence may turn completely on such a date. If satisfied that the plaintiffs mentioned the earlier date to the engineer, a court may be disposed to reject the evidence given in court of the later date. For the plaintiffs are more likely to be accurate as to the date in what they said closer to the time when such events occurred. But if the engineer has no contemporaneous note of what was said to him, his evidence of the conversation will sound uncertain. On the other hand, if the engineer can give evidence that he made a careful note of what he was told on his visit to the property, and can produce that note in court, his evidence will be extremely difficult to shake.

Rule 10: experts should provide the barrister with comments during a hearing

Whilst a witness is in the course of giving evidence, the rule is that he may not communicate with those instructing him. Indeed, he must not talk to anybody about the case. This applies over luncheon adjournments, overnight and over any longer adjournments. But before he begins giving evidence, and after he has completed his evidence, the expert can and should furnish counsel with comments as the case proceeds.

It is especially important that an expert should be present in court whilst his opposite number is in the witness box. Many cases have been won and lost on points which occur to an expert whilst the other side's expert of the same discipline is giving evidence. Almost always some new material comes out in cross-examination. Barristers will normally not ask questions of a witness unless they have some idea what the answer will be. This paradox is the reverse of the situation in ordinary life where one does not normally ask a question if one already knows the answer. But the risk to the cross-examiner if he asks such a question is that the information given in answer will prove beneficial to the other side. After all witnesses will normally be more likely to volunteer information which supports what they are saying than information which tends to weaken it. If the outcome of a barrister's cross-examination is to leave the other side's case stronger, then he is a poor practitioner of his craft. So the expert provides a quite crucial role in guiding a cross-examiner as to what an answer is likely to be and thereby to assisting the barrister to decide what to ask and what not to ask. Hurried conversations in the corridor at lunchtime and at the end of the afternoon are likely to be the order of the day whilst the other side's expert is in the box. For points which arise whilst the barrister is on his feet the best expedient is to write a note and ask the solicitor to pass it forward to counsel's bench, or to the junior if there are two counsel conducting the case. It is most unhelpful, save in a moment of real crisis or urgency to pull a barrister's gown in order to whisper into his ear whilst he is on his feet. This distracts the court and interferes with the barrister's line of thought. If the witness is speaking, the barrister may miss what the witness is saying. If the judge is speaking, it is even worse and may be regarded as a grave discourtesy to the court. So the best course almost always is to pass a note forward. The barrister will probably be adept enough at reading a piece of paper in front of him whilst talking or whilst the witness is saying something in answer.

CHAPTER 6

An Official Referee's view

His Honour Judge John Newey QC, MA, LLM, FCIArb

INTRODUCTION

Originally at common law witnesses were not allowed to give opinion evidence as it was thought that, if they did so, they would be intruding upon the roles of judges and juries whose functions were to form their own conclusions. However, problems sometimes arose which courts simply could not understand nor form judgments about without assistance from suitable experts. Gradually appropriately qualified witnesses were permitted to explain and to express personal opinions about matters which required expert evidence. Such witnesses might be the parties themselves, or their relatives or employees, or completely independent persons; the same principles would apply.

Today independent experts give evidence in many types of courts, tribunals, arbitrations and inquiries. In the criminal courts fingerprint, handwriting and now DNA experts are called; also psychiatrists to prove or rebut diminished responsibility. In Factory Acts and running down cases in the Queen's Bench Division and county courts experts give evidence as to machinery, vehicles or road conditions and medical practitioners as to injuries. Doctors also appear on pension appeals and valuers before the Lands Tribunal. Local authority planning officers and independent planning consultants give evidence at planning inquiries. Probably, however, there are no judicial proceedings in which experts are called more frequently than in construction arbitrations and in cases in the official referees' courts.

The Official Referees' courts were created in 1876 to deal with technical matters, so that it was inevitable that experts would give evidence in practically all cases tried by them. It would seem that Official Referees pioneered the making of orders requiring that parties exchange copies of their experts' reports before trials so as to prevent surprise and the possible need for adjournments. Exchange was presumably either by consent or required as a condition of leave to call expert opinion evidence.

SCOTT SCHEDULES

In the 1920s His Honour George Scott QC, Official Referee, invented the 'Scott Schedule', which requires one party to set out item by item the detail of his case and the other to comment upon it in equal detail. Parties are not allowed to make broad allegations, nor simply to 'not admit' or to 'deny'. Such schedules need to be drafted by experts or based on information provided by them. A Scott Schedule is an efficient way of sorting out a case and making it manageable, but to go through one item by item at trial can be both time consuming and costly for the parties. Nowadays, if an Official Referee orders a Scott Schedule, he usually also orders that the parties select representative items from it for trial, in the reasonable expectation that if decisions are made with regard to them, the guidance provided will enable the parties to reach agreement concerning the remaining items.

MEETINGS OF EXPERTS

In 1981 Official Referees began to make orders with the agreement of the parties that experts of the same or similar disciplines should meet 'without prejudice' before trials. At first there were differences of opinion as to whether the meetings should take place before or after the experts' reports have been exchanged, but experience has shown that generally meetings are better held before reports for trials are written. Experts are slow to reconsider their opinions after they have stated them in writing and meetings bring about more useful reports.

Meetings are intended to bring together the experts instructed in a case for a full and frank discussion, in the absence of both the parties and of their legal representatives. A meeting may result in agreement as to all or most of the technical matters involved which, when reported to the respective solicitors and clients, may bring about early settlement of the case. Alternatively, the experts may agree as to some matters, but not as to others. This, by narrowing the issues, should result in shorter reports and the saving of time at the trial. Even if no agreement can be reached, the meeting should highlight problems and result in the experts knowing and understanding the reasons for each other's opinions, so enabling them to write better informed and more relevant reports.

Experts are, of course, entitled to be paid for meeting, but the expense to the parties is nearly always worth incurring. Only if an expert is himself a party or otherwise emotionally involved in the case, or if his personality is such that he is quite incapable of even considering anyone else's point of view is a meeting likely to be valueless.

In many cases it is helpful if at the end of a meeting the experts agree minutes recording their agreements and disagreements, but since the meeting was 'without prejudice', the minutes cannot subsequently be placed before a court without the consent of all the parties. Obviously no evidence can be given at the trial, either in chief or in cross-examination, as to what has been said at the meeting.

So far as is known parties seldom, if ever, objected to orders for exchange of experts' reports and certainly there was an almost universal willingness to agree to orders for meetings of experts from their first introduction. However, the effect of Order 38, rules 37 and 38(1) of the Rules of the Supreme Court first enacted in 1974 is to give all courts power to require exchange of reports, even against the wishes of one or all of the parties, and Order 38, rule 38(3), which came into force on 1 October, 1986, gives Official Referees, and also the Chancery Division and Commercial Court, similar powers to order meetings.

COURT ORDERS RELATING TO EXPERTS

In the Official Referees' courts all interlocutory orders in a case are made by the Official Referee to whom the case has been allocated and who will, subject to his availability, try it. Orders with regard to experts are made on the summons for directions in a case, when a programme relating to preparations for trial is laid down and a hearing date is fixed. A typical order concerning experts would read:

> 'Experts: leave to call experts limited to two per party; experts of like disciplines to meet without prejudice to endeavour to narrow issues and to agree facts by not later than (a stated date); reports to be exchanged by (another stated date).'

If a case is technical in nature counsel or solicitors appearing on a summons for directions will not need to persuade the Official Referee that leave should be given for experts to be called, but, if they want more than one independent expert per party, they must give their reasons. If the costs in a case are likely to catch up, or even exceed, the amount at stake, the Official Referee will be most reluctant to give leave for more than one independent witness per party. If, for example, a party asks for one surveyor to prove defects and another to prove diminution in value, the Official Referee may well suggest that one suitably qualified surveyor might give both types of evidence. Even if the case involves very large sums of money, as in practice most Official Referees' court cases do, the Official Referee will have to be convinced of need before he will agree to more than one witness of the same discipline being called by a party. For example, if a party wishes to call an engineer, a quantity surveyor and two architects, there will have to be some difference in the expertise of the two architects to warrant both of them being called, for cases are not decided by counting heads.

The last date by which the experts are required to meet is usually about six weeks after the date when the parties may be expected to have completed inspection and probably the copying of documents in the case, so that the experts wil have had an opportunity to consider them before meeting. If there is to be a Scott Schedule the last date for meeting is often the same as, or shortly before, the date fixed for delivery of comments upon the Schedule, so that the experts will have been able to discuss the contents of the Schedule before the comments are made. Discussion at that stage may result in withdrawal of parts of the Schedule and agreement as to other parts.

In the Official Referees' courts orders under Order 38, rule 2A for statements of witnesses of fact to be cross served and to serve as evidence-in-chief are invariably made. If the experts will need information of fact, for example, as to the sequence of events, before they are able to form their opinions, the Official Referee will fix an early date for exchange of statements and a later date by which the experts must meet.

The date fixed for exchange of experts' reports is usually about six weeks after the last date given for the meeting of experts. The parties' solicitors may agree together to put back both last dates for meetings and dates for exchange of reports, but the effect of their doing so may be to deprive their clients of a proper opportunity for reconsidering the case before incurring the costs of a trial. If, in the absence of an agreement altering a date fixed by the court, a party fails to arrange for his expert to attend a meeting with other experts, or to produce his expert's report for exchange, his opponent may apply to the Official Referee, who will probably grant a short extension of time for compliance, but provide that in the event of further default the party concerned be debarred from calling expert evidence.

Investigations in cases may require the making of trial pits, taking of bore holes, laboratory analysis of products, testing of mock-ups and the like. To save time and costs and to prevent unnecessary disagreements and misunderstandings, whenever possible investigations should be carried out under the joint direction of the parties' experts. if, however, one party's expert arranges a test, for example, a loading test on a representative structure, other parties' experts should be given the opportunity to witness it. Normally parties will make arrangements with regard to such matters between themselves, but sometimes it is possible for the Official Referee to assist, for example, by providing for a specified analysis to be carried out by a named laboratory, the charges to be borne initially by the parties equally, but to be treated as costs in the action.

EXPERTS' REPORTS

Experts' reports vary enormously. All should, of course, be set out in sections and paragraphs and, if long, provided with a contents page and with sub-titles. They should be written as simply and clearly as possible. They should not be drafted with close study by a fellow expert in mind, but for reading by an ordinary, reasonably intelligent layman. When technical terms are used they should be explained. Clearly labelled illustrative sketches, drawings, sections and photographs can all aid understanding. When there is a Scott Schedule the expert may adopt sections of it or comments upon it as part of his report without the necessity for repeating them. There are cases in which long reports, accompanied by numerous documents are unavoidable, but, when possible, they should be avoided as they can impose a great strain upon the concentration and conscientiousness of the reader. In larger cases supplemental, further supplemental and yet further supplemental reports are sometimes presented. These again are often unavoidable, but, when time and costs permit, they should in the interests of clarity of presentation, be replaced by cumulative reports.

GIVING EVIDENCE

Before an independent expert gives evidence at a trial the Official Referee and all parties concerned with the case will have read his report, possibly more than once. Early in his evidence the expert will be asked to confirm that the report is his and that he presents it as his evidence. Suitable questions for counsel calling the expert to ask are: 'Are the statements of fact contained in the report true?' and 'Do the expressions of opinion contained in the report represent your genuine views?' A further question which can be asked, at least for the avoidance of doubt, is 'Is there any part of the report which you wish to withdraw?'

In evidence-in-chief, counsel will not take the expert witness through the whole of his report, but he will usually ask him questions about parts of it to emphasise their importance, or to make sure that the Official Referee has understood them, or because they are the subject of particular dispute. The expert may also be asked to comment on the contents of other experts' reports or on oral evidence which they have given.

In cross-examination the expert may be asked about any part of his report or indeed any aspect of the case. Very occasionally expert witnesses become aggressive and even discourteous to counsel in cross-examination. This is unhelpful. The expert should rely on the Official Referee prompted if necessary by the counsel who has called him, to protect him from any unfair questions and should answer as sensibly, shortly and courteously as he can. The expert, like all witnesses, should at all times speak sufficiently loudly and distinctly for the Official Referee and everyone else in court to be able to hear him without straining.

VIEWS

In most larger and some smaller construction cases the Official Referee will at the request of the parties carry out a view of the property involved either before the trial or during it. Usually he will be accompanied by an expert instructed by each party, who will between them be responsible for ensuring that he sees or feels all that is relevant. Obviously the experts have to tell the Official Referee what to look at, but nothing said at a view is evidence in the case.

EXPERTS' QUALIFICATIONS

A witness may be qualified to give expert opinion evidence by study leading to professional or other qualifications, or by experience, or by both. There are subjects which cannot be studied academically and for which experience can provide the only qualification. Most independent experts, however, belong to one or more learned professions. In deciding the weight to be given to an expert's opinion, the Official Referee will naturally take into account, among other considerations, the nature of his qualifications. To give a somewhat fanciful example: an Official Referee would be unlikely to attach much weight to the opinion of an expert as to what should have been discovered on a structural survey, if the expert, however well qualified academically, had never carried out a survey himself.

EXPERTS' DUTIES

The independent expert in investigating the facts of the case, in forming his opinions, in advising his client and his client's solicitors and counsel, and in preparing his report and evidence normally owes to his client duties of care both in contract and in negligence. The expert's duties are, however, confined to matters within his own role and competence. It is for him to advise as to technical matters, but not as to prospects of success. At the trial he is present as a witness of fact and of opinion and not as an advocate, technical or otherwise.

At the commencement of his evidence the expert witness, like all other witnesses, either takes an oath or affirms that he will speak the truth, and that he must do. He must be truthful, not only as to facts within his knowledge, but also as to the state of his opinions, and, since he will be asked to confirm the accuracy of his report, he must have been truthful in writing it. The expert's obligation to be truthful arising from his oath or affirmation is often described as his 'duty to the court'. It is a duty which prevails over the expert's duties to his client.

The question is sometimes posed: 'Does the duty of an expert to speak the truth require him to mention in court matters prejudicial to his client's case, even if he has not been asked about them?' The answer must surely be that if, in replying to a question, or writing his report on a particular topic, he gives only incomplete information, so that, while what he has said is word for word correct, the impression conveyed is incorrect and misleading, he has in substance told a lie and has acted in breach of his duty to the court. On the other hand, since the procedure in both courts and arbitrations is adversarial, an expert is not obliged to speak out, or write in his report, about matters concerning which he has not been asked at all, either by his client's opponent's counsel or by the Official Referee or Arbitrator.

An expert who deliberately lies about a material matter when giving evidence could be prosecuted for perjury, but the untruthfulness would probably have to be very blatant before proceedings would be brought. A professionally qualified expert who was deliberately untruthful could be reported to the body to which he belongs and this has happened on rare occasions.

The real safeguards against untruthfulness by experts must be their inherent integrity and their wish to be respected by other experts and trusted by Official Referees and Arbitrators. No doubt there are experts who fall below the standards required of them, but in the opinion of the writer the overwhelming majority do not.

COURT EXPERTS

In conclusion, apart from experts called by the parties, it is possible for a court on the application of a party to appoint a 'court expert' under Order 40, rule 1. When the parties intend to call experts themselves, there is little purpose in having a court expert as well and no doubt for that reason court experts are seldom appointed. If in a case the parties were prepared to agree to accept the opinion of an expert appointed by the court, it would be sensible for a court expert to be appointed to investigate and to report. In those circumstances the court expert would be acting almost as if he were an arbitrator, whereas Order 40, rule 4 envisages his being subject to cross-examination.

CHAPTER 7

View from an arbitrator

Norman Royce FRIBA PPCIArb

INTRODUCTION

An arbitrator's responsibility is to arrive at a just decision on the points at issue, and in construction disputes there are usually a number of matters requiring to be decided. In assessing the merits of the matters in contention an arbitrator, although usually appointed because of his technical expertise, often has the benefit of expert evidence to assist him. Thus one can have a situation where an architect sitting as an arbitrator listens to evidence from other architects and from other expert witnesses on matters of which he has no special expertise, such as that of structural or mechanical significance. The arbitrator, therefore, whilst conscious of his own expertise has regard to expert evidence offered by the specially appointed witnesses of the parties and being a technical expert himself he is perhaps more sensitive of the quality of the evidence than a judge might be.

The main purpose of the expert witness is to assist the arbitrator or the tribunal irrespective of who pays him. This is fundamental in any expert evidence offered, but it is my experience that in practice it is not always a requirement strictly followed by expert witnesses chosen to act in what can be quite an exacting role. Perhaps most important to the arbitrator is the ability of the expert witness to not only tell the truth but to be able to convey the truth with confidence so that it is acceptable. Many technical experts appear to lack the background to substantiate the opinions they give. I am so often left with the feeling that the opinions are a repetition of what they have been told happens, rather than what they know from experience occurs during the course of a well-run contract.

There has been a significant change in the role of the expert witness over the last fifty years in the construction industry, so much so, that a new profession, indeed, almost a new industry of experts has developed encompassing claims consultants, contract advisors and 'expert expert witnesses'. But then arbitration as a means of settling disputes in the private sector has also changed dramatically over the years, so perhaps one should examine the changes to understand a little better why the expert witness now plays a not insignificant role in assisting courts and tribunals.

Most solicitors, at the very beginning of a dispute, recommend that experts be appointed to prepare preliminary reports on the technical matters in issue in order that they can gauge the strength of their client's case. In the selection of the experts the legal advisors have regard to the reputation of the arbitrator appointed to hear the case and a great deal rests on the known experience of the arbitrator as to how many and which experts are required. This reflects, in some ways, on the ability of the arbitrator although he has it in his power to restrict the number of experts employed on either side.

It is reasonable for parties to expect the arbitrator to be experienced in the field of the dispute and have the necessary knowledge and experience of law practice and procedure so that he will be aware of what experts are talking about. It takes a lifetime in practice as an architect or engineer to master the technicalities of the construction industry and one does not expect a commercial judge to have more than a working knowledge of the intricacies of planning and constructing a building; although the official referees have acquired a grasp of a great deal of the detailed technical knowledge to enable them to interpret the technical evidence of most expert witnesses.

The solicitors advising clients have a duty to endeavour to obtain the appointment of an arbitrator with sufficient knowledge of, and experience in, the technicalities of the matters at issue to undertake the burden of the arbitration with the confidence of the parties.

If the right arbitrator is appointed he will be an expert well able to understand the evidence of the expert witnesses and will be able to give guidance in avoiding protracted cross-examination.

I believe it is reasonable for an arbitrator to bring a protracted and valueless cross-examination to a conclusion by interjecting at a convenient juncture and suggesting that a particular matter has really been exhausted.

By that stage a discerning counsel has also reached that conclusion.

I usually try to restrict the number of experts in a case for the two obvious reasons that firstly, I do not require expert evidence that lies within my expertise and secondly, the employment of experts is expensive. My advice to clients when advising on the selection of experts is always employ the best available. The best are always busy professional people actively engaged in their own practices, and they are expensive but a poor expert is a waste of money. 'To him to whom much is given, much is required.'

WITNESSES GENERALLY

An arbitrator listens generally to two types of witness. Firstly, the witness of fact or lay witness who from personal knowledge of events gives an account of what happened. A witness of fact does not normally express an opinion, but if he is the architect or engineer employed on the contract it is becoming not unusual for opinion to be invited from the professional man acting in that role.

A professional man present on a contract might be asked to give his opinion based on the facts seen by him. He would, however, be expected to give the arbitrator a fair and honest opinion—although there is often a very narrow line dividing an honest opinion from a desire to assist his client to win the case at all costs. It is a most difficult role which an experienced arbitrator from his own knowledge would require to consider carefully. Perhaps it is asking too much of the average witness, but then that is what divides the amateur from the professional.

In a building dispute a labourer might be called to give evidence on what he saw, such as signs of movement before a wall collapsed, but he would not be asked for his opinion on what caused the collapse.

A properly experienced bricklayer might, however, be asked for his opinion on the standard of the brickwork.

In many building disputes skilled workers are called to give opinions on such matters as plumbing, plastering and joinery.

The expert witness is usually appointed because of his special knowledge derived from his experience of similar work either from professional practice or the academic world enabling him to assist the arbitrator by giving his opinion either orally or by his report.

The evidence given by a witness is really information to establish facts, the facts themselves or opinions based on the facts. In arbitration as in the courts there are rules of evidence which must be observed. In arbitration, however, there is usually more informality and whilst the basic rule that the evidence must be relevant to the matter under enquiry is adhered to a great deal of laxity is usually permitted provided there are no objections from either side.

DUTIES AND QUALIFICATIONS OF AN EXPERT

It is interesting to refer to the definition of 'expert' in the Oxford Dictionary. It starts with the Latin verb *experiri* and *expertis* meaning to put to the test, to put to trial, or experiment. In the expression 'expert witness' we are not referring to somebody who is expert at being a witness, or in other words using the word as an adjective.

There are a number of expert witnesses who fall into the category of an expert at being a witness. JDJ Harvard, Secretary of the British Medical Association, recalls that he once heard Stable J address an expert witness as follows:

> Dr Jones, I recall you appeared before me some time ago on a matrimonial case as an expert in psychiatry; then I seem to remember you appearing before me in a running-down case as an expert in orthopaedic surgery, and here you are today in a medical negligence case as an expert in cardiology. I would like to know precisely what you are an expert in?

Without any hesitation Dr Jones replied:

> 'I am an expert in giving evidence in courts of law, m'lud.'

Before he was appointed Lord Chancellor, Lord Gardiner was heard to refer to a certain gentleman who had addresses in Harley Street but appeared to be permanently resident in the law courts.

In a sense expert is being used as an adjective, to describe someone who is skilled. In the expression 'expert witness', though, we are not talking of someone who is expert at being a witness, or in other words using the word as an adjective, though there are many who fall into this category, and counsel and arbitrators tend to be wary of them.

I have had many experiences of failed architects and failed engineers appearing before me as 'experts' . . . on repeated occasions over the years their performance can at best be described as falling below inoffensive mediocrity, and the limit I felt was reached when I had to dismiss an architect from my practice for gross incompetence and a month later he unexpectedly made his appearance before me as an expert in a very substantial case. His evidence did not carry a great deal of conviction with me. I believe that experts should be 'on top'—not 'on tap'. When experiencing the indifferent display of an expert witness I am reminded of the notice outside a London Park, 'Litter collector wanted, no previous experience necessary. You can pick it up as you go along.'

By the time that most parties are in dispute the opportunity for conciliation has often passed. But the experts often help by meeting on a 'without prejudice' basis to attempt to narrow down the issues.

One of the directions issued by the arbitrator in his directions is 'Figures to be agreed as figures if possible.' This gives the quantity surveyors the opportunity to meet and agree an acceptable basis for assessing quantum and this usually results in a joint document.

I have found it most beneficial to the early resolution of a dispute if the two principal experts meet, by direction of the arbitrator, and by discussion and negotiation arrive at a position where they are able to produce a joint statement under two headings—matters agreed and matters in disagreement. This should be done before experts' reports are exchanged and whilst the experts can agree the details in depth I believe that the joint statement signed by the experts should be kept simple in presentation to permit further discussion to take place.

Additional meetings may then be held to discuss and consider the matters on which agreement has not been reached so that the arbitrator can give the parties an opportunity of discussing the contentious items again with a view to engendering further possibilities of narrowing issues.

Encouragement by the arbitrator is very necessary to achieve progress and progress can only be made by capable experts with a real commitment to assist in resolving the dispute. It cannot be achieved by experts anxious to prolong the case.

I suggest that an expert should only accept an appointment if the opinions he sincerely and honestly holds will help his client's case. In the role of an expert witness:

(1) Professional integrity should be based on a regard for justice, truth and honesty.
(2) Loyalty to a client should not be at the expense of professional integrity. If an expert witness doubts his opinion he may well find that in expert cross-examination by counsel the weaknesses will be exposed and used to demolish that opinion.

There have been occasions when after listening to another expert the expert witness for the other party changes his mind. In such a case I believe he is under an obligation to notify his own client and to offer to withdraw. He is under no obligation to volunteer information which will assist the other party unless during the course of a 'without prejudice' meeting between experts both experts are happy to modify their opinions in the interests of arriving at a compromise agreement.

BACKGROUND

In the middle ages merchants became disillusioned by the legal process of resolving disputes. Even in those early days there were experts of a sort who were prepared to swear to anything and to perjure themselves for money. They were available to either party. They gave evidence on payment and many of them became well known to the courts before which they appeared.

His Honour Judge Edgar Fay in his very readable book *Official Referees' Business* describes the nineteenth-century scene:

> 'More dissatisfaction arose from the method of trial of civil litigation. Trial by jury became the usual mode of trying cases and in the Chancery although it was not only the procedures that induced Dickens to wryly observe in Bleak House, "The one great principle of British Law is to make business for itself" businessmen continued to labour under the delays and quirks of an outmoded legal system—and to complain bitterly of the expense, the delays, the uncertainties and in the case of provincial litigants, of the concentration of business in London.'

THE GROWTH OF ARBITRATION

Businessmen did more than complain. In increasing numbers they withdrew their custom from the courts in favour of arbitration. There is no statistical evidence recording the number of arbitrations year by year, but it is evident that as the nineteenth century progressed, more and more trades began as a matter of course to embody arbitration clauses in their contracts. They thus avoided the law's delays and technicalities, although as time went on it became apparent that the practice of arbitration itself was developing quirks and injustices of its own.

The Royal Commission of 1867 had already considered the position of arbitrators, and it is interesting to reflect on their findings.

The commissioners reported that arbitrators fell into two classes; they were either barristers or experts. The barristers, they found, were unable, owing to the calls of their practices, to give continuous attention to a case, and the experts, they found, owing to lack of legal training were wont to entertain irrelevant considerations and to deal unsatisfactorily with legal questions. Fees were large, adjournments were frequent, and erroneous results could not be put right by appeal.

Some of these criticisms are still valid today although arbitration as a means of settling disputes in the construction industry has been accepted as an alternative method for the resolution of technical disputes throughout the world.

THE FUNCTION OF THE EXPERT WITNESS

An ordinary witness is expected to adhere to the facts of which he has direct experience, but what sort of experience can qualify one to be an expert witness? You have to have special knowledge of the subject although it is not essential to be professionally qualified. It could even be a hobby but you should be an expert.

Experts do, however, find it a great advantage to have a relevant professional qualification. Whilst a lack of qualification will not debar him it may count against him compared with a witness having an appropriate qualification. What is more important is that an expert should be able to be impartial, to be seen to be impartial, to be able to weigh the facts based on a sound professional knowledge, to have a general knowledge of the law of evidence and to be able to express himself clearly both orally and in writing.

An expert should not normally give information in excess of that requested from him except in amplification of a question and he should not attempt to interpret the law. It would also appear that subject to having not committed perjury or fraud he has immunity from civil action against him as a result of what he says in court during the course of a trial.

In his foreword to Ronald Mildred's excellent book *The Expert Witness* the late Lord Diplock wrote:

> 'I do so for the purpose of stressing once again how much in a wide variety of cases the judiciary rely upon the candour and expertise of expert witnesses to enable justice to be done. In the very first chapter of this book attention is drawn to the function of the proper decision. Honesty in expression of his opinion on matters within the field of his expertise is a characteristic of experts with professional qualifications that I have always, and happily with justification, been able to take for granted; but order and clarity of exposition and ability to explain technical matters in terms adapted to the tribunal before whom the evidence is given, which may be entirely uninstructed in that particular subject or may share in whole or part the expert witness's own expertise, these are not gifts with which experts are endowed by nature. Like the expertise itself, they need to be learnt.'

The Chartered Institute of Arbitrators is very conscious of the necessity of the correct training of expert witnesses in the preparation of reports, proofs of evidence and on the giving of expert evidence. Proper training for this role greatly assists in the dissemination and imparting of technical expertise with advantage to both expert and tribunal alike.

Honesty of opinion should be founded on a comprehensive knowledge and experience in a particular field. Without that knowledge and experience an honest opinion could well be of limited value to the tribunal.

The proper function of today's expert witness is to assist the court or the tribunal. To that end, the expert witness is freed from one of the burdens placed upon ordinary witnesses. The expert is not confined to facts but is permitted and indeed encouraged to express his opinions based upon facts either seen or known to him or proved by other witnesses. I cannot emphasise too strongly that an expert should tell his client, right at the outset the strength of his case and he should not accept a case where his honest opinion is detrimental to his client's success.

The function of the advocate be he barrister or solicitor, is different from that of the witness. The ethics of the advocate's profession require him to accept any brief that comes his way unless there is some good reason which prevents him doing so. An advocate may not himself give evidence save in the most exceptional circumstances, and only on one occasion in the course of an arbitration has this occurred before me. It happened during an arbitration in Dominica in a case in which the parties were most belligerent. The parties to the dispute were two of the most powerful families in the West Indies and considerable sums of money were at issue. Counsel for the respondent claimed not to have seen an original document and the claimant's counsel asked leave to cross-examine him under oath regarding the matter. I ruled that the claimant's counsel be granted leave to examine the respondent's counsel on condition that he be granted a similar privilege.

Both counsel readily accepted and there followed a most spirited exhibition of advocacy. The arbitration ended in a very tense atmosphere and I was glad that I did not have to publish my award until I was three thousand miles away.

Doctor Johnson once remarked 'a lawyer has no business with the justice or injustice of the case he undertakes, unless his client asks his opinion, and then he is bound to give it honestly. The justice or injustice of the cause is to be decided by a judge.'

As long ago as 1838 Tindall LJ summarised the duties of a professional man when he said:

> 'Every person who enters into a learned profession undertakes to bring to the exercise of it a reasonable degree of care and skill and the question whether a person has exercised reasonable and proper care, skill and judgement is one of fact and appears to us to rest upon this further enquiry, viz, whether other persons exercising the same profession or calling and being men of experience and skill therein, would or would not have come to the same conclusion.'

In cases where a professional person has been accused of negligence it is usual to seek evidence from respected persons in the same profession to act as expert witnesses before the tribunal to give their opinions as to whether they would have made similar decisions to those made by the accused in similar circumstances.

This can be a very responsible role for an expert witness, so it is of interest to consider in general terms what an expert witness may and may not say. In theory—one must look first at the question of competency and then of credit, as they are often confused.

In principal any witness is competent to give evidence, in the sense that he may be allowed to. In practice the expert is usually heard, with appropriate comments being made thereafter by counsel as to, firstly, his competence, as for example, that he is an interested party, or has expressed a different opinion at other times. In the course of arbitration cases I have had the doubtful experience of 'professional expert witnesses' appearing at different times and giving quite different evidence on the same subject whilst on oath. They rarely do much good in the interests of their client's case.

There is a tendency to look with some reserve at expert witnesses generally, mainly I believe because so many expert witnesses place their responsibility to their clients so far ahead of their duty to the court.

We live in an age of increasing specialisation. The more progress that is made in science and technology, the more is the need for even greater specialisation and the need for the development of a wider range of skills. Specialists play a predominating role in most, if not all the activities of a changing society and we all tend to become specialists.

An arbitrator is more likely to give weight to a specialist of accepted status in his profession, one who is consulted by his fellow professionals, a person in practice who has specialised in the particular branch of the matter at issue.

THE EXPERT WITNESS IN LITIGATION AND ARBITRATION

In the resolution of civil disputes, the expert specialist fulfils an increasingly important, and in some cases and in some ways, even a crucial and indispensable function. The ultimate decision is so often influenced by the expert witness whose evidence is accepted.

Under the common law, in relation to the resolution of civil disputes, experts fulfil a variety of functions, which in general terms fall under the following headings, namely:

(1) experts as witnesses of the parties;
(2) experts as witnesses of the court;
(3) experts fulfilling judicial or quasi-judicial functions;
(4) experts as advocates;
(5) experts sitting with judges as assessors.

In spite of the similarities between civil litigation and arbitration there remain important differences.

THE ROLE OF THE ARBITRATOR

The arbitrator is or should be a person versed in the technicalities of the dispute, one with knowledge and experience in the particular field in which the dispute arose and he has similar powers to a judge.

In my early days as an arbitrator cases in the building industry were comparatively short—five days being a long case—and counsel seldom appeared in minor disputes. Hearings were informal and the arbitrator had regard to an early settlement at the preliminary meeting by a subtle engenderment of conciliation. Construction disputes have now grown to enormous numbers and differ from so many other commercial disputes in that the issues of fact tend to be more complex, and the issues of law tend to be intermixed and not readily severable from the facts.

John Uff QC in an article in 'Arbitration' stated:

> 'It is one of the great weaknesses in arbitration in the construction industry that so much time is wasted by calling expert witnesses to explain elementary aspects of building to an engineer or architect arbitrator.
>
> The whole process of arbitration has become far too legal and complicated, with the formal High Court procedure involving one side calling witnesses to be cross-examined by the other, and then the other party following suit. The arbitrator, like a judge, is required merely to sit and listen to the case advanced by each party and then decide which of the rival versions of fact, opinion and law, he accepts.
>
> Thus the role of the arbitrator is immediately reduced to one of an adjudicator, a task for which judges are better trained than engineers and architects.'

I believe the time has come for a short and economic arbitration procedure to be introduced into every industry and in particular the construction industry. I would also like to see conciliation introduced into the Arbitration Acts as an initial step—a prerequisite to arbitration.

THE ADVERSARIAL AND INQUISITORIAL SYSTEMS

In this country we use the adversarial system in which technical experts in theory are supposed to assist the tribunal with their opinions, but in practice each side seeks experts who are willing to support its claims. This gives the unfortunate impression that experts are always disagreeing. Judges often appear to be more confused than arbitrators at the divergence of technical evidence especially as questioning of experts is limited.

My experience of the inquisitorial system on the Continent is that the final aim of the court is the same but the system is helped by the technical evidence being listened to by an expert appointed by the tribunal. The tribunal expert can ask either side questions and be questioned so that he is independent of involvement and motive.

Court experts are required to be of a very high calibre to be effective. I would welcome the principle of the appointment of court experts and would also welcome more power being given to arbitrators to question expert witnesses in order to better understand their technical opinions. In small building disputes arbitrators tend to ask more questions, especially when parties do not have the benefit of lawyers conducting examination and cross-examination of witnesses, and it is by these questions that the arbitrator is so often able to get to the real nub of the dispute.

DUTIES OF AN EXPERT WITNESS

An expert witness is not required, or perhaps it is better to say 'is required not to' stray into a field which belongs to the court, namely the interpretation of a statute.

But what is the difference in the roles of the expert witness and the assessor? In case it is not clear to all, it may be helpful at this stage to clarify the difference between the role of the expert witness and that of the assessor.

First, let me say that the same person can perform both functions (on different occasions, of course), and both require expert knowledge and experience in a particular sphere.

The function of an assessor is to provide a tribunal with technical information, relevant to the subject of the matter under investigation, aimed to enable the tribunal to understand the expert evidence of others better and so form a reliable opinion about it. An assessor is paid by the tribunal.

The function of an expert witness is to provide a tribunal with expert opinions, deduced from facts, on technical matters which fall within his experience and technical qualifications. An expert witness is paid by the party who calls him.

In an excellent little publication entitled *Guidelines of Good Practice for Expert Witnesses*, the Chartered Institute of Arbitrators gives the following advice:

An expert witness:

(1) Should bear in mind that at the hearing his first duty will be to assist the tribunal to arrive at a just decision regardless of its effect on the interests of his client. Subject to this, he should assist his client in every possible way.
(2) Should not himself seek or advertise for, appointments as an expert witness in competition with others.
(3) Should have detailed knowledge of the theory, customs and practice of the specialist field in which he is required to give evidence of opinion together with a general knowledge of the law of evidence; of the principles of damage; of professional negligence and breach of contractual duty; and of practice in relation to the duties of expert witnesses before and during the trial or hearing.
(4) Should not refuse to disclose any relevant information known to him concerning the subject matter of his evidence. Should this information be confidential to another client, he should endeavour to obtain the latter's consent at the same time telling him that disclosure will be unavoidable if the tribunal requires it.
(5) Should give opinions which are honestly held by him personally, and are not merely the opinion of others except as reinforcement of his own.

So to come to the essential points about an expert witness. He is someone who has, if his evidence proves to be more useful than that of the other witnesses, this 'better vantage point'. He is a special kind of witness. His past and current experience is a sort of evidence though he is not expected to retain this experience as such. An ordinary witness is expected to adhere to the facts of which he has direct experience, usually by seeing or hearing the events in question and which are part of the story before the court.

PREPARING FOR THE HEARING

Having accepted an appointment the expert should:

(1) Study and read all documents, drawings and correspondence very carefully and literally prior to preparing a report in which he will give all the evidence he can that any opinion advanced as to what is a customary method of handling a particular matter, is indeed generally adopted by a reasonable practitioner. It is then so important that he is experienced as a practitioner. This might well help a witness to give a confident reply to a question from counsel, 'When did you last design and supervise the construction of a building of this type?'
(2) Endeavour to look at the dispute from the other party's viewpoint and to anticipate the points his expert is likely to raise and to see if he can refute them. In other words to think the matter through logically.
(3) Readily concede any matter for which his client is responsible or for which he is to blame. Listening to an expert witness relating a long history of his client's perfect performance unrelieved by one possible default calls for some stamina on the part of the arbitrator.
(4) Review the whole of the dispute from the point of view of each party. Consider to what extent he feels he can convey to the judge or arbitrator the strength of his client's case. If he forms the opinion that

the other party has a stronger case, advise his client to settle before the hearing. The right advice at initial report time can save a client a lot of heartache and money.

The preliminary report should be for the eyes of his client and his legal advisor only and should contain an account of the strengths and weaknesses of his case. At the preliminary meeting with client and lawyer his rationalised views should be put forward clearly and simply noting the views expressed by the other parties present. I believe that all relevant documents should be read before offering a considered opinion.

It is also vital to make a detailed inspection of the subject of the dispute. For example, if it is a building dispute it requires the inspection of roofs or the opening up of ducts for inspection. This must be done before the preparation of a report or a proof of evidence.

I remember an expert witness giving an impressive performance in his description of problems resulting from roofing defects, but in reply to a simple question from counsel he admitted that he had never inspected the roof guttering which was the fundamental cause of the problem.

PROOFS OF EVIDENCE

The 'proof of evidence' or the statement of evidence to be given at the hearing should be given as succinctly as possible and should include:

(1) the expert's personal particulars incorporating his qualifications, details of experience in the special technical aspects with which the reference is concerned together with a record of his period in practice and a list of the works for which he has been responsible;
(2) a resumé of the contract, details of the claim and defence (including any counterclaim) and a detailed opinion on the factual points which are required;
(3) a conclusion supported by clear reason.

The proof should be written in a simple, clear and unambiguous manner to convey both to counsel and the arbitrator the important points of the expert's evidence and the reasoning on which it is based. It should be borne in mind that counsel will be presenting the case so that it should be easily understood by a layman.

I cannot but emphasise the importance of keeping the proof of evidence as simple, uncomplicated and as short as possible. Too many experts prepare too many massive reports when a short report is all that is required. Appendices can be kept in a separate file. Most large reports contain unnecessary padding, the conclusion is the important message. I was present at a case in the High Court when the judge asked the principal expert to take his report away and endeavour to reduce it to a conclusion of two foolscap pages.

The expert will attend conferences with counsel by arrangement with the solicitors. But the expert should discuss the case direct with counsel who will present the case. It is all important that counsel should understand the technical strengths and weaknesses and be able to discuss them direct with the expert and the following should be achieved:

(1) It should be the expert's opinion and not that of counsel so that any amendments to the proof of evidence should be in line with the honest opinion held by the expert, and any amendments suggested by counsel with which the expert cannot concur should be resisted.
(2) There should be a thorough understanding by counsel of the finer points of the expert's evidence and of the impact of certain crucial matters which the expert wants to highlight when giving evidence.

At a recent hearing an expert produced an immaculate proof of evidence but during cross-examination he admitted that he had not prepared it. It transpired that it had been drafted by the claimant's solicitor, amended by counsel and signed by him as it represented his opinion on the matter. This became very apparent during cross-examination.

WITHOUT PREJUDICE MEETINGS OF EXPERTS

It is usual for the arbitrator to direct that the parties' experts arrange to meet on a 'without prejudice' basis to endeavour to narrow down the issues and if possible to recommend terms for settlement, although any prehearing settlement is usually negotiated by the solicitor. If there are two parties only to the dispute this can be accomplished within a reasonable time limit even if the meeting achieves only an awareness of the differences between the experts.

If there are a number of parties by joinder a 'without prejudice' meeting is far more difficult, and to endeavour to obtain some progress I have found it helpful if the experts either mutually agree that meetings shall be chaired by one of them or alternatively they agree on the appointment of an independent chairman. He should be a strong chairman. In massive disputes this is probably the only method of making progress. I have also found that more progress is made if the experts meet before the exchange of reports. Once reports have been exchanged and read it is difficult to get some experts to modify their opinion, whereas before exchange they do not feel quite so committed.

If any real value is to emerge from the meetings it is of help if the experts are persons of substance and experience and holding an important position in a respected firm. Many parties believe, mistakenly in my opinion, that if they engage a large professional firm as experts they will automatically have someone of great experience. They may have a 'name' acting for them but often the representative will be somebody of limited experience. I have found that it is usually only when one of the senior partners of a firm is involved that good progress can be made.

I consider it of paramount importance that the experts acting for parties have the full confidence of their respective clients to make substantial progress without being obliged to refer every step back to the solicitor. I find so often in these negotiations, if handled patiently and firmly, substantial progress can be made in narrowing the issues in dispute and laying down a formula for settlement. So much, however, depends on the calibre and standing of the experts concerned in the negotiations and in the confidence placed in them by client and solicitor alike.

ARBITRATION ON DOCUMENTS ONLY

With the increase in the cost of arbitration in the construction industry the resolution of disputes by 'documents only' arbitrations has become increasingly popular. They have the great advantage of speed and economy but, of course, such procedures are suitable mainly for reasonably small disputes which can so often end up at a full hearing.

The procedure of 'documents only' arbitrations has proved successful for many years in such fields as the travel industry, and the motor industry where the motor agents run a very popular arbitration scheme.

The role of the expert in presenting his evidence by means of a report in this type of arbitration is of enormous importance in assisting the arbitrator in his findings because he has to rely entirely on the written word and the expert's report accordingly has to be tailored to 'speak for itself' in its assessment of fact, opinion and conclusion. The procedure follows the usual pattern of the claimant submitting his claim supported by accompanying documents and his expert's report. Within a stated period the respondent submits his defence and counterclaim supported by documents and his expert's report to which the claimant replies. Armed with these documents the arbitrator may then inspect the subject of the dispute, consider the submission and then publish his award.

A great deal of responsibility rests on the experts to convey to the arbitrator in a comprehensive and lucid document enough information to decide on liability quantum and costs. I have found that this exercise concentrates the experts' minds into producing clear, brief and very readable reports. Lawyers sometimes have a role in the dispute where legal matters are involved, but generally this type of arbitration has greatest value where the issues are almost entirely technical.

EXPERTS FOR ENQUIRY AND REPORT

A great deal of time is wasted in the High Court in construction disputes dealing with technical matters, which could be handled more efficiently by specially appointed experts, with specialist knowledge and experience and with delegated authority to enquire and report back to the appointing judge on such matters as:

(i) measurement and rates of items in bills of quantities;
(ii) contractors' overheads and loss of profits;
(iii) final accounts and the existence of but not the cause of defects.

This is done both by judges and arbitrators at present but so often occupies a considerable amount of court time, whereas it could be handed over to a specially appointed person with specialist knowledge. A new arrangement could be by consent of the parties to the action, and a judge concerned with any technical question of fact could at any time refer the question for consideration and report by an expert or referee drawn from an *official court panel*.

The judge may accept or reject the report.

The following rules have been suggested for guidance: The reference shall state:

(a) the documents with which the expert shall be provided; and
(b) whether the referee shall
  (i) consult named expert witnesses instructed on behalf of the parties, such witnesses to be consulted in the presence of each other: and/or
  (ii) hear witnesses called by the parties, such witnesses to be heard in the presence of the other parties; and/or
  (iii) receive written or oral representations on behalf of the parties, if oral in the presence of the other parties.

I wholeheartedly support the setting up of panels of experts or special referees in various professions, the members of the panels having court recognition, and remuneration forming part of the trial costs. I believe that it would help relieve pressure on the present overburdened courts, especially the work of official referees. I would also like to see this system extended to arbitration.

THE HEARING

The expert witness is of special importance in the building industry because most disputes arise out of the running of contracts. The issues generally involved are of a technical nature even though the lawyers tend to convert technical matters into legal disputes. It often transpires at the hearing that what the parties originally considered to be a reasonably common and frequently occurring technical difference is so often decided by legal argument leaving the experts to assist in deciding quantum. This in no way suggests a diminution of the importance of the experts, it is incumbent on them to present to the arbitrator in a clear, confident and honest way the facts and opinions as they consider relevant to assist the arbitrator in arriving at a just decision when he comes to consider both technical and legal questions of liability.

In preparing for the hearing the expert should take care to ensure that his photographs and any exhibits he will refer to are agreed with other experts both on his side and the other side and carefully labelled to ensure that no unnecessary delays occur.

Proofs of evidence have already been exchanged so that at the hearing the expert witness will seldom be called upon to read his report but will have it available for reference during examination-in-chief, cross-examination and re-examination.

Provided an expert has fully prepared himself for the hearing and is a competent and experienced man at his 'trade' he has nothing to fear from his appearance as a witness so long as he is honest and does not stray out of his field of expertise.

It must be remembered that once he is on the witness stand the witness is alone, and in a long and complicated case the witness stand can be a very lonely place during cross-examination. I can recall one expert witness who stood the ordeal of being cross-examined by three leading counsel over a period of 40 days. It was a masterly effort which would have demolished a lesser man. It was the last occasion he ever wished to act in that capacity.

I support the procedure of the administration of the oath. I have experienced the unhappy occurrence at two hearings when following a relentless cross-examination the witness has admitted to telling a lie. Cross-examination of witnesses has changed and mellowed over the years. At one time there were some counsel who delighted in bullying witnesses. I do not believe it helped their client's case and it certainly did not commend them to the arbitrator.

The art of cross-examination is not that of examining crossly. The smooth, kindly and courteous barristers achieve the best results. The most convincing witnesses are those who express their opinions in very short and simple answers, avoiding embroidery and exaggeration. So many witnesses spoil their answers to simple questions by elaborating on them giving counsel an opportunity to put supplementary questions.

Expert witnesses should always remember that they have a technical expertise which counsel does not possess and provided they tell the truth and do not stray outside the field of that expertise they should have no problems. Experts should recognise their limitations and admit them, and when encouraged by counsel to reply to a question outside his professional knowledge the expert should make it quite clear that this matter does not lie within his expertise and should be addressed elsewhere.

Some over-confident witnesses attempt to score points off counsel. This is a most dangerous and unnecessary road to take. There are few F E Smiths amongst experts and counsel has usually heard it all before and immediately knows that he has the advantage which he will pursue relentlessly.

If a question is difficult to understand an expert should ask for it to be repeated and then quietly think about it before answering. Many questions call for a short reply but often with a brief qualification, and if difficulties are encountered with an over-zealous counsel an appeal to the arbitrator will be sufficient.

It is of great value if an expert is able to be present during the examinations and cross-examinations of the other parties' expert witness so that he may follow the evidence and assist his client's counsel. Unfortunately good experts command high fees and are very busy people and are often only able to be present for part of the hearing. It is therefore important that he is provided with a résumé of the evidence he has not heard, before giving his own evidence. In some awards the performance of expert witnesses is referred to in either complimentary or critical terms and it is always of interest to experts to learn what impression they had on the arbitrator and his decision.

CONCLUSION

There is a great deal of criticism of expert witnesses in the construction industry from judges, arbitrators and from the public generally. They are criticised for their lack of experience in their professions, their lack of ability in preparing and presenting their evidence—but most important—for their lack of ethical standards. It is said that you can buy any expert evidence you need for any view you desire to present.

It is regrettable that I have found, with many notable exceptions, a general deterioration in the standard and ability of expert witnesses. This I believe has resulted from the vast increase of disputes, particularly in the building world which has attracted a new school of expert witnesses who do not possess the background, experience and ability required for the exacting task of assisting tribunals.

The really good experts are either too busy in their practices or overloaded with appointments to satisfy the enormous demand and it is only too easy for anybody to set up in practice as a claims consultant or expert advisor in building.

If the wrong expert is approached at the initial stages of a dispute the wrong advice or opinion can result in a long and costly dispute which in many instances could have been settled by conciliation. So many experts make work for themselves by producing enormous reports which embark clients on a worrying and costly exercise. An experienced expert will often tell a client in forthright terms that his case is not good and should be settled out of court as quickly as possible. An expert should have a good background of experience combined with confidence and personality if his advice is to be accepted. I have had the sad experience of taking arbitrations in which there would have been a saving of heartache and money had the parties been properly advised at the outset.

Among the criticisms of expert witnesses' knowledge and ability I have heard of and experienced are the following:

(i) People are appointed as experts in areas of dispute in which they have had little or no experience. Experts whose experience has been confined to domestic work are sometimes asked to give their opinion on the management of large projects such as hotel or hospital contracts.
(ii) Lack of appreciation that the primary duty of a witness is to assist the tribunal before which he is appearing.
(iii) Lack of care in examining both the legal and the factual aspects of the subject of the evidence, including adequate inspections of real evidence.
(iv) Lack of concentration and clarification of the relationship between fact and opinion.
(v) Failure to anticipate and deal with the likely evidence of other parties.
(vi) Failure to recommend agreement with the other experts' facts and figures before the hearing.
(vii) Lack of co-ordination of evidence with that of other experts in related fields who are acting for the same party.
(viii) Inadequate proofs of evidence and exhibits.
(ix) Poor performance under cross-examination.

A tribunal sometimes comments on an expert's evidence. An expert's performance is often crucial to the arbitrator's decision. If the evidence is poorly presented and delivered and if the conclusion is weak and does not assist the tribunal it is a waste of time and money. The impression left by some expert witnesses on many arbitrators is that they often appear to be inadequately briefed on the details of the case and as a result their proofs of evidence do not appear to have been logically thought through before being committed to paper. This, combined with a preconceived view that the other parties' case has no points meriting consideration and that they could not conceivably be wrong leaves little scope for the experts to narrow down the issues.

Good and experienced experts are always worth listening to even when giving their evidence on a subject in which the arbitrator is an expert.

An arbitrator's role in respect of expert witnesses is to understand and interpret their evidence in respect of the issues concerned in a case before coming to a just and proper decision. With such a variety of experts appearing it is of enormous assistance to have had firsthand experience of the conditions and problems involved in the industry in which the dispute has arisen. An arbitrator concerned with building disputes should be experienced in the 'hurly-burly' of a building contract to be able to adequately interpret the evidence of others likewise involved. Customs and procedures vary enormously from industry to industry.

I recall in a building dispute a foreman was giving evidence and was using his own pronunciation of various words. Architect was pronounced 'artiteck', certificate was pronounced 'serstificate' and the engineer became the 'gingerbeer'. In the course of cross-examination a young barrister asked the foreman what action he had taken after a particular incident.

The foreman replied, 'I went back to my office and wrote a "resoom". (résumé).
The barrister said, 'And pray what is a resoom?'
The foreman fixed him with a rheumy eye and replied, 'You may not know what a resoom is, but I know and I am quite sure that the arbitrator knows what it is.'
They both looked at me and I said, 'Yes, I know exactly what it is.'

It is sometimes difficult to elucidate from the evidence given exactly what the point is that an expert is trying to make. Under the common law tribunals act as 'umpire', being passive with little investigating power. In the inquisitorial system evidence is clarified by an expert appointed by the court.

Both systems have the objective of endeavouring to arrive at a just settlement. Arbitrators have very wide powers which are not always widely exercised. I would like to see wider powers to enable arbitrators to take the initiative in questioning expert witnesses. It is already exercised in small cases where lawyers are not involved in order to 'bring out' the salient points of a submission. In fundamentally technical disputes it does assist in bringing about relatively speedy conclusions to the proceedings.

I would also like to see the powers of arbitrators extended to the appointment of court experts in instances where the opinions of technical experts acting for the parties are diametrically opposed; the unbiased and independent views of such experts could be of great assistance to an arbitrator, in our adversarial system, in reinforcing his views and in arriving at his decision.

Likewise the power to appoint special experts to enquire and report, if extended to arbitration, would help shorten the time of the hearing and ensure that a completely independent opinion had been obtained.

Finally what are the duties owed by the expert to any tribunal before which he appears, to his profession, to his client and to himself.

He has a duty to the tribunal of ensuring that he is an expert in the subject matter of the dispute and a duty to communicate his knowledge through the evidence he gives honestly and fairly. He has a duty to his professional integrity at all times in order to maintain the high standards that it is incumbent upon him to keep. He has a duty to his client by accepting an appointment only if he holds views which are favourable to that client, and lastly, he has a duty to himself by maintaining his personal integrity.

A number of books have been written on the subject of expert witnesses but I suggest that a study of the distilled wisdom in the pages of John Watson's *Nothing but the Truth*, and Ronald Mildred's *The Expert Witness* will prepare and fine tune the experienced witness and will assist the beginner in avoiding the pitfalls of overconfidence and unjustifiable bias.

APPENDIX

Official Referees' courts—forms

1

HEADING for writ, specially indorsed writ or originating summons commenced as Official Referees' business

(Royal Arms)

IN THE HIGH COURT OF JUSTICE 19 . . . B. No. . . .
[Chancery *or* Queen's Bench] Division
Official Referees' Business
Between A.B. . . . Plaintiff
and
C.D. . . . Defendant

2

SUMMONS for transfer of action to Official Referees' Courts

IN THE HIGH COURT OF JUSTICE, 19 . . . B. No. . . .
[Chancery *or* Queen's Bench] Division
Master . . . ., Master in Chambers
Between A.B. . . . Plaintiff
and
C.D. Defendant

LET ALL PARTIES attend [*in the Chancery Division:* before Master . . . . in Room . . . ., Chancery Chambers, *or in the Queen's Bench Division:* the Master in Chambers in Room No. . . . , Central Office], Royal Courts of Justice, Strand, London WC2A 2LL on . . . . day the . . . . 19 . . . at . . . . a.m., on the hearing of an application by the [Plaintiff] for an order pursuant to Order 36, Rule 3 of the Rules of the Supreme Court that the whole of this action by transferred to an Official Referee.

AND that the costs of this application may be costs in the cause.

DATED the . . . . 19 . . .

THIS summons was taken out by E. F. & Co. of (*address*), [Agents for (*name*) of (*address*),] Solicitors for the [Plaintiff]
To the [Defendant], and to G. H. & Co. of (*address*), his Solicitors.

3

PRAECIPE on entering action transferred from Chancery Division or Queen's Bench Division to the Official Referees' Courts

IN THE HIGH COURT OF JUSTICE
[Chancery *or* Queen's Bench] Division
Official Referee's Business

Between	A.B.	...	Plaintiff
	and		
	C.D.		Defendant

Enter this action for trial[1]

DATED the .... 19 ...

[1] With deletion of reference to Queen's Bench or Chancery Division and substitution of 'arbitration' for action this form of praecipe can be used for application to the Rota Clerk to allocate an arbitration to an Official Referee.

4

SUMMONS FOR DIRECTIONS before an Official Referee[1]

IN THE HIGH COURT OF JUSTICE
Official Referee's Business
His Honour Judge ....[1], Q.C.

Between	A.B.	...	Plaintiff
	and		
	C.D.	...	Defendant

LET ALL PARTIES concerned attend the Official Referee in Chambers, Court No. ...., Official Referees' Courts, St Dunstan's House, Fetter Lane, London EC4, on .... day the .... 19 ..., at .... a.m., on the hearing of an application by the [Plaintiff] for directions herein [including]:

(*Set out in numbered paragraphs any directions sought which are not 'common form'*)[2]

AND that the costs of this application may be costs in the cause[3].

DATED the .... 19 ...

This summons was taken out by E. F. & Co. of (*address*), Solicitors for the [Plaintiff]. To the [Defendant] and to G. H. & Co. of (*address*), his Solicitors.

[1] Insert name of Official Referee.
[2] 'Common form' directions relate to pleadings, discovery, and inspection of documents, expert witnesses, statements of witnesses of fact, plans, views and hearing date.
[3] Or any other order for costs proposed.

5

NOTICE under summons for directions[1]

IN THE HIGH COURT OF JUSTICE
Official Referees' Business
His Honour Judge ....[2], Q.C.
between A.B. ... Plaintiff
and
C.D. ... Defendant

TAKE NOTICE that the above named Defendant intends to apply at the hearing of the summons for directions herein for an order that:

(*Set out in numbered paragraphs any directions which are not 'common form'*)

DATED the .... 19 ...

This Notice was given by G. H. & Co. of (*address*), Solicitors for the Defendant.
To E. F. & Co. of (*address*), Solicitors for the Plaintiff.

[1] Notice should preferably be given at least 2 days before the date fixed for hearing.
[2] Insert the name of Official Referee.

6

TYPICAL ORDERS on summons for directions in a smaller case not involving much detail, with one defendant

IN THE HIGH COURT OF JUSTICE
Official Referees' Business
His Honour Judge ...., Q.C.
Between A.B. ... Plaintiff
and
C.D. ... Defendant

UPON HEARING Solicitors for the Plaintiff and for the Defendant IT IS ORDERED:

1. Defendant to deliver Defence by 1.2.89

2. Plaintiff to deliver Reply (if so advised) by 21.2.89
3. Each party to give discovery by lists by 21.2.89
4. Inspection on 3 days' notice
5. Leave to call experts: limited to 1 per party; experts to meet without prejudice to endeavour to narrow issues and to agree facts by not later than 1.4.89; reports to be exchanged by 15.5.89
6. Signed statements of witnesses of fact to serve as evidence in chief to be cross-served by 1.6.89
7. Hearing date 17.7.89—3rd fixture—estimate 4 days
8. Liberty to restore generally
9. Costs in cause

DATED this 12.1.89

7

TYPICAL ORDERS on summons for directions in a smaller case involving considerable detail: one defendant

IN THE HIGH COURT OF JUSTICE

Official Referees' Business

His Honour Judge . . . ., Q.C.

Between A.B. . . . Plaintiff

and

C.D. . . . Defendant

UPON HEARING Solicitor for the Plaintiff and Counsel for the Defendant IT IS ORDERED:

1. Defendant to deliver Defence and Counterclaim by 1.3.89
2. Reply and Defence to Counterclaim by 1.5.89
3. Defendant to deliver Scott Schedule[1], setting out each defect alleged and cost of remedying by 1.3.89
4. Plaintiff to comment on Schedule by 1.5.89
5. Each party to give discovery by lists by 1.5.89
6. Inspection on 3 days' notice
7. Experts: limited to 2 per party; experts of like disciplines to meet without prejudice to endeavour to narrow issues and to agree facts by not later than 15.6.89; reports to be exchanged by 31.7.89
8. Signed statements of witnesses of fact to serve as evidence in chief to be cross-served by 1.10.89
9. Parties to agree representative items from Scott Schedule for trial by 15.9.89. In default of agreement application to be made to Official Referee

10 Any view to be held after Plaintiff's opening

11. Hearing date 13.11.89—5th fixture—estimate 8 days
12. Liberty to restore generally
13. Costs in cause; special allowance for Solicitor; certificate for Counsel

DATED this 21.1.89

[1] See Forms 9–11 post.

8

TYPICAL ORDERS on summons for directions in a larger case: three defendants

IN THE HIGH COURT OF JUSTICE

Official Referees' Business

His Honour Judge . . . . , Q.C.

Between A.B. . . . Plaintiff

and

(1) C.D.

(2) J.K.

(3) L.M. . . . Defendants

UPON HEARING Counsel for Plaintiff and 1st and 2nd Defendants and Solicitor for 3rd Defendant

IT IS ORDERED:

1. Defendants to deliver Defences and any Counterclaims by 15.2.89
2. Plaintiff to deliver Reply and Defences to Counterclaims by 1.4.89
3. Plaintiff to deliver Further and Better Particulars of Statement of Claim requested on 5.1.89 by 1.2.89
4. Each party to give discovery by lists by 15.5.89
5. Inspection on 3 days' notice
6. Experts: limited to 4 per party; experts of like disciplines to meet without prejudice to endeavour to narrow issues and to agree facts by not later than 15.7.89; reports to be exchanged by 1.10.89
7. Signed statements of witnesses of fact to serve as evidence-in-chief to be cross-served by 15.11.89
8. If view desired in advance of hearing to be arranged with Official Referee's clerk
9. Pre-trial Review 8.12.89 10 a.m. (2 hours)—Counsel for Plaintiff to circulate to other Counsel suggested list of issues by 1.12.89—Defendants' Counsel to inform Plaintiff's Counsel of any suggested additional issues by 7.12.89
10. Hearing date 4.4.90—2nd fixture—estimate 24 days
11. Liberty to restore generally
12. Costs in cause; Certificates for Counsel; Special allowance for Solicitor

DATED this 12.1.89

9

SCOTT SCHEDULE in action for defective work

IN THE HIGH COURT OF JUSTICE
Official Referees' Business
Before His Honour Judge ...., Q.C.
Between

19... B. No. ...

A.B. ... ... Plaintiff
and
C.D. ... ... Defendant

pursuant to the Order of the Official Referee date .... 19....

1 No of Item	2 Full particulars of each item of work alleged to have been improperly or unskilfully performed, stating the defects complained of	3 Plaintiff's estimate of the cost of remedying the defects complained of, and, where the remedial work has been done, the cost thereof, identifying the relevant documents	4 Defendant's estimate of the cost of remedying any admitted defects	5 Defendant's observations	6 Column for Official Referee
1	DRAWING ROOM The paintwork on all wooden surfaces is peeling off, owing to insufficient preparation of the surfaces. Only one coat of paint was applied, instead of two as specified. It will be necessary to strip off the paintwork and re-paint with two coats	£1,000.00	[*Either:* Nil *Or:* £40.00]	[*Either:* The work of preparation was properly done. The defects complained of have been occasioned by hard wear in the two years which have elapsed since the work was done. *Or:* It is admitted that a small area of paintwork in the N.E. corner of the room requires re-painting.]	

Served by the Plaintiff on the Defendant on .... 19....   Served by the Defendant on the Plaintiff on .... 19 ....

10

SCOTT SCHEDULE in action claiming extras and omissions to fixed-price contract

IN THE HIGH COURT OF JUSTICE — 19... B. No. ...
Official Referees' Business
Before His Honour Judge ...., Q.C.
Between

A.B. ... ... Plaintiff
and
C.D. ... ... Defendant

pursuant to the Order of the Official Referee date .... 19....

EXTRAS

PART I

1 No of Item	2 Full particulars of each item of extra work claimed	3 Price claimed by Plaintiff	4 By whom ordered, and date	5 Price, if any, admitted by Defendant	6 Defendant's observations	7 Column for Official Referee
1	On excavating the foundation trenches the District Surveyor required them to be carried down a further 0·9 metres at the N.E. end over a length of 10 metres	£750.50	Defendant, on being told of District Surveyor's requirement on .... 19....	Nil	The item is not an extra. The Defendant was not consulted	

OMISSIONS

PART II

1 No of Item	2 Full particulars of the item omitted	3 Allowance offered by Plaintiff	4 Allowance claimed by Defendant	5 Defendant's observation	6 Column for Official Referee
1	DINING ROOM Alterations to fireplace	£285.50	£420.00	The allowance offered is insufficient.	

Served by the Plaintiff on the Defendant on .... 19.... Served by the Defendant on the Plaintiff on .... 19 ....

II

SCOTT SCHEDULE: specimen column headings

1. Work done and materials supplied

(*The Plaintiff completes columns 1–6 of Part II; the Defendant completes column 7 of Part I and 9 of Part II*)

LABOUR

PART I

1 No. of Item	2 Week ending	3 Name of workmen	4 Rate of pay	5 No. of hours worked	6 Total amount claimed by Plaintiff	7 Defendant's observations	8 Column for Official Referee

MATERIALS

PART II

1 No. of Item	2 Full particulars of any materials used	3 Name of supplier	4 Date purchased	5 Supplier's invoice no.	6 Gross cost	7 Trade discount	8 Net price	9 Defendant's observations	10 Column for Official Referee

2. Work done and materials supplied: alternative form

(*The Plaintiff completes columns 1–3; the Defendant completes columns 4 and 5*)

1 No. of Item	2 Full particulars of each item executed	3 Price claimed by Plaintiff	4 Price admitted by Defendant	5 Defendant's observation	6 Column for Official Referee

3. Dilapidations

(*The Plaintiff completes columns 1–3; the Defendant completes columns 4 and 5*)

1 No. of Item	2 Full particulars of each item of disrepair complained of	3 Plaintiff's estimate of cost of repair	4 Defendant's estimate of cost of repair of any admitted item	5 Defendant's observations, stating whether the need for repair is admitted, and, if so, whether the work has been or will be done	6 Column for Official Referee

4. Goods sold and delivered
(The Plaintiff completes columns 1–6; the Defendant completes columns 7 and 8)

1 No. of Item	2 Short description of the goods	3 Invoice No.	4 Date of Invoice	5 Amount of invoice	6 Date of delivery	7 Amount, if any, admitted by Defendant	8 Defendant's observations	9 Column for Official Referee

5. Agent's commission
(The Defendant prepares Part I and completes columns 1–5, leaving column 6 to be completed by the Plaintiff, who is the agent. The Plaintiff prepares Part II and completes columns 1–4, leaving column 5 to be completed by the Defendant)

PART I

1 No. of Item	2 Name of customer who purchased the goods	3 Date and no. of invoice	4 Amount of invoice	5 Commission due to Plaintiff	6 Plaintiff's observations, stating whether it is alleged that further goods were delivered to the customer, giving the best particulars thereof	7 Column for Official Referee

PART II

1 No. of Item	2 Names of any customers which it is alleged have been omitted from the account	3 Date and no. of invoice in respect of any goods which it is admitted were sent to the customer	4 Amount of invoice	5 Defendant's observations	6 Column for Official Referee

12

NOTICE of application for further directions given pursuant to liberty to restore

IN THE HIGH COURT OF JUSTICE
Official Referees' Business
His Honour Judge .... Q.C.
Between A.B. ... Plaintiff
and
C.D. ... Defendant

TAKE NOTICE that the above named [Plaintiff *or* Defendant] intends to apply to the Official Referee in Chambers, Court No. ...., Official Referees' Courts, St Dunstan's House, Fetter Lane, London EC4, at .... a.m. on .... day the .... 1989 for further directions in this action as to

(*Set out in numbered paragraphs directions sought*)

AND that the costs of this application may be costs in the cause.

DATED the .... 1989.

This summons was taken out by E.F. & Co. of (*address*), Solicitors for the [Plaintiff].
To the [Plaintiff *or* Defendant] and to G.H. & Co. of (*address*), his Solicitors.

13

TYPICAL DIRECTIONS on a pre-trial review

IN THE HIGH COURT OF JUSTICE
Official Referees' Business
His Honour Judge .... Q.C.
Between A.B. ... Plaintiff
and
(1) C.D.
(2) J.K.
(3) L.M. ... Defendant

UPON HEARING 2 Counsel for Plaintiff, 2 Counsel for 1st Defendant and Counsel for 2nd and 3rd Defendants

1. Liability only to be tried commencing 4.4.90—estimated length of liability only, 20 days
2. Assessment of damages (if required) to be on 4.10.90—3rd fixture—4 days
3. For trial of liability Plaintiff's Counsel to provide Court and other Counsel with written summary of opening at least a weekend before 4.4.89

4. Defendants' Counsel may each make short statements after Plaintiff's opening—written summaries to be provided
5. Parties' Solicitors will agree 'key' volumes of documents
6. Volumes of literature and of photographs, each with index, to be provided
7. Parties will arrange daily transcript; cost of which will be in cause
8. Directions with regard to assessment of damages hearing to be given after judgment as to liability
9. Costs in cause—Certificates for 2 Counsel each for Plaintiff and 1st Defendant and 1 Counsel each for 2nd and 3rd Defendants

DATED this 9.12.1988

14

NOTICE OF APPEAL from Official Referee

IN THE COURT OF APPEAL 19......... B. No. ....
On Appeal From The High Court Of Justice
Official Referees' Business
Between A.B. ... Plaintiff
and
C.D. ... Defendant

TAKE NOTICE that the Court of Appeal will be moved on .... day, the .... 19......, at the sitting of the Court or as soon thereafter as Counsel can be heard, by Counsel on behalf of the above named [Plaintiff] for an order that the judgment directed to be entered herein by His Honour Judge ...., Q.C., Official Referee, before whom the action was tried as appears by his Order dated .... 19....., be set aside on the grounds that

(*insert grounds*)

and that in lieu of the said judgment, judgment be entered for the [Plaintiff] for £........., with interest, and with costs of this action, and the costs of and occasioned by this appeal be paid by the [Defendant] and for such further or other order as to the Court of Appeal shall seem just

DATED this .... 19.....

of (*address*)
Solicitors for the above named [Plaintiff]

To G.H. & Co. of (*address*)
Solicitors for the [Defendant]

Index